Carthage

A New History of an Ancient Empire

EVE MACDONALD

EBURY
PRESS

EBURY PRESS

UK | USA | Canada | Ireland | Australia
India | New Zealand | South Africa

Ebury Press is part of the Penguin Random House group of companies
whose addresses can be found at global.penguinrandomhouse.com

Penguin Random House UK
One Embassy Gardens, 8 Viaduct Gardens, London SW11 7BW

penguin.co.uk
global.penguinrandomhouse.com

First published by Ebury Press in 2025

2

Typeset in 11.7/16 pt Calluna by Six Red Marbles UK, Thetford, Norfolk

Printed and bound in Great Britain by Clays Ltd, Elcograf S.p.A.

The authorised representative in the EEA is Penguin Random House Ireland,
Morrison Chambers, 32 Nassau Street, Dublin D02 YH68

A CIP catalogue record for this book is available from the British Library

Hardback ISBN 9781529911671
Trade Paperback ISBN 9781529911688

Contents

Introduction: The Burning Pyre

The city is aflame, burning in a Roman blaze after three long years of siege. The last holdouts take refuge in the great citadel known as the Byrsa hill. Among these desperate few is the wife of the commander of Carthage. Her name is not recorded but we know her husband was Hasdrubal, and she had their two children with her. Dressed in her finest clothes, she stands on the ramparts gazing down on the carnage below. She sees her beautiful city in flames, and images of unimaginable chaos, death and suffering. She is witnessing the final scene of Carthage, the very last moments of the city, in the year 146 BCE. For six days and nights Roman soldiers have fought and slaughtered their way from the ports, across the marketplace, to the top of the hill, street by street, facing resistance from the Carthaginian population. So fierce has the resistance been that the Romans had to send in sweepers, whose only job was to push the dead out of the way as more and more reinforcements piled in. The heavily armed infantry, the famed legionaries of the Roman army, have been unrelenting in their destruction. At this moment, the wife of Hasdrubal, looking down from the citadel, spots the Roman commander, Scipio Aemilianus, adopted grandson of the famous Scipio Africanus, conqueror of Hannibal. She looks closer and sees that her husband Hasdrubal has surrendered to him and now kneels at Scipio's feet.

The wife of Hasdrubal addresses Scipio directly from the ramparts and, as quoted by a later historian named Appian, says, 'For you, Roman, the gods have no cause of indignation, since you exercise the right of war.' With these words, she absolves her enemies and their destruction of her city. She continues to call down to the Roman commander but trains her eyes on her husband, who gets no such absolution: 'Upon this Hasdrubal, betrayer of his country and her temples, of me and his children, may the gods of Carthage take vengeance and you be their instrument.' For Hasdrubal's betrayal is both public, in his role as chief magistrate and defender of Carthage, and personal, as her husband who has failed in his duties. Hasdrubal has forsaken his oaths to the city and her gods, and has left his wife and children to fend for themselves. She calls him a wretch and a traitor and taunts him with his future of 'decorating a Roman triumph', being paraded through the streets of Rome as a trophy of war. And finally, she accuses him of being the 'most effeminate of men' and one who has left his family to be engulfed in flames. With these final words, the last ever spoken by a Carthaginian, she turns and kills her own terrified children, throwing them down into the fire. In her final act, she flings herself after them. The end of Carthage comes with this ultimate statement of death over enslavement, of suicide over capture.

What was Carthage and who were the Carthaginians? Why did the Romans destroy them so completely? From the first time I set foot on the place that once was ancient Carthage, near the modern city of Tunis in the country of Tunisia, I was fascinated by these questions. The beauty of the place captured me, along with the haunting memories that reside there and all the many faces of the city. For 600 years Carthage was a dominant player in the history of the ancient world and a foundational power of the western Mediterranean, but its importance was largely erased by the Romans over the centuries after their conquest. Here I have set out to explore the city and lives of its citizens across its long and illustrious history, bringing their stories to the fore after two millennia in which their tales have been told by those who destroyed them. In doing so, we uncover a civilisation that was a fundamental part of the ancient Mediterranean, whose cultural presence is still felt across the whole of the North African coast, Portugal and Spain, mainland Italy, and the islands of Sicily, Sardinia and Corsica.

There are challenges in trying to address these questions of who the Carthaginians were, and even what Carthage was. Theirs is a fragmented history, distorted and rearranged, a puzzle with key pieces missing. The final lines of the dramatic scene set by Appian above captures the problem. Much that we know of the Carthaginians is filtered through a lens created for us by their enemies. So Hasdrubal's wife condemns her husband for posterity, and with it, all Carthaginian men are condemned, for this idea of the effeminate man was a great insult in the Roman and Greek male mind. The Carthaginian Hasdrubal does not act like a man, and he is willing to suffer humiliation, even slavery, rather than protect his wife and children, his city and gods or to take his own life. Not so his brave spouse, whose final act, the hurling of herself and her children on to a funeral pyre – while possibly a scene entirely invented by the Romans – is admired by the Roman historian. Appian sums up the scene with the line, 'in this way the wife of Hasdrubal died, an end that would have been more fitting to himself.' Even this most famous of stories is told, in the traditional narratives, with a Roman slant.[1] With this book, I aim to interrogate the Roman sources and draw on new archaeological evidence to allow a much more nuanced Carthage to take shape.

The dramatic story of Carthage and its rise and fall has fascinated people for millennia. The tales of Dido and Hannibal, of great wealth, total war and ultimate tragedy make for a compelling narrative. Only now can we weave them into a story that includes new information and greater depths of understanding produced by the leaps in archaeological research over the past 20 years. New DNA and stable isotope analysis of human remains from mass graves at the site of Himera in Sicily give us insights into the far-flung origins of the people buried there. Archaeologists from Tunisia and the Netherlands have used radiocarbon dating on samples from deep excavations at Carthage that confirm the foundation of the city in the ninth century BCE. The ongoing studies, excavations and research from across the Mediterranean have begun to provide a foundation for the real story of Carthage that takes us beyond the Roman story and is underpinned by technological advancement, industrial innovations and multicultural populations. We can now tell of new perspectives on the city and its place in the wider world.

At its height in the third century BCE, Carthage was a technologically advanced culture and a city of possibly 250,000 people – although this number is likely inflated. It sat in a geographically perfect location on the north coast of Africa linked to points east and west across the Mediterranean Sea, and north and south reaching into the African continent (see page 10). Carthage was also founded in the midst of rich agricultural land and abundant natural resources, which the Carthaginians fully exploited. In fact, the only piece of Carthaginian literature that the Romans preserved from its libraries after their destruction of the city was the text of a man named Mago who wrote about agricultural techniques and innovation, how to cultivate the best wine and what species of plants thrived in the landscape. So advanced was the Carthaginian agricultural technology and land, so rich was Carthage as a place of connectivity, that it was in conquering Carthage that the Romans came to be the power that went on to rule the entire Mediterranean. Many would argue, including the ancient Romans, that without Carthage, there would have been no Roman Empire.

The people of Carthage and the culture that existed there are often referred to as 'Punic', a word commonly used to refer to people who were part of a large Phoenician-speaking diaspora and whose cultural focus was the central and western Mediterranean. Punic Wars, Punic behaviours and all things Punic are described by the Roman sources. 'Punic' is a difficult word; its origins rest in a cultural stereotype that the Romans created about their old enemy. The word comes from the Latin word *Poenus*, which is believed to derive from the Phoenician origins of the Carthaginians. Being Punic was not a compliment in the third-century BCE Roman mind, but it is the name that has stuck and been used for the Carthaginians since. For a lack of anything better, I use the word 'Punic' here too, with some distinction between Carthaginian and west Phoenician identities especially in the earlier periods of their history.[2]

Many books have been written about Carthage and its history over the centuries, starting with lost ancient Roman epic poems such as Naevius' *Bellum Poenicum* about the First Punic War and works of other writers whose stories are some of the earliest surviving examples of Latin literature, written in the third and second centuries BCE. So Rome's wars with Carthage were the events that shaped early Latin literature, and became a fundamental part of the city's memories and construction of an epic past.[3] The second-century history by the Greek Polybius is an essential part of any narrative of Carthage and was hugely influential on later histories written in the early Roman Empire, such as Livy's monumental work in Latin on the story of Rome, *Ab urbe condita* ('From the Foundation of the City'). Also important were Latin imperial epics like Silius Italicus' *Punica* and the later works by the Greek-language authors of Roman history like

Appian, who we saw above, and Plutarch. In the centuries that followed the destruction of Carthage, the Romans continued to be fascinated by the events of the wars and to tell these as formational tales. Many different sources, ranging from classical Greek writers like Herodotus and Thucydides to late Roman historians, will be used as we unfold Carthage's story. The ancient views are essential, but we always must consider that Carthage was ultimately projected as 'the other' in almost all of these texts. This 'othering' of Carthage continued well into the post-antique period when the memory of Rome and its empire was mused upon by Arabic geographers, medieval scholars, Renaissance writers and early modern composers.[4]

Today we still find this perspective, especially in the ways that Carthage appears in the history of Rome, often only as its ultimate enemy. Here I have told the history of Carthage and its citizens through key individuals or places and the seminal events that shaped the civilisation's history and destiny, always trying to keep a Carthaginian view at the fore, wherever possible. We begin with the Phoenicians and the foundation of Carthage as a colony of Tyre in Chapter 1. Here we meet the beautiful founder of the city, the queen Dido, and look at the myths and legends that survive of this deep past in the ninth century BCE. The early chapters look at the way that Carthage was drawn into the politics and power struggles of the eastern Mediterranean, where the Achaemenid Persian Empire and the archaic Greek cities struggled for dominance. We will examine how Carthage engaged with its neighbours and developed its own cultural and religious identity over the sixth and fifth centuries BCE and will explore Carthage as it begins to flex its muscles in the western Mediterranean within a multicultural and competitive world of Greeks, Phoenicians, Etruscans and Romans. Chapters 4 and 5 look at Carthaginian interactions with Greek cities on Sicily and show how Carthage's history was intricately linked to larger geo-political shifts and the ideas created from the conquests of Alexander in the fourth century BCE. By the height of Carthaginian power in the third century BCE, individual actors and the politics of the 'Hellenistic' successor kingdoms became the model by which to see famous Carthaginian generals like Hannibal.

In the latter half of the book, we meet with Carthage as an empire and follow the continuum of rivalries and expansion of power through the third and into the second century BCE. Chapters 6 and 7 look at the conditions for a western Mediterranean-wide war and the battle for Sicily that became known as the First Punic War. The Second Punic War – arguably the most renowned episode in Carthaginian history – is covered in Chapters 8 to 10, and we follow Hannibal as he leads his elephants into Italy and challenges Rome to its very core. In Chapters 11 and 12 we look at the final 50 years of Carthage, as the battle with Rome leads to Carthage's last gasp and its final annihilation. After Carthage's destruction, in the final chapter we follow the vestiges of the Carthaginians that survived the destruction and the long memory of the city. We will see how the residues of Carthage can be found across the Roman Mediterranean and still exist right up to the present day.

Underlying so much of the story of Carthage is its identity as a North African city. On North African soil were its closest allies, its bitterest enemies, shared myths and local traditions. The indigenous people of North Africa, today's Amazigh, were referred to as Numidian/Libyan or sometimes Berber in ancient and medieval texts, and they were an essential part of Carthage's make-up and history. From the beginning to the end of Carthage's history we will explore the stories of the African communities – as allies of Carthage, and in terms of the intermarriage and identities that created the distinct people that we call Carthaginians.

Here I either use the word 'Numidian' or 'Libyan' for the indigenous North Africans unless referring to a specific people by the name of their kingdom or city.

My ambition with this book is to tell a story of Carthage that is both an epic tale and an account that helps us to gain a better understanding of the real people who lived and thrived in this beautiful city on the sea in the centuries before Rome. The Romans didn't want anyone – their people or their adversaries, their citizens or their descendants – to fully understand or see Carthage or its citizens as real people; they wanted the Carthaginians to forever be seen as the enemy. My aim, and the journey of this book, is to reveal, as much as is possible, what the Romans tried to make us forget: that Carthage has always been one of the foundational cultures of the ancient western Mediterranean. And if we look hard enough, we will see that without all that Carthage was, there would have been no Rome.

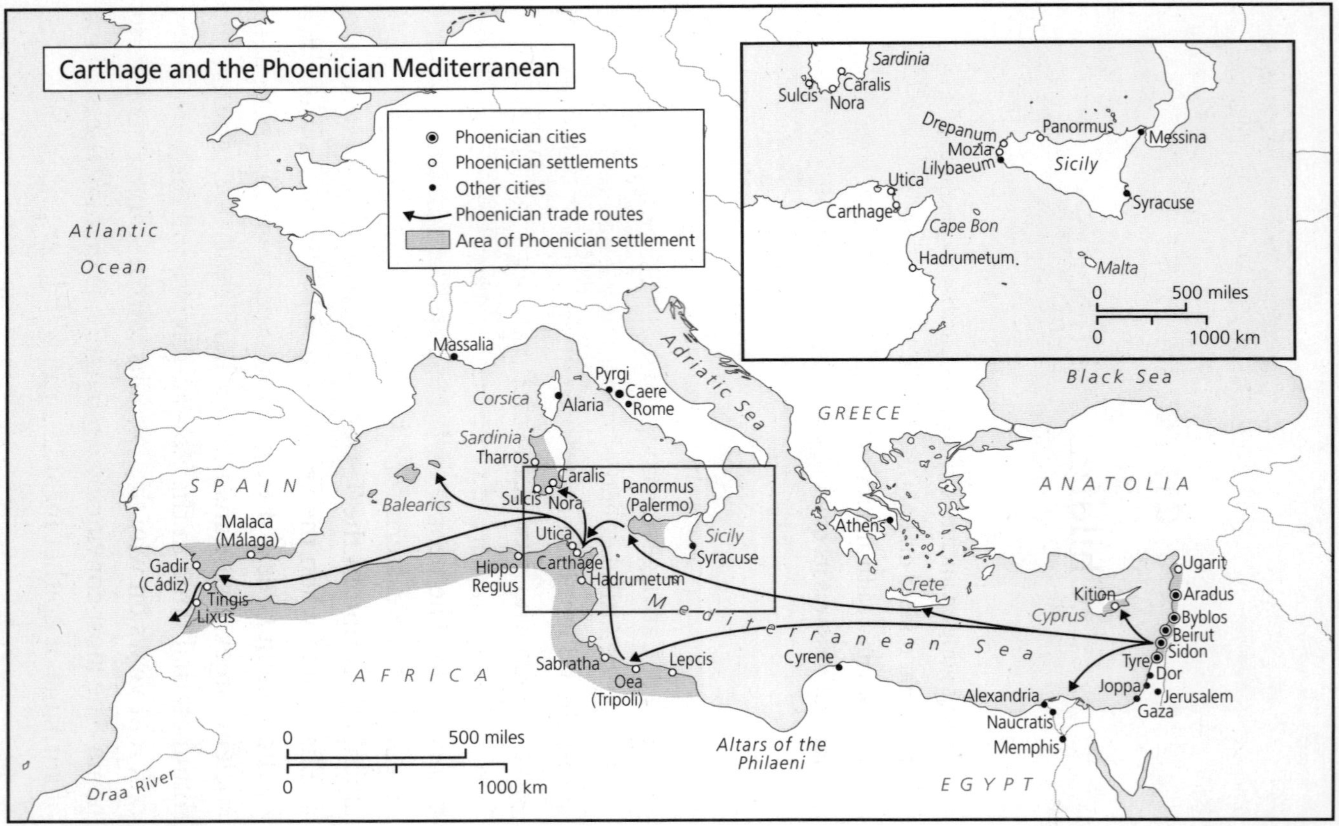
Carthage and the Phoenician Mediterranean
Phoenician cities
Phoenician settlements
Other cities
Phoenician trade routes
Area of Phoenician settlement
Atlantic Ocean
SPAIN
Gadir (Cádiz)
Malaca (Málaga)
Tingis
Lixus
Draa River
Balearics
Massalia
Corsica
Alaria
Sardinia
Tharros
Sulcis
Nora
Caralis
Pyrgi
Caere
Rome
Adriatic Sea
Panormus (Palermo)
Sicily
Syracuse
Utica
Carthage
Hadrumetum
Hippo Regius
Sabratha
Oea (Tripoli)
Lepcis
AFRICA
Mediterranean Sea
Altars of the Philaeni
Cyrene
GREECE
Athens
Crete
Black Sea
ANATOLIA
Cyprus
Kition
Ugarit
Aradus
Byblos
Beirut
Sidon
Tyre
Dor
Joppa
Jerusalem
Gaza
Alexandria
Naucratis
Memphis
EGYPT
0 500 miles
0 1000 km
Sardinia
Sulcis
Caralis
Nora
Drepanum
Mozia
Lilybaeum
Panormus
Messina
Sicily
Syracuse
Utica
Carthage
Cape Bon
Hadrumetum.
Malta
0 500 miles
0 1000 km

CHAPTER I

Children of Phoenix

In ages gone an ancient city stood – Carthage – a colony of Tyre,
from afar it faced on Italy and on the Tiber's mouths;
vast was its wealth and revenues
and ruthless was its quest of war.

Virgil, *Aeneid* 1.12–14[1]

Any story of Carthage must begin with Dido. In myth, she was an enduringly beautiful queen whose tragic life has been recounted across the millennia in literature, art and music. In history, she was a woman who lived in the ninth century BCE and came from Tyre, a city in modern-day Lebanon. And she was not really named Dido. The people of Tyre spoke Phoenician, a Semitic language of the eastern Mediterranean that was written in an alphabetic script. In the Tyrian native tongue, she was known as Elishat and when the Semitic name Elishat was transcribed by the ancient Greeks it turned into Elissa, which is how some ancient Greek historians refer to her. It was as Dido that she found eternal fame in the Roman stories, and there are many different views on why the Romans took to calling her by this name. The most convincing explanation is that Dido was a kind of surname or epithet meaning 'the wanderer', which may be a nod to how she travelled across the Mediterranean before she reached the place where Carthage was founded.

The Roman poet Virgil immortalised the most famous version of the foundation legend of Carthage in the *Aeneid* in the first century BCE, but this was eight centuries after the event itself and over 100 years since Carthage had been destroyed. Virgil took a pre-existing story of Dido/Elissa and wove it together with one of the foundation myths of Rome – entwining the two cities for posterity. In Virgil's epic, the Trojan hero Aeneas, after escaping the burning city of Troy, takes refuge on the north coast of Africa, at Dido's Carthage, just as the city is being constructed. Aeneas' sorry tale of Troy's destruction plays on Dido's sympathies and the two become star-crossed lovers, doomed by the gods to be separated. Dido is seduced by Aeneas before he abandons her, leaving the Tyrian queen heartbroken and full of remorse. Aeneas carries on to Italy, as he follows a destiny prescribed by the gods. This Roman tale turns Dido into the very archetype of a rejected, abandoned and vengeful woman. For this was a profound humiliation for a noble woman, who is left with little choice but to take her own life. It is with her dying breath that she hurls a curse down upon the departing Aeneas and all his descendants. Dido implores that in the future there will 'Rise some avenger of our Libyan blood', and in this story a Roman justification was created for the subsequent wars between the two great cities.[2]

Virgil's Dido has resonated throughout the ancient and modern worlds, with the tragic queen portrayed in theatre, opera and novels across multiple languages and cultures. But this is not the only version of the story of Carthage's foundation, and in the other surviving tales there are perhaps more tangible details of the woman who inspired these stories. The earlier versions omit the Roman Aeneas from the story altogether and tell us of the Phoenician queen Elissa. Originating from a Sicilian Greek writer named Timaeus of Tauromenium (modern Taormina in Sicily), this tale dates to at least the late third century BCE, but it probably existed even earlier. Only fragments of Timaeus' history still exist, teased out from pieces preserved by later ancient writers, so the complete pre-Virgilian story of Carthage's foundation remains somewhat unclear. In this version of the story, Elissa was a Phoenician princess from Tyre seeking refuge on the North African coast. She had been forced to flee her home city because of the political turmoil caused by her brother, the young king Pygmalion. Pygmalion killed Elissa's husband, who had been king regent and chief priest to the Tyrian patron god Melqart. After the murder of his brother-in-law, the young Pygmalion seized the throne of Tyre for himself, but his grip on power was shaky and many of the nobility were not convinced by his rule. This included his sister Elissa, who was horrified by her husband's death and sacrilege to their gods, and who became a focal point for opposition to the new king among the ruling elites.[3]

Elissa and her group of rebels fled the city by night, taking sacred artefacts that belonged to the god Melqart with them. They began a long journey across the Mediterranean, heading west to settle in the new colonial lands. The Roman historian Appian echoes these details when he tells us that Dido/Elissa 'set sail for Africa and took with her property and a number of men who wanted to escape from the tyranny of Pygmalion'.[4] The rebels' first stop was the island of Cyprus, where they collected young women to join their party as brides. The women came from a renowned temple at Kition dedicated to the goddess Astarte (equivalent to the Greek Aphrodite or Roman Venus); this was a place where a young girl might be sent by her family to serve time as what we have conventionally called 'a temple prostitute' in honour of the goddess. After their time in the temple, we are told these young women were considered very eligible brides.

Thus the noble Tyrians and their brides left Cyprus together and voyaged across the sea, stopping in Greece and Sicily before arriving at the place that we know as Carthage.[5]

What to do with these fragments of a long-ago myth, filtered through the lens of Carthage's enemies? And how do we interpret them? The essential elements of the story that survive, from the gathering of women and the appropriation of sacred objects, suggest this was no mad flight across the sea but a planned expedition. This fits into what we now understand about early Phoenician settlement and the evidence from other sites like Cádiz in Spain that show urban foundations and organised city planning.[6] The fact that Carthage would continue to pay tribute to the temple of the god Melqart at Tyre throughout its 600-year existence makes it clear that this was a move with colonial intentions; an annual tithe points to a close and very specific relationship with the mother city. There are hints in the stories of Elissa/Dido's relationship to her dead husband, as well as his worship of Melqart and her enduring fidelity to him, that give us building blocks for the ideas behind the foundation of the city of Carthage. The name Melqart literally means 'king of the city', and he would play an important role through the whole history of Carthage. Melqart's role was as protector of the city and its new colonists. He was part of the divine pantheon of the religion of Carthage but also associated with other Phoenician cities in the west. This made him a focal point for a community identity and one that would spread across the whole western Mediterranean. So, embedded in these myths of the founding queen Dido and her idealised female virtues is information about the choices made by the Tyrians who settled in Africa.[7]

Carthage's mother-city Tyre was a vital centre in antiquity, a regional power with monumental architecture and a sophisticated port. The later Greeks and Romans have left us various descriptions of it, like Quintus Curtius Rufus who notes in his *History of Alexander* that Tyre was 'memorable among all the cities of Syria and Phoenicia for its renown and size'.[8] It was a dominant force in the eastern Mediterranean Sea and hinterland regions, and the Tyrian population would have carried this fame and pride in their origins with them to establish their new cities in the western Mediterranean. Set just off the coast of the Levant on an island, Tyre was a classic location for a Phoenician city: protected from the mainland, easily accessible by sea and offering good shelter for ships. Carthage too shared these attributes. In fact, the name Carthage in the Phoenician language was *Qart Hadasht*, which means, literally, the New City.[9]

Carthage was not the first Phoenician city on this coast of Africa. Just 30km to its north was Utica (see page 10), founded, according to ancient historical sources, some centuries before Carthage. But our archaeological evidence from Utica does not match up with these earlier recorded dates and the city may have been there for only a few decades when Carthage was established. The pottery, mostly drinking cups and plates, found in excavations at Utica are stylistically dated to a contemporary period, the ninth century BCE, and the results of radiocarbon dating make it possible to push the occupation back slightly earlier – into the tenth century. One spectacular recent find uncovered the remains of a whole feast held by the people who lived in Utica in these early years. The population had slaughtered, roasted and consumed goats, oxen, pigs, horses, turtles and a domestic dog in a communal meal. Then, after the dining and drinking, all the plates and cups were gathered up and deposited – along with the animal remains – in a deep well. The reason for the feast and deposit made afterwards may never be known but the theory is that the community held some kind of ritual closing of the water source. Thousands of years later, these remains found by archaeologists provide all kinds of insights into the early African city and the engagement of the population with the world around them.[10]

The pottery and tableware used at the feast at Utica came from across the central Mediterranean and tell us that the people there in these early years were in contact with neighbours to the north in Sardinia and in central Italy, and to the east in Greece and the Levant. They were very well connected and had been busy trading across the seas. So, we have to ask, why was Carthage built just some 30km to the south? The answer lies in its location. Although an inland site today, Utica sat on the coast in the ninth century BCE where the course of the Bagradas (Medjerda) River met the sea. The river's annual flow meant that the harbour of Utica, right at the river's mouth, constantly suffered from silting and the likelihood is that Carthage was chosen as a more easily accessible and functional port.[11]

Once the new colonists arrived in Carthage, the local inhabitants, referred to variously in our ancient sources as Numidians or Libyans, seem to have been somewhat resistant to another settlement. The indigenous peoples would have already had dealings with the settlers from the Levant in Utica and were not welcoming to Dido and her followers. In fact, Dido and the new arrivals are believed to have tricked the locals into giving up their land. In the myth, which is recorded by a much later Roman source called Justin, Dido bargains with a local king for a piece of land, asking only for 'as much land as could be covered by a single hide of an ox'. Dido tells the king that she is only going to use the land to rest her people who are tired after their long journey from the east. Then, she secretly has the oxhide cut into the thinnest possible strips. Laying each thin strip end to end, she encircled as much land as she could, and in doing so acquired a lot more land than she had first seemed to ask for. The piece of land acquired by the lovely queen was afterwards called the Byrsa, and this became the citadel of Carthage – for *Byrsa* in Greek etymology means 'hide'. Justin doesn't tell us about the Libyan king's reaction, but he could hardly have been thrilled at the deception.[12]

The story of the oxhide seems outlandish to us but was frequently repeated by ancient writers to showcase Dido's clever ruse in outwitting the local king. The Carthaginians would be eternally characterised as tricky, deceptive and untrustworthy, but some scholars believe there may be a modicum of truth in the tale. It may be that the oxhide story echoes a contemporary legal process of land acquisition we have no knowledge of, and mixed with it is a much better-known concept of using an ox to plough an area of land to mark out boundaries. But questions about the story remain. For instance, why would Tyrians, whose language was Phoenician, use a Greek word like *Byrsa* for their citadel? Here we can see the layers of text and traditions at work as a story from a prehistoric past is woven into the tale of the foundation of Carthage. The Phoenician word for fortress is *barsat* and some experts argue that Byrsa is a corruption of the original Phoenician word made sensible for a Greek audience. This version of the story shows us how ancient Greek writers tried to understand the Carthaginians within their own mythical and linguistic frameworks.[13]

In all versions of the myth, death comes to Dido by her own hand. The city she founded grew and prospered so much that a neighbouring king named Iarbas took the opportunity to seek out marriage to the queen. Dido refused his offer, claiming she could never break the vow she had made to her long dead husband. More realistically, her decision likely reflected the vulnerability of women rulers at the time, and she did not want to hand over her autonomy and power to Iarbas. The elites of Carthage had other ideas and Dido's followers were, as the story goes, supportive of the marriage proposal. This tale reveals a lonely queen who struggled for power and needed to secure the city through the support of a man. The population would have wanted a leader to produce heirs, and here is the timeless tale of a reigning childless queen pressured from all sides. It began to look as though Dido would be forced to marry, that the elites around her were ready to overthrow her if she refused. In the legend, Dido chose to kill herself rather than be forced into this unwanted marriage. In the final scene, she throws herself on to a burning pyre and in her self-immolation embraces a symbolism of great sacrifice, female virtue and modesty.

These many stories of Dido have left a complex and conflicted image of a woman who is both virtuous and self-sacrificing, powerful and creative, but at the same time someone whose passion and love led to her destruction – at least in Virgil's story. Can the variant versions of Dido tell us anything about Carthage or are they only useful for understanding Roman ideas of female power and virtue? There are parallels in the story with one of the only other Carthaginian women we know anything about, the wife of Hasdrubal, who we talked about at the very beginning of the book and who dies in the same way, and on the very same spot –the Byrsa hill. There are layers of literary construction underpinning the story, resting in the ideal of a self-sacrificing woman and even similarities to the character of the noble Lucretia from early Roman mythology whose suicide set in motion the creation of the Roman Republic.[14] The contrasting version of Dido in Virgil's *Aeneid* presents a less-than virtuous queen who uses emotional and sexual temptation to try to lure the proto-Roman Aeneas away from his destiny. The depiction of a temptress Dido, leading a noble Roman astray, has been frequently linked to the figure of Cleopatra, who loomed large in the mind of Virgil's contemporaries when this story was written down in the late first century BCE. This is the most enduring of the Dido myths and was written with the approval of the first Roman emperor and great propagandist, Augustus, who had just come to power by defeating the forces of Cleopatra and Marcus Antonius at Actium in 31 BCE.[15]

In the mythology of Dido, then, there is a mix of component parts that combine later Roman characterisations of Carthaginians as tricky and untrustworthy with the strength of character and nobility of action that we see more commonly in stories of great Roman virtue. The depiction of Dido's life captures all the issues that a history of Carthage must contend with, for what the Carthaginians believed about their own foundation is not recorded and how the Carthaginians saw their own history has long been erased from memory.

Beyond the myth, the facts about the foundation of Carthage are only slightly less dramatic. A trail of early Phoenician-speaking merchants and travellers from the coastal cities of the Levant leads to the western Mediterranean over the ninth to seventh centuries BCE. The reason behind this movement was a complex combination of the shifting need for resources, population pressures and external political factors. The city-states of the Levant that made up the region we refer to as 'Phoenicia' turned to trade and colonialisation as a way of alleviating issues at home. This led the population of these places to establish many cities in the western Mediterranean, and chief among them was Carthage. Deep excavations into the earliest layers of Carthage now confirm that a city was founded at a time that corresponds with the ancient sources who claimed these events occurred in circa 814 BCE.[16]

Carthage sat on a prime location for a connecting city: midway along the north coast of Africa near the island of Sicily, which formed a kind of natural land bridge across the central

Mediterranean linking Africa to Europe. Since successful maritime navigation in antiquity was based on the winds and ocean currents that could be devastating if miscalculated, ships moved from port to port and always kept land in sight. From Carthage there were easily predicted currents and visible land that carried ships from Carthage to Sicily in the best sailing months. The location also meant that whoever occupied Carthage could control the comings and goings across the Mediterranean's central zone (see page 10).

If you go to Carthage and stand on the Byrsa hill looking out to the Bay of Tunis today, you immediately see that the geography was ideal, as it is both open and protected. The city sits out on a small peninsula, tucked away to face slightly southeast but at the same time with full access to the sea.[17] In antiquity, the peninsula was entirely surrounded by water and the link to the land was much narrower than what we see today. Much of what is currently visible to the north and the south of the narrow peninsula is reclaimed, silted-up land. There was the ideal mix of sea, shelter and agricultural land and as a location for a city it was perfect – and also perfectly Phoenician. In the early period of Carthage's existence, from the ninth to the seventh century BCE, the sea was a very dangerous place to be settled upon and coastal towns were vulnerable. So there needed to be a balance of location that allowed for maritime travel and protection from the potential damage caused by piracy, invasions and the equally destructive power of storms.

In fact, every time I have visited another Phoenician city culturally linked to Carthage, places like Cádiz, Palermo, Tyre or Motya, I have had that same feeling of being both a vulnerable coastal site, but also a location protected by the very sea surrounding it. There is an inherent similarity between these cities founded by early Phoenician explorers in the Mediterranean, and the only way to really understand early Carthage and its foundation is to look more closely at the other Phoenician-speaking peoples and their role both in North Africa and across the seas. Since in these early years Carthage was only one of many cities in the western Mediterranean, how it evolved out of a group of related Phoenician settlements, colonies and trading posts to become a power is a key part of the story. To understand Carthage, we need to understand who the Phoenicians were and why they moved into the Mediterranean and settled in these regions.

The people we call Phoenicians are believed to be related to those called the 'Canaanites' of the Hebrew Bible, from the land of Canaan of the second millennium BCE. In the late Bronze Age, the Canaanites played an integral role in the movement of goods around the eastern Mediterranean and the Aegean. Evidence for this travel and trade comes from shipwrecks, one in particular found just 50m off the shore near the town of Uluburun along the southern coast of Turkey in the Bay of Antalya. At a depth of close to 50m but clearly visible to divers in the blue Antalyan sea was the ship's cargo, scattered across the seabed. The detritus of a Bronze Age ship can tell us about the people on board and the routes taken by these intrepid travellers over 3,000 years ago. On board this ship were 10 tons of copper ingots, ceramic jars full of wine from Cyprus and oil from the Levant, glass beads, an Egyptian scarab of Queen Nefertiti of Egypt, and Aegean pots. From the range of these objects, we can tell that the ship had been on a circular route around the eastern shores of the Mediterranean, picking up and dropping off cargo. The Canaanites disappear from historical view in the late second millennium BCE. The theory is that at the beginning of the new Iron Age (i.e. in the tenth/ninth centuries BCE), they re-emerge in the historical record as the people we now call Phoenicians. These 'Phoenicians' lived in cities along the east coast of the Mediterranean and would have referred to themselves by their city of origin, including the flourishing urban port centres such as Sidon, Tyre, Beirut and Byblos.[18]

We only call them Phoenicians because the later Greeks did – they never referred to themselves that way. The name comes from the Greek word *phoinike*, which is associated with the colour purple and linked to the extremely valuable purple-red dye they were known to produce. The manufacturing of this dye was a key industry in ancient Phoenician cities, with the precious ink coming from a process of grinding the now almost extinct murex shell. There are references to the word *Phoenix/Phoinix* very early in Greek literature, and a man named Phoinix turns up in Homer's *Iliad* as an elderly councillor of Achilles. Elsewhere Phoinix is, in the Greek tradition, the eponymous founder of the Phoenician peoples.[19] In the earliest Greek texts, Phoinix was also the father of Europa, who, in mythology, was a princess, raped and carried off by Zeus and brought to the island of Crete. Europa is another of the female Phoenicians of myth and legend who has resonated through Western culture and art. These stories show how contemporary Greeks came to understand and embed Phoenicians, their culture and practices into their mythology.

Early in the first millennium BCE these Phoenicians living along the coast were expanding westwards. Evidence of a rapid growth in cities between the twelfth and eighth centuries BCE and of food shortages as early as the tenth century BCE suggests that the population may have outstripped the productivity of the land. The narrow fertile strip that formed the Phoenician cities' homeland runs about 200km north–south along the coast. It is well watered and protected from the east by mountains known as the Lebanon Massif and the Anti-Lebanon Range that extend over 3,000m high. The geographical features block the coastal strip from any easy eastward land expansion. These mountains had always supplied plenty of fresh water and famously excellent-quality timber in the form of Lebanese cedars for building ships. As a result of finite agricultural potential and a growing population, the people we call Phoenicians set out for new horizons into the Mediterranean. They were the earliest to reconnect with traditions of interstate economic activity that had flourished in the Bronze Age and began to take advantage of what we see as growing commercial links in the Mediterranean in the early Iron Age (tenth to ninth century BCE). They moved westward out of the eastern Mediterranean and Aegean to the very edge of the Mediterranean, and perhaps beyond.

The Phoenicians acquired a reputation as great seafarers and developed some of the first decked warships in antiquity. There is a famous image of a bireme, from a relief found at the Assyrian palace at Nineveh (in modern Iraq, near Mosul), that clearly illustrates the use of a decked warship with two levels of oars (see Fig. I, in plate section). So, in this period we have Phoenicians becoming known as traders and also merchants, artisans and farmers, but even more significant was their role in navigation and naval warfare in the eastern Mediterranean.

At the beginning of the Iron Age, Phoenicians set out westwards, searching for valuable natural resources to be brought back and traded in the urbanised world of the eastern Mediterranean. They acquired raw materials that were then brought east, both as essential commodities and for the production of luxury goods such as gold amulets and carnelian scarab rings, jewelled earrings, bracelets and armbands. New technologies and industries of the Iron Age had shifted the supply chain and demand for raw materials. The iron-ore deposits of the western Mediterranean became key to the prosperity of those civilisations in the east. Exploration in the western Mediterranean, particularly in the Iberian Peninsula (modern Spain and Portugal), Sardinia and Etruria (central Italy), led to the Phoenician exploitation of rich natural resource deposits and an increasing reputation for great wealth.

A combination of all these factors seems to have driven the settlement of the western Mediterranean by Phoenician-speaking peoples. The early Iron Age kingdoms of Assyria, Egypt, Israel and Judah, and their relationship to the Phoenician cities, underlie our understanding of these events. There is a famous relief from the palace of the Neo-Assyrian king Ashurnasirpal II (ninth century BCE) at Nimrud (ancient Calah or Kahlu on the east banks of the Tigris) where we can see what is thought to be a Phoenician paying tribute to the king (see Fig. 2 in plate section). Accompanying him are two monkeys, one carried on the man's shoulder and the other led by hand. Are we looking here into the face of an early Phoenician ruler bringing exotic gifts to the great Assyrian king? We can't know for sure, but we can see how the Phoenicians became associated with these ideas of exotic animals and exploitation of resources from faraway, with the foreign, all symbolised by the monkeys from the west of Africa being presented as tribute.

The nature of the early Phoenician expansion is much simplified in some literary sources where well-known passages in the Hebrew Bible note the wealth available in far-off lands: 'Tarshish was thy merchant by reason of the multitude of all kind of riches; with silver, iron, tin and lead, they traded in the fairs,' says the book of Ezekiel.[20] By the sixth century BCE, when the Hebrew Bible was written down, the sources of their great wealth are listed as silver, iron, tin and lead; many of these were to be found in the western Mediterranean, in Spain (tin, silver) and in Etruria (iron ore, copper).

The best way to think about this complex web of Phoenicians is to look at the sea routes taken by sailors and merchants around the Mediterranean in these years. The way it worked is that a ship would move from port to port, region to region, dropping off and picking up goods along the way, never straying far from land. The process is called *cabotage* and the merchants who plied the shores of the Mediterranean not only drove trade, but also increased interactions between cultures. This shows a circular, counterclockwise navigation of the sea that accommodated winds and currents (see page 10). The location of the place called Tarshish in the Hebrew Bible is thought to refer to Tartessus, a region in modern Spain beyond the Pillars of Herakles (Strait of Gibraltar) northwest of the early Phoenician colony of Gadir (Cádiz). This, the Rio Tinto region, is an area set around the Guadalquivir (River Baetis in antiquity), rich in mineral ores even today. This land of great value was prized for its resources, and it is no coincidence that centuries later it would see some of the fiercest fighting between the Carthaginians and the Romans in the Second Punic War: two powers battling for the abundant natural resources of this wealthy region.

The locations of the first Phoenician colonies and settlements were on Cyprus and then Crete, Greece, then on to Sicily, Sardinia, the Balearic Islands and on to Gadir. The return route crossed the north coast of Africa and to Utica, Carthage, the cities of the 'emporia' (in Libya today), the Nile Delta and back to the east coast cities of the Mediterranean. Spain, Portugal, Italy, Malta, Greece, Cyprus, Turkey, Morocco, Algeria, Tunisia, Libya, Egypt, Israel, Palestine and Lebanon all have sites with Phoenician origins. Phoenician cities are often still cities today: they chose the locations for them so well that across the Mediterranean there are thriving modern cities from Beirut to Palermo and Cádiz that rest on their Phoenician foundations.

The Phoenicians' reputation as traders and merchants stuck with them across the centuries, and ancient sources often comment on their connections to wealth, and gold and silver. Along with these come insinuations and claims of greed and corruption and exploitation. An ancient author named Diodorus Siculus, who wrote in the first century BCE, provides a story of how the Phoenicians came to acquire such great wealth through exploitation of less technologically advanced cultures. Diodorus claims that the Phoenicians would use their sophisticated knowledge of metals and trick the indigenous peoples into exchanges: 'they purchased silver in exchange for other wares of little, if any, worth.' Diodorus writes that this was the reason why the Phoenician peoples became so wealthy. They transported the silver to Greece and Asia and 'acquired great wealth'.[21]

This age-old tale of colonial exploitation captures how the Phoenicians were perceived by much later writers. Diodorus' story goes even further and emphasises the idea of extreme wealth when he explains that 'so far indeed did the merchants go in their greed that, in case their boats were fully laden and there still remained a great amount of silver, they would hammer the lead off the anchors and have the silver perform the service of the lead.' The image of silver-hewn anchors stuck, and Diodorus' story emphasises so many of the classic Phoenician/Carthaginian stereotypes told by their later enemies. These stereotypes of greed and dishonesty occur again and again in the Greek and Roman sources in discussions of Carthage.

The Mediterranean in the tenth to seventh century BCE often gets explained by scholars using modern terminology like sea commerce, cabotage or maritime trade, and this presents a false picture of a world that is structured by rules and organised inter-state bodies and national governments. Much of what was going on was much more free form, involving individual ships crews heading out to sea to try their luck, and underlying many of the descriptions is the act of what we now call piracy. The early Greek texts often called the Phoenicians pirates, and it seems likely that if we had similar texts to describe the Phoenician view of the Greeks, they too would be called pirates, symbolised by the Greek god Zeus in the form of a bull carrying off Europa, daughter of the Phoenician king Phoenix, to Crete. Zeus acting for his own pleasure underlies the evolutionary tales of small groups raiding foreign shores, carrying off women. This is embodied in the great Homeric epic of the *Odyssey*, and many would argue that Odysseus was the greatest pirate of them all. The story reflects much of what was going on across the Mediterranean: men in ships sailing off for adventures and explorations. So, when we read about the foundation of cities and movement of peoples across these seas it is important to understand that the Mediterranean societies of the ancient world we often think of – Carthage, Rome and Greek city-states especially – are being formed in this period, and their DNA is deeply embedded in an identity that combined maritime expansion, myth, legend, piracy, trade and violence.

At this critical moment in the Mediterranean, the Phoenicians' contact with Greek-speaking peoples creates a spark of cultural fusion we can still see evidence of today. The first place of cultural exchange between Greeks and Phoenicians was undoubtably on Cyprus and there is evidence of this at the site of Kition (see page 10). Geographically, Cyprus was a natural place of dialogue between the Greeks and Phoenicians and is a site of fundamental importance. As we have already seen, at Kition was a renowned temple set up for the worship of a goddess. We refer to her as Astarte, a near eastern deity, who became identified with a local goddess by Phoenician speakers on Cyprus. Over time, the deity worshipped transformed into the Greek goddess of love, Aphrodite. We saw that in one of Dido's myths, the young women from the temple of Astarte/Aphrodite on Cyprus become wives for the new city to be found in Africa by the Tyrian queen.

The love goddess Aphrodite (the Roman Venus) was said by the Greeks to have come from the east, as set out in poetry in the origin myths of Hesiod written down in the eighth century BCE.

> She came to sea-bound Cyprus, and came forth an awful and lovely goddess, and grass grew up about her beneath her shapely feet. She who gods and men call Aphrodite. (Hesiod 194–5)

This is a vision that still permeates our conceptualisation of the goddess, with the many representations of Botticelli's Venus surfing on a shell towards the shore (see Fig. 3 in plate section). So, Astarte was an eastern goddess whose transformation into a Greek deity, worshipped as a fertility and sex goddess, gives us a taste of the kind of cultural transformations that were ongoing over the early Iron Age. And even further west, on Sicily, there was a place where Phoenicians and Greeks and indigenous Sicilians interacted and worshipped the goddess at the hilltop site of Eryx (Erice today) on the far west coast. This too would become a place of contention between Carthage and Rome in their later wars.

It was probably on Cyprus that the Greeks adopted the Phoenician alphabet, and there is evidence of this by the eighth century BCE in both Greece and beyond. The connection between the Phoenician cities and alphabetic writing is embodied by the fact that the name of the Phoenician city-state Byblos becomes the word for book in Greek and Latin. In Greek mythology, Cadmus, mythical founder of Thebes and patriarch of the family that gave us the tragic stories of the Oedipus cycle, brought, in the words of Herodotus, 'letters to the Greeks'.[22] The heroic prince Cadmus was known to be a native of the Phoenician city of Sidon.

There is evidence for the transformation from the Phoenician to the Greek alphabet found even further west, in the form of a famous, tatty-looking cup from Pithekoussai (modern-day Ischia, off the coast of Naples). As the first Greek colony in the western Mediterranean, Pithekoussai was a place where cultures mixed and merged during the eighth century BCE. Researchers have found pottery showing Greek geometric forms, along with Levantine 'Phoenician' amphorae and central Italian luxury items. But there is also a small, unique ceramic cup that was discovered in a simple cremation grave of a young child, a ten-year-old boy, and which preserves just a few lines of poetry scratched on its side. It is called Nestor's cup, from these lines that read: 'I am Nestor's cup, good to drink from. Whoever drinks this cup empty, straightaway desire for beautiful-crowned Aphrodite will seize him'. This is thought to be a direct reference to a story told in the *Iliad*, which would have circulated around the Mediterranean as an oral epic, sung by travelling bards and entertainers who plied the shores, following those who settled in the coastal areas. The inscription on the cup is both poignant and self-effacing, in that this little ceramic cup from the grave of a young boy references the heroic Nestor's golden urn, which was so heavy only a strong warrior could lift it. Even more incredible is that the words are written on the cup in the nascent Greek alphabet, which was, at this early date, still being written from right to left like the Phoenician.[23] Here is a captured moment of cultural fusion (see Fig. 4).

In these formative years, we have a Phoenician alphabet being transformed into a Greek one and eastern deities adopted into the pantheon of the Greek world. Just these few examples, stories and myths from the early Iron Age and the archaic western Mediterranean world hint at the vibrant environment of trade, exchange and exploration that was going on. The Phoenicians were vitally

Fig. 4 Nestor's cup (c. 750–700 BCE) at the Museo Archeologico di Pithecusae

important players in connecting cultures and carrying ideas across this landscape.

So, beyond the myths and stories, these are all the facts that underlie the foundation of the city of Carthage in the ninth century BCE. There is little specific detail from this proto-historic period; during the first three centuries of its existence Carthage barely registers in deep legend. But these stories of early Phoenicians and their interactions across the vast reaches of the Mediterranean nevertheless contain the origins of the city and seeds of its people and its power. Over the next few centuries, we know very little about what happened at Carthage, much less who succeeded Dido and how the city was governed, how many people lived there or what they thought of themselves. This is true not just of Carthage but of the whole Mediterranean; most of what we know from these formative centuries is steeped in the myths and creation stories of Greeks and Romans written down hundreds of years after the events. We will have to wait until the sixth century BCE before we can differentiate between Carthaginians and Phoenicians and can begin to say who her people – the first real Carthaginians – truly were. To fill in the gaps, I think that looking more carefully at archaeology will help to give us a tangible idea about what was happening in Carthage, about who lived there and what they might have believed and valued. This kind of information, while not necessarily tied directly to a historical figure, can enrich the story with ideas of people who lived and breathed in the city, and the houses they lived in, their contacts and trade, their career options and religious beliefs and hopes for the afterlife. It is archaeology that helps us to link the mythical beginnings with the rise of the city that would become the great power of Carthage.

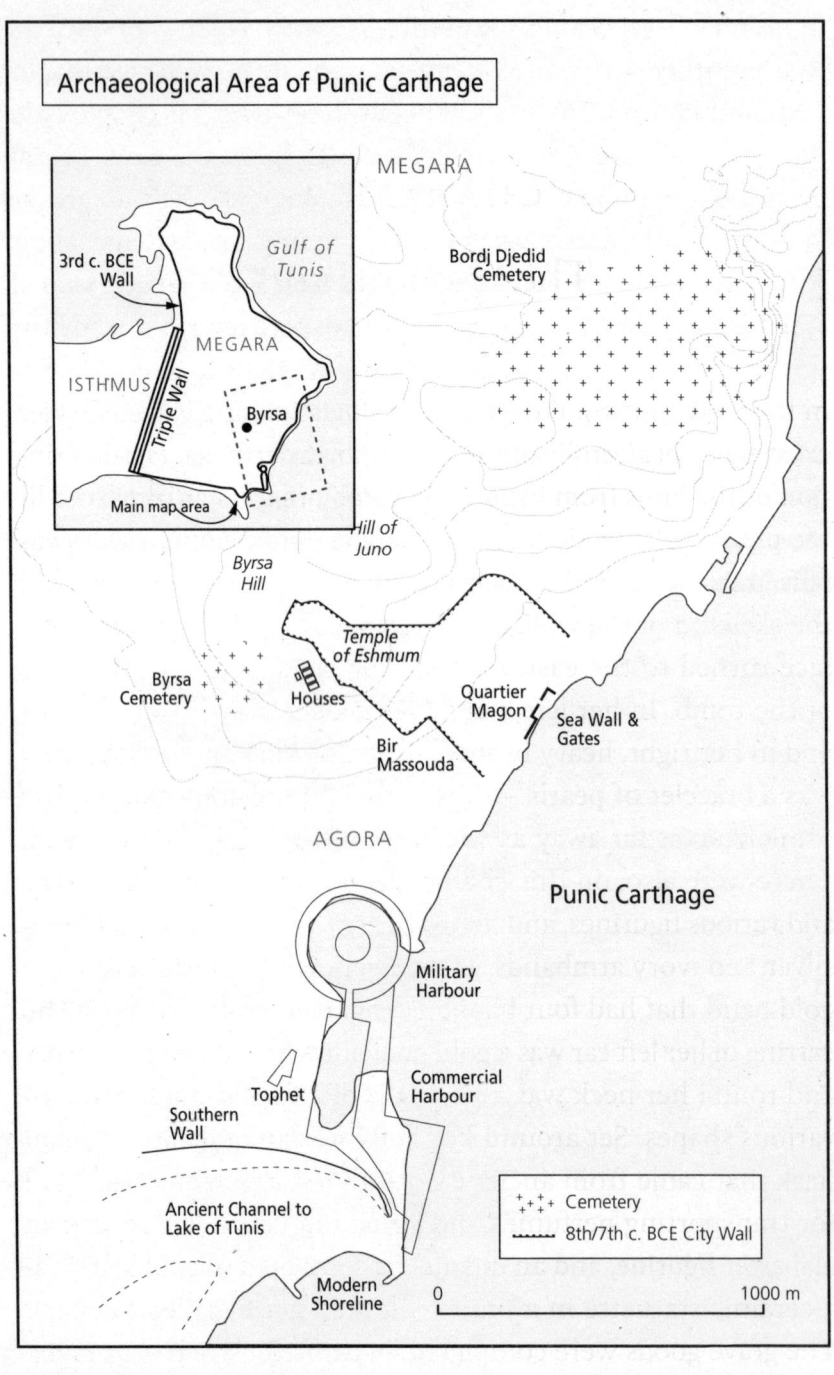

Archaeological Area of Punic Carthage

3rd c. BCE Wall

Gulf of Tunis

MEGARA

ISTHMUS

Triple Wall

Byrsa

Main map area

MEGARA

Bordj Djedid Cemetery

Hill of Juno

Byrsa Hill

Temple of Eshmum

Byrsa Cemetery

Houses

Quartier Magon

Sea Wall & Gates

Bir Massouda

AGORA

Punic Carthage

Military Harbour

Commercial Harbour

Tophet

Southern Wall

Ancient Channel to Lake of Tunis

Modern Shoreline

Cemetery

8th/7th c. BCE City Wall

0   1000 m

CHAPTER 2

The Sign of Tanit

In the early 1900s, a French archaeologist named Paul Gauckler excavated a beautifully preserved tomb at Carthage. His description of the finds from inside that tomb presents an almost still-life picture of the identity of a Carthaginian woman who was buried in the seventh or sixth century BCE. Gauckler describes the skeleton of the woman stretched out on her back with her face turned to the east, towards the rising sun and the door of the tomb. In her left hand she holds a large bronze mirror and in her right, heavy bronze cymbals. Worn on her left wrist was a bracelet of pearls – those rare and precious objects that came from as far away as the Persian Gulf and Indian Ocean. There were also, on this charm-like bracelet, Egyptian scarabs and various figurines, and her right arm was encircled by several silver and ivory armbands. Her fingers wore silver rings and a gold band that had four baboons engraved on the setting. The earring in her left ear was a gold pendant with a tau-shaped cross and round her neck was a necklace of 40 solid-gold pieces of various shapes. Set around her body was an aryballos, a small flask that came from ancient Corinth in Greece and was used for transporting perfumes and ritual unguents. There was an alabaster figurine, and an enamel flask covered in gold leaf with a ceramic statuette in a multi-coloured glaze (called faience). The grave goods were completed by painted ostrich eggs and a lamp, along with other pottery.[1] This chamber tomb of a Carthaginian woman and the finds in it tell us that she was of the elite, wealthy enough to have gathered about her many varied objects of luxury from far-off lands. Gauckler thought she might have been a priestess. We can interpret these funerary goods as messages about what was cherished by the person buried inside, and about deities worshipped by the dead; they convey hints of beliefs in an afterlife.

The most significant aspects of any ancient culture rests in their religious beliefs – they tell us what people thought about their world, their city, the lives they lived, their families and the environment. Our interpretation of the beliefs of the Carthaginians often rests on the Roman and Greek conceptions of their culture as different – they were 'not like us'. The reality was not so simple; the Carthaginians had so much in common with different groups of people in the wider Mediterranean world. The pantheon of Carthage included myriad gods with a hierarchy that saw the Lord, Ba'al Hammon and his consort the Lady, Tanit at the top alongside Reshef (a god of war). These big three were deities who functioned at a state, or governmental, level; they were evoked and connected to Carthage as political and military entities. Also important were their civic and community functions too – the success and wellbeing of the city. At a site southwest of Carthage, called Dougga, a surviving temple to Ba'al Hammon eventually became equated with the Roman god Saturn. While Tanit is mentioned briefly in the old Phoenician world as an aspect of the goddess Astarte, she then takes on her own persona in Carthage, an old-world deity transformed in the new environment of the colonies through their local experiences. One of the most recognisable symbols of Carthage, found on early mosaic floors, jewellery and funerary stelae (commemorative stones including tombstones), is a triangular shape with a horizontal bar at the top and a circular form above. Looking much like a stick figure and similar to the better-known Egyptian ankh, which symbolises life, the Carthaginian symbol is known as the 'sign of Tanit' (see Fig. 5 in plate section).[2]

On the next rung down in the pantheon of Carthage were three gods, two of whose names are by now familiar: Astarte, Melqart and Eshmun. The significance of these three varied over time but their association seems to be to individuals rather than the city-state itself so we might assume that these deities were more linked to the personal aspects of religious belief. Although Eshmun was a civic god, he also had healing attributes, and the fertility goddess Astarte and the colonial god Melqart both played an important part in the beliefs of individual citizens who considered them as patrons and protectors. In the third century BCE, when Carthaginian history becomes clearer, the role of Melqart as the patron god of Hamilcar and Hannibal Barca was emphasised; these famous Carthaginian men personally connected their military exploits and adventures to those of the deity Melqart, as we will explore in Chapters 8 and 9.

At Carthage, gods and goddesses from the wider Mediterranean world were also formally adopted into the cults of the city. We see this in other cultures across the Mediterranean where worship was transported into a place and the veneration of new deities came into the religious practices of the local population. This could happen through preferences and personal beliefs or more formally through state intervention. Late in the fourth century BCE, for instance, when a Carthaginian general was laying siege to the city of Syracuse on Sicily, his army sacked a temple to the goddesses Demeter and Kore outside the city walls. This was sacrilege and the magistrates of the city of Carthage, to try to make up for it, officially adopted the cult of Demeter and Kore and installed it in the city. There is even a passage from the

Roman historian Diodorus Siculus that describes the event in detail:

> They [the magistrates of Carthage] unanimously decided to appease the offended gods by all possible means. They had neglected to honour Kore and Demeter in their ceremonies, so they selected their most esteemed citizens as priests for these goddesses and with great solemnity, they consecrated statues of Kore and Demeter and performed rituals in accordance with Greek customs. Additionally, they appointed distinguished Greek residents to serve the goddesses. (14.77.4–5)

Demeter and Kore were the goddesses of fertility and grain, and they would have been especially relevant in times of famine and war. The presence of Greek residents in Carthage mentioned by Diodorus adds another layer of multiculturalism to a city already comprised of Numidians and Phoenician speakers from the eastern Mediterranean as well as other North Africans, Iberians and Sicilians.

We know from inscriptions hung on the walls of temples at Carthage that citizens organised sacrifices in the city. These inscriptions were detailed instructions, and included specifics about how the Carthaginians arranged their religious dedications in the city. These public documents outlined who was owed what by whom and how the offerings and sacrifices were to be accounted for. One very specific inscription described its origins as being from the Temple of Ba'al Ṣaphon. The word 'Ba'al' here is used as a title to mean 'the lord'; Ṣaphon was a deity worshipped at Carthage whose function was possibly related to aspects of the great storm god.[3] The inscription included a list of instructions on how someone might make an offering to the god. The priests who worked in ancient temples across the Mediterranean were both religious figures and community butchers, expert at killing and carving, dividing up the animals that were offered by individuals as sacrifices. These priests would be paid for their services, and at the temple of Ba'al Ṣaphon there was a 'tariff of fee which [the 30 men in charge of fees] set up'. These '30 men' were obviously citizens whose job was to regulate sacrifice, and the inscription was carefully dated to the rule of a specific magistrate whose name was recorded as 'Ḥilleṣba'al the sufet, son of Bodtinnit son of Bodesmun' and their colleagues.[4]

The inscription includes lists of the types of sacrifices made, the animals involved and the prices charged. A person could choose an ox, deer or calf, and the tariff amounts were given in silver shekels – for the Carthaginians used the Tyrian shekel as their main currency standard. Rams and goats, lambs and kids and birds were also listed and given a value. Mixed flour and oil or milk could be offered to the deity as well, at much less expense, and provision was made for those who could not afford to dedicate an animal and pay a priest with the line that reads 'for each sacrifice which a person poor in cattle or in birds sacrifices the priests shall not receive [a thing]'.

The meat of the sacrifices would most likely have been shared out with the community after the priests who performed the rituals took their share for the gods. Room for abuse of the system was obviously a problem, as a line was included in the inscription that warned 'any priest who takes a fee against what is set in this tablet shall be fined.' Both individuals or groups could make an offering if they followed the rules, so that 'any association, any clan, any fellow-drinkers association in honour of a god, and any men who sacrifice . . . these men [shall pay] a fee for each sacrifice according to what is set in the document.'[5] The community and animal sacrifices were central to communal festivals, consumption of meat and the sharing of the wealth of the larger population, and at Carthage, like across the Mediterranean, this was regulated. Carthaginians belonged to associations bonded by family traditions and occupations that would offer community appeasement of the gods.

At one of the oldest and most controversial religious sites of ancient Carthage, often called the Tophet, there are thousands of small stone stelae, some of which were inscribed with the words 'because he/she heard our voice'. The stelae were deposited atop ceramic urns that contained the cremated remains of very young children, infants, neo-nates and some animals. All these are crammed together into a space in Carthage that spans the whole history of the city from its earliest foundations through to the end of its existence. These urns are the most controversial religious offering from Carthage that we know about. From the moment this place was discovered just over a century ago in 1921, there has been a storm of debate over its meaning. What was this place? Was it really the spot that some Greek and Latin authors wrote about where the barbaric Carthaginians sacrificed their children to the gods? Or was this site a place they used to revere the children lost naturally, reflecting the high infant mortality rates of the ancient world? There are no unequivocal answers to these questions, but there is so much more information about this incredible place and what it may have meant to the early citizens of Carthage that it is worth exploring how the site helps to shape what we know about the city and its citizens.

Today the area is called the precinct of Tanit, after the Lady Tanit, goddess and consort of – and sometimes on inscriptions referred to as the 'face of' – Ba'al. Sometimes it is simply referred to as the Tophet, which is a misleading name but the one that is the most well-known. The name Tophet comes from two passages in the Hebrew Bible and was used by the first Europeans who came to excavate at Carthage and who discovered the site. The word derives from a place found in the Hebrew Bible called *Tofet*, in the valley of Ben Hinnom in Jerusalem, where the Philistines were said to 'sacrifice their children through fire'.[6] The use of the Hebrew word was imposed by early European scholars, and the interpretation was also deeply influenced by a nineteenth-century French novelist, Gustave Flaubert, whose novel *Salammbô* imagined scenes of child sacrifice at Carthage. So, the 'Tophet' of *Salammbô* has no real relationship to the function or meaning of the place but I use it here because it is the conventional name.

The Tophet was an open-air sanctuary filled with deposited urns and stelae. The very earliest offerings were made by the first citizens of Carthage and are buried deep in the ground, 4 to 5 m below the surface. The first offerings are very simple: cremated remains placed in a small ceramic urn usually just 20 to 25cm tall, sometimes covered by a pile of small stones. Over time commemorations became more elaborate. As the citizens of Carthage became more prosperous, so too did the stones that mark the place of their offerings. Some of the cremated remains were found beside bits of jewellery or an amulet, and occasionally ceramic masks, shaped into grimacing facial expressions, were found among the stones. These are thought to have been used to ward off evil spirits (see Fig. 6).[7]

Some of the stone stelae are decorated, and others carry inscriptions that tell us that the deposit has been made in the fulfilment of a vow, because the deity had 'heard their voice'. This all matters because it tells us that citizens from all different parts of society deposited remains here – it was not just one ritual or type of deposit. Wealthy people could afford more elaborate materials or decorations, and could add in grave goods, while poorer families deposited very simple urns and stones.

Fig. 6 Ceramic mask from Carthage at the Bardo Museum

There is one stele in particular that tells us a visual story. It dates to the fourth century BCE and is a long narrow shape made of hard limestone, decorated with incised figures. The main scene shows a man dressed like a priest with a hat and robes who steps forward with his right hand raised. This arm gesture indicates prayer and is something seen on other artefacts and representations at Carthage and across the ancient Near East as well – it was a universal symbol. The left arm of the man encircles a small child, who is curled in the crook of his elbow. The child looks like it is sleeping, or perhaps is dead (see Fig. 7).[8] The stele is also decorated with various crescent shapes, and especially the crescent and disc combination that are believed to be symbols of the god Ba'al. This object was the first – and so far, only – one that seems to tell the story of the place, and its discovery was what first led excavators to the site where we find these remains.

How do we understand the people of Carthage through this space of religion and sacrifice? Who were the parents who dedicated their cherished children to the gods and deposited the bones of their newly born offspring into the earth, fulfilling a vow? We have

Fig. 7 Priest's stele

some of their names and know that they were not all one ethnic group but Carthaginians and Libyans and Greeks. The parents of ancient Carthage cared as much for their children as the Greeks and Romans of antiquity, and to sacrifice a child was beyond comprehension. Yet there were very high levels of infant mortality in the ancient Mediterranean – some estimates put it as high as 50 per cent – which means that viable children were even more precious then than they are today. So to dedicate a child for the wellbeing of the city and to ensure its flourishing was the greatest surrender of all. The precinct was a visible and obviously important part of the city, and somewhere that citizens, and those who were not from Carthage too, chose to set up votives and make offerings.

There are many theories about the significance of the Tophet. Some scholars suggest it was a ritualised means of population control. We know that in contemporary Roman and Greek societies, and all through the ancient world, children were exposed and left to the elements to die if they could not be cared for, or by those who wanted a boy rather than a girl, or because of disfigurement or disability. Some argue that at Carthage the ritual was perhaps more formalised. But this does not ring true, for the votive inscriptions tell us clearly that these are deposits made in the fulfilment of vows and prayers answered. The implications are that a family would have made their request of the gods before the child was born or perhaps even conceived, and the ritual sacrifice would have to be performed well after the promise had been made.

Very recent excavations of the site at Carthage have employed the most up-to-date techniques and analysis. They show us that the children were often only a few days old when cremated and that both male and female children were given as offerings. The substitution of animal bones in some cases also tells us that the ritual was not consistent; what it started as in the very first years of Carthage's existence and what it became were not necessarily the same.

The Tophet at Carthage is not the only one in the central Mediterranean. It is one of several similar sites that we know of that have been excavated. They exist on Sardinia and Malta, at Motya on Sicily and in other sites in North Africa too, such as Hadrumetum (modern Sousse). The presence of a Tophet in a city can perhaps tell us about direct connections and links between Carthage and its various satellite settlements. Perhaps it identifies the core of what was the Punic/west Phoenician world. The Tophet sites across this zone always contained a small chapel for the cult and a large number of pottery urns, with stelae, with or without inscriptions on them. Since they are essentially a Carthaginian phenomenon, there has been a lot of thought on whether it is possible to understand the site from a Carthaginian point of view. Is it possible to see these Tophets as they were and how they were used, rather than how they were received by ancient Romans and Greeks or even today? Human sacrifice was not unknown among the ancient Mediterranean cultures that rivalled Carthage. Evidence that it was carried out by Roman and Greek societies and others at various times exists, so it would have been much more normalised in the ancient world than we can perceive of in the modern.[9]

The Tophet is located within the walls of the ancient city, and this is relevant because in ancient cities cemeteries were almost always outside the walls for hygiene and health reasons. The location at the heart of the city is key to understanding the Tophet as fundamentally attached to the urban life of Carthage (see page 32). The place dates to the first establishment of the city when it was founded on the east, sea-facing, slope of the hill known as the Byrsa. The remnants of the early city are deeply buried metres below the surface – first, beneath centuries of thriving occupation, then the destruction and rebuilding of the city in the Roman period all the way to the current residential suburb of Tunis that occupies Carthage – so our knowledge is not complete. We know the apex of the city, the Byrsa, comprised the citadel and was the centre of government, law and state religious life. The rest of the urban centre spread out across four different zones. In the early city there were zones of habitation, an industrial area, a number of cemeteries where the very first occupants were buried and the Tophet, the most enduring religious site at the city.

In the last 40 years, parts of the earliest phases of the first city have been excavated, providing a much better understanding of how people lived and what their homes were like. The earliest habitation zone was on the east slope of the Byrsa hill, in a neighbourhood with well-built sea-facing structures made of rubble walls with floors of crushed limestone. The occupants in this archaic period lived in shared accommodation complexes made up of four rectangular buildings with a communal paved courtyard. It is likely that multiple, or extended, families lived together in a block. By the end of the eighth century, these communal dwellings show signs of reworking into single family homes, with four rooms made of simple mud-brick walls resting on a rubble foundation, and a private courtyard. There were sometimes three other spaces that were open towards the street that probably functioned as workshops and retail. People living and working in the same space was very common in pre-modern housing.

By the time Carthage reached the seventh century BCE, two centuries after its foundation, it had developed into a densely built city that covered about 60 hectares. Family homes had evolved into a more standardised pattern. These constructions are based on urban traditions from the eastern Mediterranean of a four-room house, and perhaps the new house styles came to Carthage with new populations from the cities of the Levant in this period. Carthaginians now lived in houses with three parallel rooms and a central corridor or lightwell with an oblique room lying in front. Archaeological remains show us that people were using more pottery from the home cities in the eastern Mediterranean. This could mean that there was greater contact between the two regions through formal trade and Carthage was producing more goods to export, bringing back oil, wine and other goods in ceramic vessels from the east. Or perhaps the harsh realities of life in the eastern Mediterranean in these years was the reason. For Tyre, these were difficult years. The city was regularly under siege by larger forces such as the Neo-Assyrians and Babylonians, right through the seventh and sixth centuries, and political turmoil in the mother city may well have led to increased immigration to Carthage.

At the same time, multistorey buildings appear, and these structures reflect a sturdier kind of construction process and one that would become famous across the Mediterranean. The masonry technique that allowed multistorey construction was admired by the later Romans, and they called it 'African style' (Latin *opus africanum*). It was put together with vertical ashlar blocks set at regular intervals with the area in between filled with rubble or mud brick (Fig. 8). The African style of building was a very stable construction method and was innovative as it allowed for walls that could bear a substantial load, and for the buildings to be built higher. Like today, an urban environment growing upwards to accommodate an increasing population usually means there are issues around space. Carthage's growth was constrained by geographical factors: the sea lay to the east, cemeteries to the north and southwest, and to the south, the Tophet. The result was that for the first few centuries Carthage existed within these boundaries but eventually, by about the end of the sixth or the early fifth century BCE, the city grew outside of the original spatial constraints.

Success for the population at Carthage was largely dependent on the goodwill of the city's neighbours for the first few centuries of its existence. In the very early years, most of what was being consumed was grown locally, and only in rare instances

Fig. 8 Schematic of African-style masonry

do imported goods show up in the archaeological record. This means that the Carthaginians lived and thrived in conjunction with the indigenous peoples on whose land they had founded their city. They must have relied on close familial contacts, inter-marriage and connected families. This was how the Carthaginians developed as a people, mixing populations and accepting new groups of people who moved there and brought new ideas, gods and traditions. The ancient sources identified the population who lived outside the city, from this mixed environment, as Libyphoenicians. These were the families who, for generations, farmed and fought for Carthage through its history, and played a crucial part in its survival and eventual success.

There is now good evidence that the early settlers at Carthage brought advanced technological processes with them to the city as well. These technologies continued to develop in the industrial zones of the city.[10] At the foot of the Byrsa hill from the eighth to the fifth century BCE there were blacksmiths working in forges that produced metals for the people of Carthage and for export as well. There is evidence of iron production and, from the seventh century BCE, crucible steel being fabricated in these locations. Archaeometallurgical analysis of the forge material found at Carthage implies that blacksmiths were producing metal objects not only for local consumption. There was enough surplus material that could be used to trade and build networks both in Africa and across the Mediterranean. Once there is evidence of surplus goods to trade, and tools and technologies allowing for building expansion along with aiding in efficient agricultural production and advanced weapons of war, the city can be seen to be thriving. These features are all present at Carthage and by the fifth century BCE the early forges had to be moved further from the centre of the city as urban expansion took place.

Tying the tangible material of Carthage with the historical

46

narratives of the Mediterranean allows us to add another layer to life in the city. A place so well-connected east and west meant that its location alone led to it being impacted by events in the wider Mediterranean. In the sixth century BCE, upheaval in the east brought change to the west. From the time the Achaemenid Persians took over Mesopotamia and the coastal regions of the eastern Mediterranean (539 BCE), Tyre and the other Phoenician city-states were no longer independent, self-governing cities but part of a much larger empire. The impact on Carthage, one of Tyre's chief colonies, must have been significant. Here again we can imagine an influx of refugees coming west to settle, bringing new ideas and people into the city. The power shift would also have served as a link, joining Carthage through Tyre to a much wider world. The Achaemenids created the world's first global empire, with peoples from across the Middle East, Eurasia and the Arabian peninsula all ruled by one power. This is a period that correlates to fundamental change at Carthage, where a ruling monarchy was replaced by a republic-style oligarchy. The sixth century BCE also presents us with the first actual Carthaginians in the historical record after Dido.

Malchus was the name of one early Carthaginian leader and his story was recalled by a much later Roman historian named Justin.[11] Malchus was described as a Carthaginian 'general' but his name itself is, in the Phoenician, *mlk*, meaning 'king'. Because of the generic nature of the name, he may have been a composite character, one based on many different individuals in a deeply remembered past of Carthage. There are similar figures in early Roman history like the Etruscan king Numa from this same period. The story is important because Malchus is our first historical Carthaginian after Dido and we find him at war in the central Mediterranean. The tale is sparse on specifics, contested in date and very odd in the telling, but I repeat it here because of its significance. Malchus was, at first, celebrated as victorious while campaigning with his army in Sicily, presumably against some of the Greek city-states there, before he was then defeated in a battle in Sardinia. Sardinian settlements by the Phoenicians thrived on the southern and western shores of the island where iron ore and other resources were valued. The indigenous Sardinians lived in many inland hilltop towns and were often in conflict with the coastal settlers. Because of his defeat in Sardinia, Malchus was exiled by the Carthaginians, but he then returned to Carthage and laid siege to the city.

Malchus was camped outside the city walls with his soldiers, who are described as his personal army rather than a military force of the state. As Malchus laid siege to Carthage, his son Carthalo appeared. The young man had been on a mission to Tyre where he had taken the tribute to the great temple of Melqart from the wars in Sicily. Carthalo continued with his religious duties despite the siege going on around him, and eventually returned to his father's side only after he was discharged from his official tasks as envoy. The Roman historian who narrates this story claims that Malchus was so outraged at his son that he crucified him, then and there, emphasising that he was still dressed in his priestly robes. This great sacrilege did not stop Malchus from taking Carthage by force and killing ten of the ruling senators. He then pardoned the rest of the citizens. Malchus was eventually defeated by another faction in the city and brought in front of the courts in Carthage. He was prosecuted for treason and for the murder of his son.

This curious vignette, staged both outside and inside the walls of Carthage, creates more questions than it answers. The bare bones of this tale imply a civil war at Carthage between different familial factions, or a usurpation of power in the city. The Roman retelling is certainly confused and muddled, but perhaps there was something important in the symbolism of the ruler and the sacrifice of his son. There is, in this story, the idea of military and religious powers of Carthage in conflict and the possibility of some kind of separation between the two strains of rule resulting from it. The tale also touches on the harsh treatment of failed generals and how intolerant the state of Carthage was to military defeat in the field. These themes will be repeated again and again in the long history of the city.

Malchus was referred to as a *sufet* and the plural of this word, *sufetes*, was the name for the leading magistrates in the administration of the city of Carthage. There were two annually elected *sufetes*, and their rule began an era of marking time in the city. There is a votive inscription from Carthage dated from the late sixth century BCE that reads 'in the twentieth year of the rule of the *sufetes* in Carthage'.[12] The story of Malchus and this written inscription showcase how a transition at Carthage from monarchy to oligarchy may have taken place. These magistrates held the power of a king, but for a limited time. There seem to have been magistrates with this title in Tyre, too. The word *sufet* is linked to the Hebrew term *shophetim*, with the underlying idea of a magistrate with judicial powers, a judge. The role then, by the historical period at Carthage, was that of head of the governing body of the state, held by two magistrates who were chosen from a council of aristocratic elites that functioned as a kind of senate. By the end of the sixth century the oligarchic government that ruled Carthage through the rest of its existence seems to have been, more or less, in place.[13] The successors to Malchus were called the Magonids, a powerful elite family that would dominate Carthaginian magistracies and military command for the next century but of whom little is known.[14]

The citizens of Carthage then lived in multistorey houses, worked the jobs associated with urban life, practised medicine, forged iron and steel, cultivated crops and piloted boats in the ports. They were parents, farmers and scholars, legal experts and musicians, generals, admirals, priests and priestesses. It was these people who made Carthage. People who were less than citizens must have lived and worked in the city too. We know very little about the way Carthaginian society dealt with the unfree or enslaved. We assume, because the enslaved were a key part of all contemporary ancient societies across the Mediterranean, that people with less status worked in many industries in Carthage, but they are largely invisible in the recorded history and the archaeology.

The Greek philosopher Aristotle, when he analysed the Carthaginian constitution in his *Politics*, described the rules of employment of the people of Carthage. Aristotle mentioned the role of pilots in the ports, of sitting magistrates in the markets, of Carthaginian ideas around social drinking, and social interactions and reproduction. At Carthage, drinking alcohol was banned if you were working on pilot boats in the ports, if you were sitting as a judge and if you were trying to conceive a child – all sensible ideas to the modern mind. The Carthaginians seemed to like to drink good wine. They produced it, exported and imported many vintages from the eastern Mediterranean as well. Especially popular was wine from the island of Rhodes, as is evidenced from the presence of a large number of imported Rhodian amphorae.

There was rarely any separation between religious observance and civic government in the cities of the ancient Mediterranean. Gods, civic identities and warfare were all mixed together into the personality of a place, its people, government and prosperity. In the second book of Aristotle's *Politics* he discusses 'other' forms of government outside of those of the Greek city-states. Aristotle was duly impressed with how things were run at Carthage in his day (fourth century BCE), noting that the Carthaginians 'are also considered to have an excellent form of government'.[15] This one mention is the only historical source that directly rates the government of Carthage as an overall system, but we can add many other fragments from later Greek and Roman historians too that contain offhand comments about the state and its function. These come with their own set of problems, the most important of which, as one scholar of Carthage noted, is that these sources, coming later and also from outside of Carthaginian society, have a diminishing effect on our understanding. They reduce the system of Carthage into their own frame of reference, and therefore make comprehending it more remote.[16]

The organisation at Carthage that functioned as the seat of power for the elite oligarchy was called the '*drm* (adirim) and functioned like a senate. These men (as far as we know there were no women) met at the Temple of Eshmun, which sat on the apex of the city at the Byrsa hill. The sacred meeting place was used for the important occasions that drew the men of the city-state together to discuss policy, wage war and make treaties. This Eshmun is as a city god of Near Eastern origin and he is often equated to the Greek healing god and son of Apollo, Asclepius. Other Carthaginian-founded cities across the western Mediterranean may have had the same set-up, and there is good evidence that one of these places, Cartagena (New Carthage) in the Iberian Peninsula, was crowned with a temple to Eshmun, as described by an eyewitness account of the Greek historian Polybius. It may be that colonial foundations often assumed a standardised urban structure that reflected back to Carthage as a kind of template.[17]

The underlying support for the oligarchy at Carthage came from its assembly of the citizens, called '*m* (pronounced like ham). The people's assembly is referred to by Greek and Roman writers who note that, by the third century BCE and the Punic Wars,

Carthage had become more democratic, with the 'people' having too much say in matters of state (ancient writers such as Polybius were no great fans of democracy). It is unclear how one became a member of the citizens' assembly and what made someone a citizen of Carthage. Birthright for certain, but it doesn't seem to have been necessary for both parents to be citizens. For example, two military commanders whose fathers were from Syracuse on Sicily and whose mothers were from Carthage were Carthaginian citizens who fought with Hannibal in Italy. This implies that a maternal link to citizenship may have been important, or perhaps having just one Carthaginian parent was enough. The citizens' assembly may have voted in neighbourhoods, organised by sectors of the city. This is an assumption made from an inscription from the city of Dougga, to the southwest of Carthage, where voting groups seem to have been based around the different gates of the city.

In the Carthaginian state the equivalent to a general or proconsul was called *rb mhnt* (rab mahanet), which literally translates as the chief/head of the camp. The position was considered among the top in the state, as Aristotle mentions, 'for the Carthaginians choose their magistrates, and particularly the highest of them – their kings [*sufetes*] and generals – with an eye both to merit and to wealth.' Here we can see that military duties were separated from the civic magistracies, which is unlike Rome where military leadership was predicated on holding a civil magistracy. The early evidence we have seen suggests the ruling magistrate may well have been in charge of the army, like Malchus. A separation seems to have developed over time and the generals of Carthage may have been chosen from the governing landowning elite, although we have evidence that they could have come from farther afield as well. A military commander could go into the civic magistracies but did not necessarily evolve out of them.

A Carthaginian general did, however, exercise real autonomy while on campaign. The Carthaginian commander in the field oversaw negotiating treaties, making decisions on settlements, judicial matters in camp and minting coinage. They were also held personally responsible for the success or failure of a campaign and severe punishment for failure was inflicted. Sometimes, like Malchus, they were exiled and in several instances in the First Punic War (264–241 BCE) generals deemed to have been too easily defeated were crucified – without trial. Others were brought in front of a 'council of 104' and tried, and if convicted the punishment could be crucifixion or exile. There does not seem to have been a fixed term for a commander, but the position was for the length of the war he fought. The appointment to general was a whole project at which the commander either succeeded or failed.

Over the ninth to sixth centuries BCE, the city grew from a small colonial outpost to become a central power in the western Mediterranean. Locally made pottery, containers to hold olive oil and dry goods from neighbourhoods in and around Carthage, point to the growth of the agricultural industry and domestic food production in the fertile plains. From these pottery fragments we learn that, quite early on in Carthage's history, Carthaginians became agriculturally self-sufficient. These details highlight the vital fertility of the lands that surrounded the city of Carthage, and its agricultural self-sufficiency and then surplus, along with commerce and communication, all led to the growing success of the city.[18]

As Carthage materialises as a more perceivable entity in the historical record, we see its government was admired across the Mediterranean and the city was considered to be prosperous. It was not a smooth trajectory but one of stops and starts. The legends of Dido and the early Phoenicians had shifted to the reality of a growing city that began to control much of the trade and commerce across the central Mediterranean zone. By the fifth century BCE there was a specific Carthaginian identity, with Carthaginians living along the North African coast; a city-state with its own republican-style government moulded from a mix of influences that, along with the city's prime location, led to the flowering of a new civilisation in the west. A tangible history of Carthage begins in these years – we hear of Carthage founding its own colony on the island of Ibiza (c. 564 BCE) and of Carthaginian fleets involved in major sea battles. As the western Mediterranean becomes increasingly more crowded and competitive, Carthage will reach out to its neighbours in friendship, in alliance and in conflict.

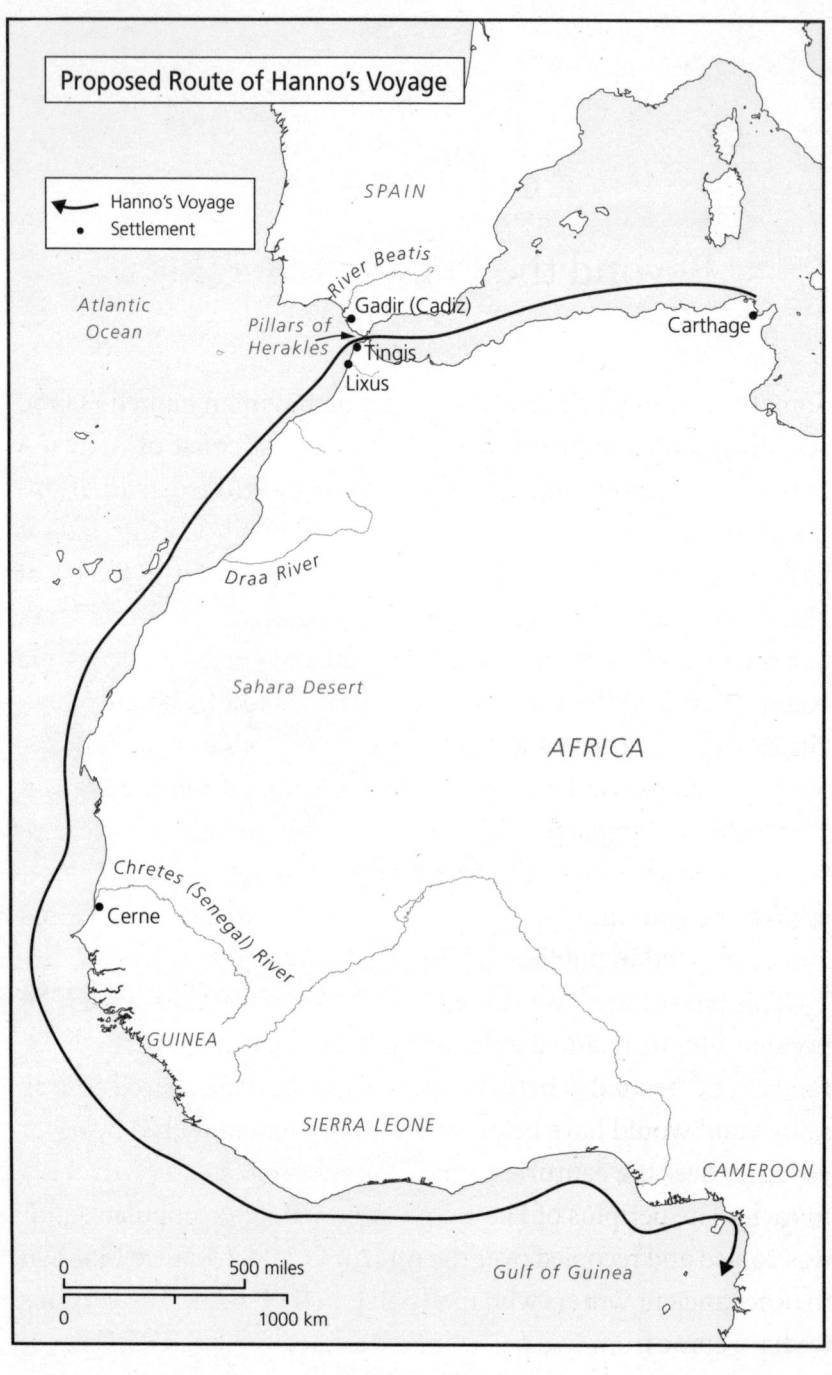

Proposed Route of Hanno's Voyage

→ Hanno's Voyage
• Settlement

SPAIN

*Atlantic
Ocean*

River Beatis

Gadir (Cadiz)

*Pillars of
Herakles*

Tingis

Lixus

Carthage

Draa River

Sahara Desert

AFRICA

Chretes (Senegal) River

• Cerne

GUINEA

SIERRA LEONE

CAMEROON

Gulf of Guinea

0   500 miles

0   1000 km

CHAPTER 3

Beyond the Pillars of Herakles

Sometime in the fifth century BCE a Carthaginian named Hanno set off on an expedition to explore the west coast of Africa. A partially preserved logbook of this journey still exists in an 18-line document called the 'Navigation of Hanno, a Carthaginian nobleman, along the coasts of Africa beyond the Pillars of Herakles'. The author may have been the ship's captain Hanno, but the tale is written as a third-person account, so some people believe that a scribe recorded what happened on the journey – either way it is an eyewitness account.[1] The original document, we believe, was written down and fixed to a temple wall in Carthage not long after the voyage took place. Hanno's successful return to the city would have been commemorated with offerings to the gods and an official version of the journey recounted and celebrated in public.

This type of work was called a *periplus* and was both a genre of popular literature and a guide for sailors in the ancient Mediterranean and beyond. These navigation guides were shared among sailors and would have been copied, translated and used by other voyagers over the centuries. That Hanno's story survives at all is a miracle. The periplus of Hanno must have been so popular that it was copied and recopied over the millennia, and it was well-known to other ancient writers who mention it in their texts. The versions we have come from two partial manuscripts, written in Greek and dating back to the ninth and the eleventh centuries CE – so over a thousand years after the events they record. The Byzantine scribes who made these new copies are unknown, but the earliest version now rests in Heidelberg University and the other is divided into two parts with one in the British Museum and the other in the Bibliothèque nationale in Paris.[2]

The periplus of Hanno is an adventure story, an ethnographic exploration based on this expedition sent out from Carthage. The intention of the voyage seems to have been to explore and settle along the coast of Africa, and the leader, Hanno, is referred to as a *sufet*, a magistrate of the city. Hanno and his fleet sail west along the south shore of the Mediterranean and, exiting the Pillars of Herakles, they turn south, travelling along the shore, stopping to trade and interact, to settle and to learn. The story is full of the crew's encounters with rivers full of crocodiles and hippopotami, wild indigenous peoples and a landscape of active volcanoes, good forests and a wealth of resources. Studying the surviving manuscript is like following written directions, a pathway across the seas taken by the ship, noting each place they pulled into harbour or anchored off the shore. It often includes place names we no longer understand. The story of Hanno is remarkable because it tells us that at the same time as Carthage was establishing its city and economy in the central Mediterranean, its citizens were setting out on ships to explore the world around them, to colonise, to exploit and to understandthe people and the lands beyond their borders.[3]

Before the Carthaginians launched ships to investigate the wider world, their Phoenician forebears had been celebrated for navigation skills and seamanship, and Hanno was not the first to explore the coastal regions of Africa beyond the Mediterranean. While Hanno's tale is unique as the only surviving personal account that claims to have been written originally by a Carthaginian, a story from the sixth century BCE pre-dates it. The earlier tale, told by the Greek historian Herodotus, recounts a Phoenician ship that circumnavigated Africa on an expedition funded by the Egyptian pharaoh Necho II of the 26th dynasty (r. 610–595 BCE). Necho belonged to the last native dynasty to rule Egypt, which ended with the Achaemenid Persian conquest in 525 BCE, and this tale of exploration was one of his crowning glories. Herodotus explains that

> Libya's geography [Africa is called Libya here] is surrounded by the sea on all sides except where it meets Asia. A detail initially observed and communicated by the Egyptian king Necho. After completing the construction of a canal linking the Nile to the Red Sea, he dispatched Phoenician sailors along it, with instructions to keep going until the journey passed through the Pillars of Heracles on their return voyage and reached the northern sea and eventually Egypt.[4]

Herodotus' account is sketchy on the details but describes how the voyage took place with the ship sailing along the east coast of Africa, around the south and back up the west. This was slow going, and each autumn that the ships were at sea the expedition would put into a harbour, plant seeds to grow a harvest and then take their food and carry on. There were many sophisticated ancient societies along the east coast of Africa in this period, those that were linked across the Indian Ocean through trade.[5] The Phoenician ships had first passed through the canal heading into the Red Sea and then down the coast of Africa. What is curious about Herodotus is that he questioned the validity of his own tale – and ironically, buried in this assertion, is our confirmation of the journey. 'There they said (what some may believe, though I do not) that in sailing around Libya [Africa] they [the Phoenicians] had the sun on their right-hand side.' For the ships heading south of the equator and around the southern point of Africa, today called the Cape of Good Hope, would indeed have kept the sun on their right in the southern hemisphere. Herodotus did not know the world was round.[6]

The triumphant Phoenician ships returned to Egypt and their grateful pharaoh after three years of journeying. There are many questions about this voyage that we cannot answer, but the mystique and legends of the Phoenicians and their navigation skills remained celebrated by the later sources. Some modern scholars question the validity of the story because of the fact that later maps of the world, drawn by Roman geographers like Ptolemy in the second century CE, do not reflect the knowledge of this voyage or the understanding that Africa was surrounded by the sea and could be circumnavigated. A medieval map based on an ancient version by Ptolemy shows this most clearly: the landmass of Africa is drawn as limitless to the south.[7] The idea is that there is no way the Romans did not know what the Phoenicians did – which is a perfect example of the extreme Roman biases that still dominate so much of our thinking about the ancient world. This attitude belies what we understand about the connectivity that existed in the sixth to the fourth century BCE in the eastern Mediterranean, Middle East and western Asia. This was a period of great expansion when the Achaemenid Persians built the first global empire, one which joined together the Mediterranean, the Persian Gulf, Asia and the Indian Ocean by land and sea. The Phoenicians and their Carthaginian descendants were agents for change in this period. They linked the eastern Mediterranean with all its interdependent relationships to the west and extended this into the coastal regions of Africa. Knowledge and understanding of the Phoenicians at the height of their navigation skills, and the subsequent story of their cultures, scripts and stories, have been largely overlooked and forgotten in the centuries that followed on from their conquest.[8]

Narratives around ships, naval technologies and travel form the basis of much of what is understood about the Phoenicians and Carthaginians. Tall tales and facts mix, making the realities of the stories difficult to ascertain. The ancient Roman geographers and natural historians, whose work is the dominant narrative, wrote about their world through the optic of centre and periphery. The further one moved away from the centre (in this case the Mediterranean), the wilder and more outlandish things became as the landscapes and their peoples were imagined as monstrous and dangerous. We can also see this perspective in the story of Hanno. There is a stage-by-stage voyage down the west coast of Africa that may have gone as far as Senegal and possibly all the way to the modern Gulf of Guinea (see page 56). The text reads:

> The Carthaginians ordered Hanno to sail out of the Pillars of Heracles and found a number of Libyphoenician cities. He set sail with sixty fifty-oared ships, about thirty thousand men and women, food and other equipment.[9]

This was no minor expedition but one of real ambition, even when we consider the ancient tendency to exaggerate numbers. This was a big investment of thousands of people, finances and 60 vessels. These were families of Carthaginians and certainly other west Phoenicians, sent out to settle in new regions and establish new networks of contact. There is good evidence for settlements of Phoenician/Carthaginian origin dotted along the north coast of Africa, along the coastal regions of the Iberian Peninsula and around the tip of the continent into the Atlantic and down the western coast to Mauretania (Morocco) at least. Sequences of settlement and expansion had been the way the Mediterranean functioned all through these early centuries, when Phoenicians and Greeks (and later Romans) expanded, sent out surplus citizens, settled in new areas and won land through negotiation or warfare.

One of the possible reasons for Hanno's voyage, beyond just the expansion of settlements, is about resources, and especially access to gold. The Carthaginians traded across the Sahara with the indigenous people of the oases there, and one of the key commodities they traded for was gold. Carthaginians were aware that the source of this gold lay in the region of what is today called the Niger Delta, and that this could also be accessed down the west African coast, by sea. Their expedition may well have been an attempt to cut out the desert middlemen by establishing direct links themselves, travelling by sea and setting up a network of contacts and colonies to facilitate this trade. These are the timeless actions of colonialists, cutting out the middlemen and getting directly to the source of their interests. Ancient authors like Diodorus Siculus and Herodotus describe how the Carthaginians operated while on trading expeditions and the descriptions fit a well-known template of exploitation by a culture with technological superiority. Equally fascinating here is a curious silent trading between cultures who do not share a language, as Herodotus described:

> they [Carthaginians] come here and unload their cargo; then, having laid it out along the beach, they go back aboard their ships and light a smoking fire. The people of the country see the smoke, and, coming to the sea, they lay down gold to pay for the cargo, and then withdraw from the wares. Then the Carthaginians disembark and examine the gold; if it seems to them a fair price for their cargo, they take it and go away; but if not, they go back aboard and wait, and the people come back and add more gold until the sailors are satisfied.[10]

The periplus of Hanno provides a detailed description of the journey and especially the variety of exotic and unknown animals the ships encounter and men who can run faster than horses.

When the Carthaginians reached Mogador, an already established Phoenician colony near modern Essaouira in Morocco, they pressed on. Like a Carthaginian version of *National Geographic*, the story is part wonder and part commerce. Hanno describes how they made allies with new peoples and then 'reached the Lixos, a large river flowing from Libya. The Lixites, a nomadic tribe, were pasturing their cattle beside it.' The expedition stayed a while with the Lixites and new friends were made. The Lixites supplied the expedition with guides and interpreters to lead the ships further south. The location here is thought to be south of Agadir in modern Morocco, close to the kingdom of Tazzarult (possibly modern Tazeroualt), a region that once controlled caravan routes across the Sahara to Sudan and would certainly have been useful allies for the Carthaginians. The expedition moved further south, past the river referred to as Chretes and around the 'horn of the west'. They were met with hostility by stone-throwing locals and regions inhabited by 'Ethiopians', which is the generic Greek word for anyone with dark skin – the word means 'burned'. There were mountains covered in trees with a colourful and aromatic wood, and finally they reached a volcano that some believe to be Mt Cameroon. Hanno and his fellow sailors describe an encounter with what the manuscript calls 'gorillas'. The Carthaginians attempted to bring back specimens alive but failed to capture any. The sailors ended up killing two females of the species – the terrified females could not escape the Carthaginians while all the males had fled – and these were skinned and brought to Carthage as trophies. The skins were hung in the temple of Ba'al Hammon on the return of the voyagers.[11]

The voyage of Hanno was remembered as a great deed in other ancient sources too. It was a renowned tale and Pliny's *Natural History*, written centuries later (first century CE), briefly mentioned Hanno when he commented, 'while the power of

Carthage was at its height, Hanno published an account of a voyage which he made from Gades to the extremity of Arabia.' Pliny's claim is that Hanno circumnavigated the continent of Africa to return back to Carthage, travelling all the way to Arabia, but this does not reflect the existing text.[12] The extant periplus fits well into other stories that circulated that were part myth and part history, with the Greek legends of Perseus and the Gorgon or the Odyssey coming to mind, a hero on a quest underlying a people exploring their world, settling in new regions and encountering all sorts of wild animals and perceived monsters in what they could not understand. The realities of this trip may well have been conflated with other explorations of the ancient Mediterranean and beyond. It is difficult to know much more about it from a Carthaginian perspective, but the story helps us model how Carthage grew and expanded, explored and extended its reach, and shows us how the continent of Africa was a part of their growing world.[13]

And of course, as we've already established, ships were a crucial part of this, with Carthage inheriting a reputation for shipbuilding from their Phoenician founders. The very early decked warships of the Phoenicians visible in the Neo-Assyrian relief sculpture had given way to the famous trireme of the Greeks by the sixth century BCE. Building on this, Carthage, according to Aristotle, created a quadrireme, a ship with two banks of oars and two rowers per oar (see Fig. 9). In this age of technological innovation, Carthage was at the centre, building bigger, faster and better ships, expanding its knowledge of navigation and contacts for trade.

In the sixth century BCE, Carthage begins to appear on the geopolitical scene as its own distinct entity – as opposed to just being a colony of the Phoenicians. This is the first time that the Greek sources for the period, like Herodotus, used the word 'Carthaginian', instead of 'Phoenician', in their texts – and

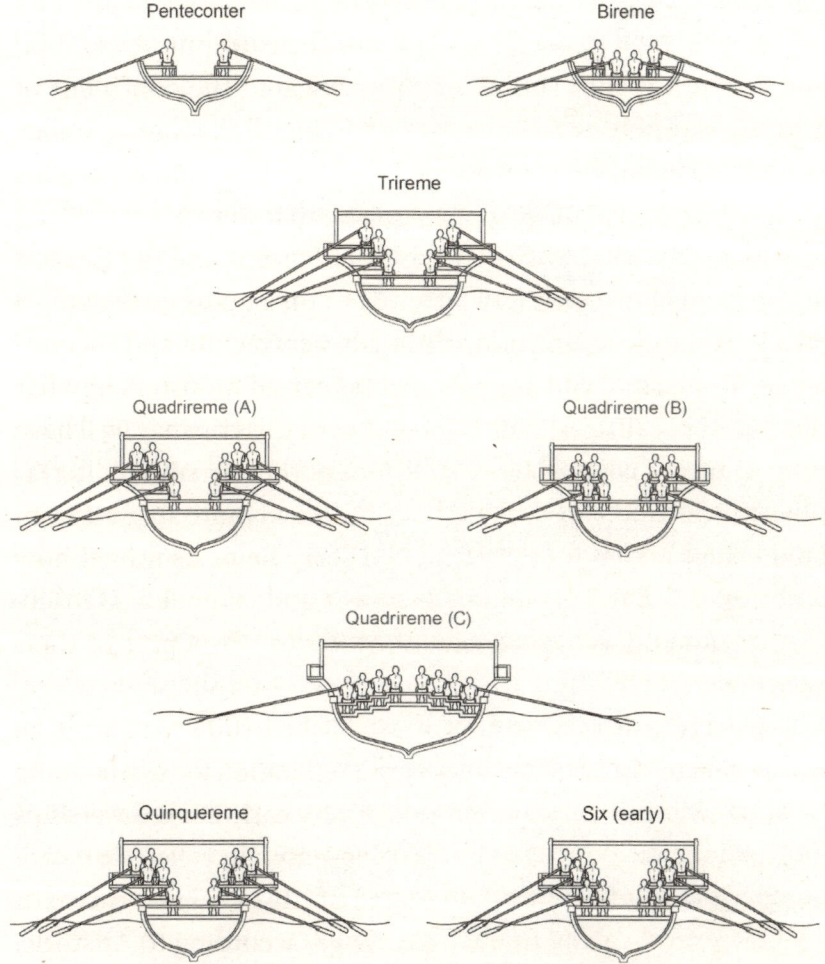

Penteconter

Bireme

Trireme

Quadrireme (A)

Quadrireme (B)

Quadrireme (C)

Quinquereme

Six (early)

Fig. 9 Hypothetical schematic shows variations in ship sizes

words matter. While the two terms still get mixed up by the Greek historians, this implies that the city and the identity of its citizens were becoming distinct. Carthage gradually grew and extended its influence over the pre-existing nexus of Phoenician cities in the western Mediterranean. These were areas with a shared cultural and linguistic heritage. Diodorus Siculus believed that Carthaginians had established a colony on Ibiza

(Ebusus) as early as 564 BCE, although the details are disputed. Either way, we find Carthaginians heading out into the central and western Mediterranean zones, and the city's superb geographic location helps it to become a natural fulcrum for the world around it (see page 80).[14]

Carthage's geopolitical expansion correlates to the physical growth of the city. The original foundation outgrew its limits and expanded in a slow and non-linear process that took almost 300 years. But, along with their innovation, expansion and exploration came conflict. As Carthage grew, so too did settlement in the central Mediterranean by other peoples. The beginning of bigger geopolitical conflicts was focused on the control of strategic places of connectivity in this region that formed a land bridge across the sea from North Africa to Sicily, Sardinia and Corsica. The Carthaginians found both allies and enemies in this zone and formed an alliance with the Etruscan city-states, which were flourishing in central Italy around the same period as Carthage. Both regions began to feel encroached upon from an ever-growing presence of Greek colonial settlements in the western Mediterranean. As populations grew, interactions between the various cultures intensified, and there was increased competition for resources and access to strategic ports.

One event, dating to circa 535–530 BCE, relates to a specific battle off the port of Alalia (Aléria) on Corsica's east coast. The conflict was a pivotal moment in the history of the western Mediterranean, marking a shift from what seemed to be a peaceful coexistence of the main players – various Greeks peoples, Etruscans and Carthaginian/Phoenicians – towards a more aggressive stance. The expansion of Greek-speaking peoples into the western Mediterranean saw city foundations such as Massalia (modern Marseille) and Emporion (Empúries in the Iberian Peninsula). There were many factors underlying Greek expansion, and many of them linked back to the same events that had shifted the relationship between Carthage and the Phoenician city-states of the Levant in the sixth century: the conquests of the Achaemenid Persian Empire and its extension of control into Asia Minor, Egypt and all along the Mediterranean coast. The Achaemenid superpower status, which lasted from the sixth century BCE until its demise in the late fourth century BCE, meant that some populations of Greek speakers along the Asia Minor coast who resisted their rule ended up expelled or fled of their own accord when their resistance had failed.

Herodotus is the main source for this crucial battle. It is the story of a naval engagement between ships from the east and central Mediterranean. At Alalia there was a settlement of Phoceans, Greek-speaking people from Phocaea in Asia Minor (Foça in modern Turkey) who had recently settled at this spot and began to wreak havoc on the seas. In Herodotus' description they were quintessential pirates:

> When they reached Corsica, the Phoceans resided there for five years alongside the original settlers, establishing temples and settlements. However, they engaged in plundering neighbouring territories, prompting the Tyrrhenians [Etruscans] and the Carthaginians to form a coalition against them. Each faction assembled sixty ships and set sail to confront the Phoceans. In response, the Phoceans also mobilized sixty ships and confronted their adversaries in the Sardonian Sea. Although they [the Phoceans] emerged victorious it was a Cadmean victory that came at a cost; they lost forty ships, rendering the remaining twenty ineffective due to damage. Subsequently, the Phoceans sailed to Alalia, where they embarked their families and belongings onto their ships. Departing from Corsica, they voyaged to Rhegium. (*Histories* 1.165–6[15])

The tidy number of 60 ships per fleet – exactly the same as the number that set out with Hanno on his voyage around Africa – raises some suspicions of exaggeration, or perhaps reflects a generic number of ships needed to make up a fleet. In either case, this would have been a large naval battle for the time and a massive investment by the main players. Triremes (whose name derives from having three banks of oarsmen on each side) were crewed by 200 men (including 170 rowers), which means that each side with 60 ships had supposedly put 12,000 men at sea. Given the probable sizes of the potential populations during this period in the western Mediterranean, this number, 36,000 men in all, is unlikely unless there were many other settlements and peoples engaged in the fighting – a much broader coalition on both sides. Herodotus also refers to a Cadmean victory. Cadmus was the legendary Phoenician king from Sidon who ruled in Greek Thebes and whose descendants included famous kings of epic and legend like Oedipus. Polyneices and Eteocles, the two sons of Oedipus, had fought each other for the rule of Thebes and both ended up dead, thus neither side won – a Cadmean victory became the catch phrase for this kind of destructive, hollow win.[16]

Alalia is not mentioned in other sources specifically and may even be conflated with sea battles we know nothing about. Herodotus' contemporary Thucydides mentions only briefly that 'Finally the Phoceans, on their way to found Marseille, won a naval battle over the Carthaginians.' But not clear is whether this refers to the same battle as Alalia or to an earlier encounter between Phoceans and Carthaginians over the foundation of Massalia circa 600 BCE.[17]

So, what do the lessons from Alalia reveal about this time? That there was increasing conflict and competition over control of strategic ports and sea lanes between the growing powers in the western Mediterranean and that Carthage was in the middle of it. As we have seen, the Phoceans moved into the western Mediterranean due to increased pressure from the growing Achaemenid Persian Empire. Their activities – harrying and plundering – in the circular zone of the central Mediterranean provoked a reaction from the Etruscans and the Carthaginians. A look at a map illustrates how the location of Alalia, sitting right across the sea from the Etruscan ports, would give the Phoceans the ability to disrupt shipping and commerce coming in and out of the Etruscan cities (see page 80). It may well be that the presence of a new Greek threat in the region saw the Etruscan cities call on the Carthaginians in alliance to protect their shared interests. What ended with the Cadmean victory of the Phoceans led to their retreat from Corsica entirely and they eventually resettled themselves by force in Velia on the southern Italian coast. This makes us think that the reported victory for the Greeks is overstated, adding in the fact that the battle of Alalia marks the end of Greek colonial expansion westward. The outcomes certainly favoured the Carthaginian/Etruscan alliance and perhaps lines were drawn here around spheres of influence, which were important for Carthage and its future; this would not be the last time the city's fleets played this role and operated in the Tyrrhenian Sea. Increasingly Carthage would come to the aid of allied city-states that were threatened by Greek expansion.

Etruscans, much like the contemporary Phoenicians and the Greeks, were never one unified entity but were from city-states that occupied the region of modern Tuscany, and were linked by a shared language and culture. As allies of the Carthaginians at the battle of Alalia they were called only Tyrrhenians, the generic name for the Etruscans. There is other, more specific evidence, which exists in written form, of the alliance between Carthaginians and the Etruscan city of Caere.[18] Three spectacularly inscribed bilingual gold sheets discovered at the port city of Pyrgi have intrigued since they were excavated in 1964. The inscriptions on the sheets are in the Phoenician and Etruscan languages (Fig. 10 in plate section).

Pyrgi was the port of the powerful inland city of Caere. These sheets date to the late sixth century, to the same period of the alliance mentioned in Herodotus. There are three texts on the sheets, two in Etruscan and one in Phoenician, which describe the dedication of the gold tablets by the chief magistrate of Caere, who is named as Thefarie Velianas, to the sanctuary. Worshipped at this temple was a goddess presented in the inscription as both the Phoenician Astarte and the Etruscan Uni. The Etruscan texts are longer and the Phoenician translation is not literal but seems to convey the same meaning. The sheets are a clear link between the two cultures in terms of a shared worship of the goddess; they tell us of the presence of both cultures in this popular and wealthy port and sanctuary, and that they were on friendly terms, allying together in times of need. Carthage's merchants and fleets were welcome there and its citizens would have been able to worship at the sanctuary and seek protection from the goddess. The inscribed hammered gold sheets would have been hung, probably on the door or wall of the temple, as an offering to the goddess worshipped there. The still visible holes in these golden sheets along the edges, and the golden nails that were found nearby, confirm that this is how they were displayed.

The most incredible thing about these gold sheets is that they survived at all. When discovered in 1964 these priceless hammered gold sheets had survived for thousands of years only because they had been rolled up and hidden away in ancient times. The sanctuary must have been covered with similar dedications and littered with wealthy donations from across the Mediterranean; it was renowned for its international patronage. Coincidentally there is a surviving written story that might provide the context for the hiding away of the sheets – the attack on Pyrgi by the tyrant of the Sicilian Greek city-state Syracuse, Dionysius. Dionysius sacked the sanctuary and this was perhaps the catalyst for one of the priestesses to hide the sacred sheets away.

> Dionysius, in need of money, set out to make war against Tyrrhenia with sixty triremes. The excuse he offered was the suppression of the pirates, but in fact he was going to pillage a holy temple, richly provided with dedications, which was located in the seaport of the Tyrrhenian city of Agylle, the name of the port being Pyrgi. (Diodorus Siculus 15.14.3)

Although this text jumps ahead to a period of intense warfare in the late fifth and fourth centuries BCE, it is still relevant. Dionysius had been marauding around the Mediterranean trying to raise funds to put together a big fleet to launch an attack on Carthage, so the significance of his raiding target, the Carthaginian-allied Pyrgi, may have been intentional.

There is another, even more intriguing, piece of evidence for a close association between Etruscan cities and the Carthaginians in the form of a guest card (*tessera hospitalis*) found in a tomb at the St Monique cemetery in ancient Carthage. Inscribed on a wild boar-shaped ivory card were the words 'I am Puinel from Carthage', in the Etruscan language. This fragmentary inscribed figurine tells us so much. I like to imagine it as a kind of ancient ivory business card that would have allowed two sides in a negotiation or deal to connect over long distances. A merchant in Carthage or an Etruscan city would send one half of the card with an associate who travelled to different ports and negotiated deals. Then, once an agreement was made, the other half of the card was included with the shipment as a guarantee of the product when the goods met the buyer.[19] A Carthaginian merchant, buried at

71

Carthage with a calling card in the Etruscan language in his tomb, illustrates a significant link. This was a relationship deemed important enough to literally take to the grave. The meaning of the words on the card are slightly ambiguous to us now and we can't tell if the *Puinel* on the card may be an ethnic label, related to Punic, or a proper name. I have read this as a proper name here, so our merchant from Carthage, Puinel, arriving in one of the Etruscan port cities with his card, which explained for the locals in those few words who he was and where he was from. This is such a clear and personal vestige of how Carthaginians operated in the Mediterranean and also how Carthage itself had developed into an identity and a defined place. It had arrived as a significant power in the western Mediterranean.

The relationship between Carthage and the Etruscan cities of central Italy was a long-standing connection. Etruscan pottery was imported to Carthage in large quantities as early as the seventh century and through to the fifth century BCE, and there is evidence of exchange and cultural fusions travelling in both directions. Another stunning piece of evidence comes in the form of a sarcophagus lid of a man named Laris Portunus, an Etruscan name, from a necropolis in Tarquinia, Italy. The image of the man is displayed on the top of the sarcophagus and he is depicted wearing distinctive Carthaginian dress, the long tunic likely made of fine linen. There is a similar and well-known figure from Carthage on the so-called 'Priest's sarcophagus': it has an almost identical man on the cover (see Figs. 11 and 12). Both men hold up their hand, a common gesture on Carthaginian iconography that is thought to suggest prayer. To widen the circle even more, the Etruscan sarcophagus is made of imported Parian marble, luminous white stone from the island of Paros in the Cycladic Islands of Greece. This was an expensive and expressive burial. A Greek marble sarcophagus decorated with a distinctive Carthaginian figure and carrying the remains of a man with an Etruscan name: here is the perfect example of the fluid and ephemeral nature of cultural exchange in this period in the western Mediterranean. These cultures were not siloed but constantly mixing and the labels we sometimes assign, 'Carthaginian', 'Etruscan' or 'Greek', may not have reflected how people saw themselves. Who was this man Laris Portunus, whose multivarious sarcophagus leaves us so much to think about? We don't know and the hypotheses vary from his being a merchant, a mercenary soldier or a priest to someone else entirely.

In the midst of these three powerful cultures, Carthaginian, Etruscan and Greek, all vying for dominance in the central Mediterranean, came the rise of the city of Rome. Around the same time as Carthage was extending its interests, a revolution at Rome saw the Romans overthrow their Etruscan kings and establish a new Latin republic in 509 BCE. This is the same year that the very first of many treaties between Carthage and Rome began.[20] The two city-states were in direct diplomatic contact from this date onwards, in peaceful alliance and trade that lasted for centuries before they ever engaged in warfare. The text of the late sixth-century BCE treaty tells us about how Carthage defined itself and Rome in a period of fledgling interstate relationships. Rome

Fig. 11 (left) Sarcophagus of Laris Portunis (Tarquinia); Fig. 12 (right) Priest's sarcophagus (Carthage)

was already, by the late sixth century BCE, a significant force in central Italy. It was a large city with monumental temples and an active river port on the Tiber – but it was not, yet, a naval power.[21] The preservation of the treaty forms part of a digression that the Greek historian Polybius wrote to explain the backstory of the Punic Wars, and it is important to keep this context in mind. Polybius was an eyewitness and contemporary to the destruction of Carthage by the Romans in 146 BCE. In contemporary history this kind of digression is referred to as the *hinterland* – the background to the events that are being witnessed. So, Polybius described the story of Carthage from the point of view of its destruction and from the point of view of Rome's rise, asking all along – how did it come to this?

The text of the first treaty demonstrated that Carthage was the more powerful partner in the negotiation and the terms seemed to reflect their interests. Most of the details concern areas in which Carthaginian and Roman merchants and their allies could do business and trade, and ports in which they would be welcome. The geographic range of commerce included in the Carthaginian sphere extended across part of the North African coast and Sardinia:

> To Carthage itself and all parts of Libya on this side of the Fair Promontory, to Sardinia and the Carthaginian territory of Sicily the Romans may come for trading purposes, and the Carthaginian state engages to secure payment of their just debts. (Polybius 3.23)

The two sides agree to respect the stated allies of the other and the terms are set out clearly, although Polybius, writing 350 years after the original treaty, says he has trouble deciphering the archaic style of the language. The overlying intentions of these treaties likely display the same terms and ideas in similar texts and agreements with other city-states too. The key ideas are reflected in the words '[the] Romans may not make either marauding expeditions, or trade, or found cities' in Carthaginian-controlled areas. This reveals the underlying realities of life in the Mediterranean in these centuries when piracy, colonial foundation and trade were all part of everyday life. The treaty shows an attempt at quasi-regulation of this behaviour, even if it was not always effective. Tantalising questions about what drove this initial treaty remain open to speculation. Did the Carthaginians reach out to the new Roman Republic, the breakaway state which had overthrown its Etruscan kings, in order to secure its interest in the zone of trade that was important to it? Or, on the other side, did the Romans reach out to the Carthaginians in order to establish some kind of recognition of their fledgling state by the larger power? Did Carthage treat with the Romans because they were supported by some of the Etruscan city-states in their existing alliance? Any of these scenarios, or perhaps all of them, seem likely.

Polybius explains that in his view:

> this treaty shows that the Carthaginians looked on Sardinia and Africa as their own domain, but that it was not the same as regards to Sicily, where part of the island subject to Carthage was explicitly distinguished.[22]

These were the central areas of their hegemony to which Carthage saw its sphere of influence extend, though be it direct or indirect we cannot really be sure. One ancient legend that focused on the expansion of Carthaginian cultural hegemony across Africa may provide further clues. The story of the establishment of a border zone or frontier between the extended influence of Carthage and that of the Greek city-state of Cyrene in the region of Cyrenaica (eastern Libya to the border of Egypt) forms the backdrop (see page 80). Cyrene and the Greek cities of the region were prosperous and important throughout the whole of the classical period and into the early Christian era. Cities like Berenike (modern Benghazi), Apollonia, Ptolemais and Teucheira made up a region referred to in Greek as the Pentapolis, the five cities. Cyrene was the most prominent of them all and had been founded as a colony of Thera (modern Santorini) in the seventh century BCE, itself a colony founded by Sparta.

The tale recounts the origins of a place called the Altars of the Philaeni, the border zone between the two cultural spheres of influence, and believed to be where the Carthaginian and Greek powers met.[23] The two cities, Carthage and Cyrene, were supposedly weary of battling each other over territory and their magistrates agreed that on a specific day and at a specific time their best and strongest warriors would set out from each city towards the other. The spot where the men met would become the settled boundary between the two powers. Now, a quick glance at the map shows that the location of the place where the two teams met, the Altars of the Philaeni, was much closer to Cyrene than Carthage (see page 80). The Cyrenaicans accused Carthage of cheating, and the two Carthaginian brothers, named in the tale as the Philaeni brothers, were so deeply offended at being accused of dishonesty that rather than redo the race, they accepted being buried alive on the spot.

In the ancient world and forever after, two columns sat at this very place as boundary markers. This was a very popular story in ancient times, appearing also in the geographer Strabo and natural historian Pliny the Elder's writings, but there is also something of a natural geographic boundary at this place that may be reflected in the tale.[24] It seems more than a coincidence that in recent history the strategic significance of the altars has been emphasised too. Ajdabiya, a location just east of the altars, was the site of much more modern battles, such as in March 2011 when the former Libyan dictator Muammar Gaddafi and the rebels who were fighting to bring him down clashed there. It was also the site of a significant battle in the Second World War in late December 1941 and early 1942 between the forces of Bernard Montgomery and Erwin Rommel.

The legend of the Philaeni brothers is folklore – their name is Greek and means 'lovers of praise'. The landscape between the two areas of population is and was sparse and barren. If the Carthaginians made it so much further than the Greeks in their footrace, they did not acquire a great deal of arable or valuable land in the deal. In fact, land acquisition may not have been what the territorial claims were about at all. One recent thoughtful interpretation of this story by Josephine Quinn suggests that the altars must have been markers to be viewed from the sea and were much more relevant for coastal navigation.[25] This implies that the location of the Altars of the Philaeni marked the boundary of coastal waters between the Greeks and the Carthaginians along the stretch of North African coast that runs across modern Libya and around the Gulf of Syrtis.

What we can interpret from the story of brothers and foot-races between the Greeks in Cyrenaica and the Carthaginians is that there was competition for resources along the coast of Africa. This was an area of important and wealthy cities, especially focused on three settlements known in the ancient world as Sabratha, Oea and Lepcis Magna. These three were all Punic/Phoenician foundations that were referred to as the *emporia* by the Greeks, a word that simply means 'marketplace'. The cities of the emporia were all linked to Carthage through cultural and economic relationships. This long thin region along the coast of what is the western part of Libya today was renowned for olive-oil production in the ancient world. The cities were independent but culturally Punic/Phoenician and key stopping points on the sea route that circumnavigated the Mediterranean. They were also some of the northern termini for caravans that traversed the Sahara through a series of oases, so their connectivity east and west by sea and south into Central Africa made them extremely wealthy and coveted. Access to these ports was protected by Carthage, and the treaty terms expressed by Polybius banning Romans from travelling beyond the 'Fair Promontory', the North African cape facing Carthage, may have been geared at limiting access to these prosperous port cities and the markets.

In these heady days, Carthaginian naval power gave them the authority to found colonies, dictate treaty terms and to rely on economic protectionism when it came to strategic cities. All of this took place along the coastal zones, but we should not think of Carthage as only a power of the sea. The land of North Africa, especially around where Carthage was founded, was rich and prosperous and populated. The indigenous peoples of inland North Africa were also the story of Carthage, and the land they farmed and the populations they produced became the backbone of the Carthaginian military. The Numidians were the key allies of Carthage and, eventually, their great nemesis (as we will see in Chapter 12). They were friends, allies, relations, their royalty intermarried with Carthaginian elites, and the settlement of Phoenician/Carthaginians along the central regions of the Bagradas River and into the fertile lands of the Sahel and Atlas foothills created a whole new people that the ancient authors called Libyphoenicians.

There is such complexity to Carthage as a place, as a people and an identity in these formative centuries and the little evidence we have offers only tantalising snippets of insight. By the fifth century BCE, the Carthaginian cultural presence across North Africa and through the central Mediterranean was significant but not dominant. Carthage was one of many important and thriving city-states that had benefited from closer links between neighbours, and an expanded realm of contact and trade. It was a place essential in the process of bringing the east of the Mediterranean and the west into closer contact. By the fifth century BCE, the people of Carthage regulated their relationships with neighbouring entities through treaties, protected their interests and waged war to do so. Nowhere would this become more significant than on the island of Sicily, and our next chapters will relocate there, as Carthage becomes embroiled in a long period of conflict that will occupy its attention and resources.

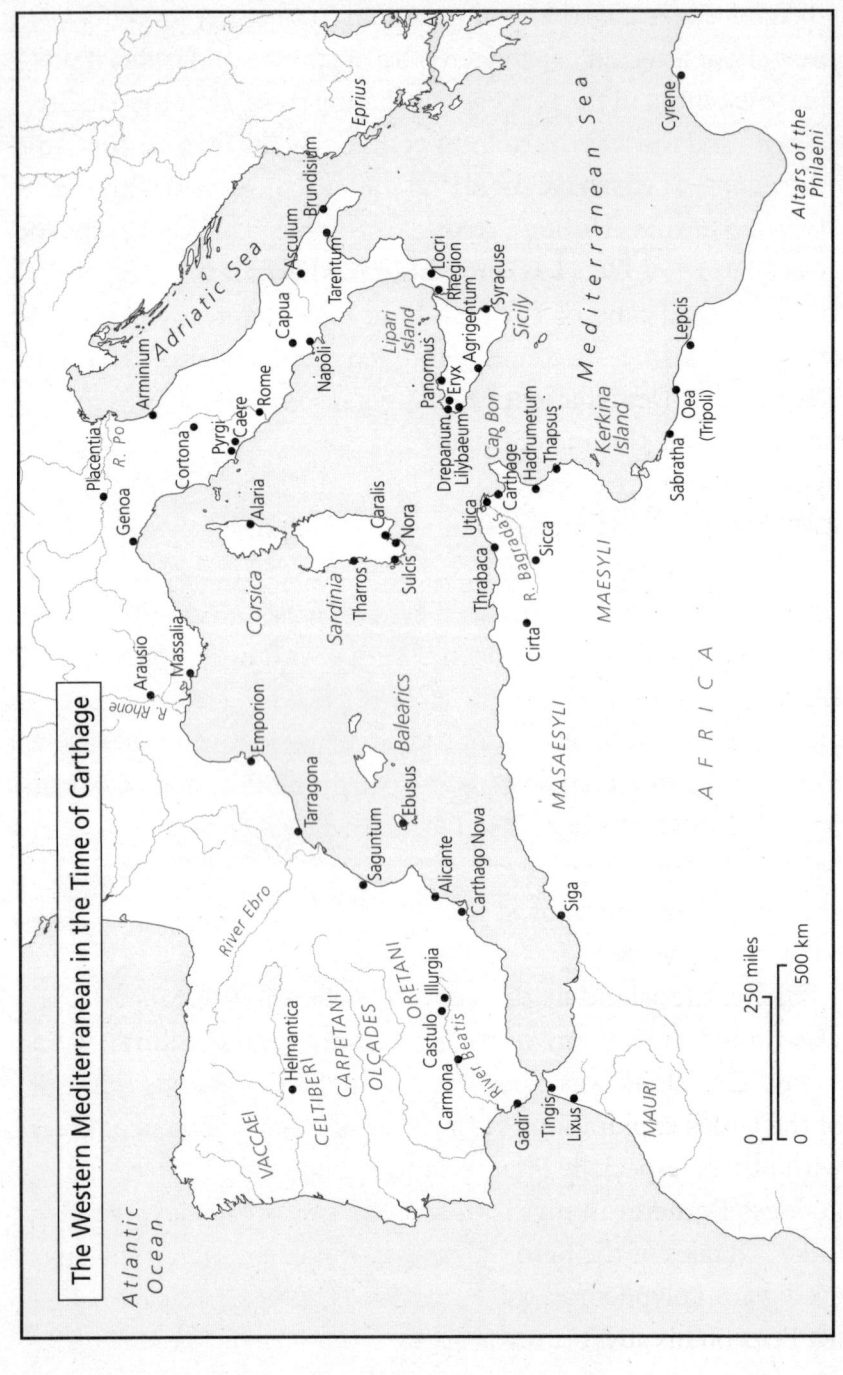

The Western Mediterranean in the Time of Carthage

Atlantic
Ocean

Adriatic Sea

Mediterranean Sea

Epirus

Cyrene

Altars of the
Philaeni

Brundisium
Asculum
Tarentum
Capua
Napoli
Rome
Caere
Pyrgi
Cortona
Placentia
Arminium
Genoa
Placentia

R. Po

Locri
Rhegion
Syracuse
Agrigentum
Sicily
Eryx
Panormus
Drepanum
Lilybaeum
Cap Bon
Carthage
Utica
Hadrumetum
Thapsus

*Lipari
Island*

Lepcis
Oea
(Tripoli)
Sabratha

*Kerkina
Island*

Thabraca
Sicca
R. Bagradas
Cirta

MAESYLI

AFRICA

Caralis
Nora
Sulcis
Tharros
Sardinia
Alaria
Corsica

Arausio
Massalia
R. Rhone

Emporion
Tarragona
Balearics
Ebusus
Saguntum
Alicante
Carthago Nova

MASAESYLI

Siga

River Ebro

Helmantica
VACCAEI
CELTIBERI
CARPETANI
OLCADES
ORETANI
Castulo
Illurgia
Carmona
River Beatis
Gadir
Tingis
Lixus

MAURI

250 miles
500 km
0
0

CHAPTER 4

The Three-Sided Island

The goddess Demeter lost her daughter Persephone on Trinacria, which was the ancient name for the island of Sicily. There, by the shores of the sacred lake Enna, the beautiful young girl was kidnapped and raped by the god of the underworld, Hades. The powerful fertility goddess Demeter raged across the world searching for her lost daughter, all the crops failed, and famine set in. It was only when Zeus intervened with his brother Hades that Persephone was released, but her taste of one pomegranate seed in the dark reaches of the underworld meant she would forever have to return down to Hades for half of each year. The pomegranate is the last plant in the Mediterranean to bear fruit before the onset of winter and marks the end of the growing season – the moment of departure – when Persephone returns to the underworld.[1]

Sicily, the island at the centre of the Mediterranean Sea, was rooted in so many of the myths and stories still repeated today. The island was closely associated with legends that tell of the Greek explorations of the Mediterranean and encounters with others, especially Phoenicians. Sicily was connected to the goddess Demeter in myths of fertility and prosperity, but also linked to tales of the hero Odysseus, who encountered the one-eyed giant Polyphemus, the monstrous Cyclops, in a cave below Mt Etna on his adventures after the sack of Troy. The adventure story told by Homer of monsters and wild beasts reflected the memories and myths of the diverse Greek-speaking peoples and their encounters in new and strange lands. So too on Sicily was a temple of a powerful goddess who had been worshipped on a sacred mountain by the indigenous Elymi peoples, and where a temple to Astarte was founded by Phoenicians. On that mountain the goddess would be worshipped as Astarte by the Carthaginians, as Aphrodite by the Greeks and as Venus by the Romans. Her place of reverence was the mountaintop shrine at Eryx (modern Erice), just inland from Trapani on the northwest coast of Sicily. She was many things to all the various peoples who lived and travelled through Sicily, and to call her one or the other of the deities is too reductive.[2] Like the goddess herself, Sicily was many things to many different peoples all living there together and at the same time.

The power and wealth of the sanctuary at Eryx on Sicily was well known. Pan-religious shrines were visited by people from all over the Mediterranean who came to worship the goddess and dedicated gifts and vows. Prayers were offered and payments made to fulfil these vows. A line in Thucydides provides a glimpse into the great wealth available at a pan-religious sanctuary like Eryx. In the context of the doomed Sicilian expedition of the Athenians at the end of the fifth century BCE, Thucydides described a moment when the Segestans were trying to entice the Athenians into war and to use Athens to protect themselves from their closer Greek neighbours. The Segestans impressed the Athenians with tales of the great wealth available in Sicily and took the envoys to the temple on Eryx to show them all the loot that could be theirs if only they would come to their aid. The Athenians were 'brought into the temple of Aphrodite in Eryx' and there they were shown all the 'holy treasure, goblets, flagons, censers, and other furniture, in no small quantity'.[3] The richness of the material impressed the Athenians enough to commit to intervention, and this led to a military disaster. This moral tale told by Thucydides about how chasing great wealth leads to calamity showcases the shrine's significance in the region.

The three-sided island of Sicily, at the very centre of the Mediterranean, would become the crux of much of the story of Carthage in its last centuries and was the chief location for the rivalry between Carthaginian and Greek cultures. This placed Carthage firmly into the epic stories of the Greek world and created a lasting narrative for the island of Sicily as well. Over the course of the eighth to fifth centuries BCE, Sicily became a mix of Phoenician settlements and colonies in the west, Greek colonial foundations in the east and important indigenous cities inland with several pan-Mediterranean religious shrines – places that belonged to all the different cultures. Connected to the east and west, Sicily strategically controlled movement across the central Mediterranean. Early colonisation by the Phoenician city-states of the Levant took place in the eighth century BCE at the island city of Motya just off the west coast. Motya is a small, flat, roughly circular island measuring 895m long by 700m wide, covering an area of about 62 hectares. You can still visit this fascinating island that lies low in salt pans between a larger island to the east and the west coast of Sicily, just over 500m away (see page 102).[4] It is perfectly protected from capricious seas and has a location that was not unlike Tyre itself. Motya contained a sacred spring – natural fresh water, around which grew up an important temple to Ba'al and a religious complex approached directly from the sea with a sacred lake. There was excellent agricultural land and a safe harbour. Access to Motya was by boat, but there was also a paved underwater causeway that could be traversed on foot or by chariots and other vehicles with large enough wheels and which ran north from the island to the mainland. The causeway is still visible under the sea in the lagoon that surrounds Motya.

Phoenicians had settled on Motya and along with the already existing population of people who we call Elymians there developed, as at Carthage, a distinctive culture – one that we sometimes refer to as west Phoenician. Like Carthage, at Motya there was a Tophet, with urns containing cremated infants and stelae marking the dedications, situated on the northwest edge of the island which was important throughout its history. Motya's location allowed for easy contact and travel between North Africa and Sardinia and the Iberian Peninsula. The island functioned as the node for a network of allied peoples that in the early centuries included Carthage, along with other Phoenician settlements on the west of Sicily such as Panormus (Palermo), Soluntum and Drepanum (Trapani), and also those on the south of Sardinia (see page 80).

On the east coast of Sicily, also in the eighth century BCE, Greeks from Euboea established a colony at Naxos and then the city of Syracuse was founded by people from Corinth (see page 102). The city of Corinth had grown during this century to become a major centre of production and contact with its two harbours – one facing east and one west – and was located on the isthmus that joined Attica to the Peloponnese. Corinth sent out and settled many colonies, with Syracuse among the most important. Thucydides detailed Syracuse's foundation as an act by Archias, a member of one of the ruling families of Corinth, and his followers. By ancient accounts the Syracusans arrived fighting. The centre of the city of Syracuse was the ear-shaped island of Ortygia, which had been occupied by indigenous Siculians when the Corinthians arrived. Archias and his followers drove the Siculians off this strategic island and took it for themselves.[5] On Ortygia was a sacred spring called Arethusa which had sweet water, and soon a temple to the god Apollo was founded there. By the seventh century BCE, the town had expanded its holdings on to the mainland, encompassing the region across from the island as part of the urban fabric of the city and gaining access to good agricultural land in the process. Syracuse grew and became prosperous, with harbours on both sides of the central island. It sustained agricultural growth and visible prosperity along with the conquest of neighbouring territories of the indigenous peoples of Sicily.

Like their Phoenician counterparts in the west, the Greek colonial foundations flourished and grew, extending satellites north to the very tip of the island at Messina (called Zancle originally and then Messana), south along the coast to Gela and Agrigento (Akragas), and even further west to Selinunte (see page 102). By the sixth century BCE, Syracuse had become the most powerful of many successful and culturally linked Greek cities of Sicily. These city-states warred chiefly among themselves and also with the western Phoenicians on the island, and with the powerful Elymian and Siculian cities like Segesta and Enna. Loyalties and alliances shifted, not easily fitting into the clear ethnic boundaries or simple narratives of Phoenicians/Carthaginians vs Greeks that our later sources like to depict. The populations in these cities were mixed; the west of Sicily shows Greek inscriptions on Punic-style tombs and temples with multivarious themes appealing to broad audiences. There was no one ethnicity in any Sicilian city, no one language spoken, but the population often reflected prevailing traditions of that place, be it Phoenician, Greek, Elymian or Siculian. Fighting took place over strategic locations and resources like for access to good agricultural land and for control of sanctuaries and ports. Sicily, in these years, was a restless and vibrant place, and that is still reflected in the amazing cultural hybridity visible in the landscape and the culture today.

Carthage became embedded in Sicily and Sicilian issues from early on in its history, although the evidence is sparse beyond obvious associations visible in pottery shapes and religious practices. The tale already discussed of the Carthaginian Malchus (in Chapter 2), thought to date to the sixth century BCE, refers to a victory for Carthage in Sicily before defeat in Sardinia. By the fifth century BCE, Thucydides links Carthage to Sicily in his brief account of the settlements there:

> the Phoenicians dwelt here and there all over Sicily, after occupying the headlands overlooking the sea and the islets near to the coast . . . Then, when the Greeks came from overseas in large numbers, they [Phoenicians] left the greater part of the land and were concentrated at Motya, Soluntum and Palermo, where they lived close to the Elymi, reassured by alliance with the Elymi themselves and by the fact that this point of Sicily was very near to Carthage. (6.2)

Our earliest written histories tie Carthage and Sicily together and so too do the day-to-day utensils, found by archaeologists, that people used for consuming food, including plates, cups and carriers for wine and oil (amphorae). Specific-shaped amphorae with goods from Carthage have been found in the west of Sicily and these date back to the seventh century BCE with their production continuing until the third century BCE.[6] This tells us that over those centuries Carthage supported and traded with the city-states of the west of Sicily – just as Thucydides implied. The examples we have clearly show that Motya was a close ally of Carthage. When boundary struggles or conflicts arose with its neighbours, it looked south across the sea to Africa for support. Carthage would have been protecting its own interests in doing so as well, and the significance of military campaigning on Sicily is best visualised through early Carthaginian coinage that reflected its relationships on the island. The earliest coins of Carthage are minted on the drachm standard, the Euboean Greek coinage widely used across the Mediterranean (as opposed to the Tyrian shekel standard coins we find at Carthage slightly later), and were modelled on Syracusan design prototypes. These are beautifully crafted coins but do not appear in circulation until the late fifth century BCE and often bear the legend 'in camp', signifying they are being minted in the field, in a military camp. These coins were being used to pay for supplies, soldiers and support for the army. Minted to a Greek weight standard and carrying a Punic legend, with a Greek goddess head on the obverse and a reverse with a horse's head (sometimes being crowned with a victory figure) and a date palm, the coins illustrate the fluid and multiple identities on Sicily (see Fig. 13).[7]

The city of Himera most strongly evokes the history of Carthage in Sicily and there were two important clashes between Carthaginian allies and the Greek city-states there in the fifth century BCE. Himera was a strategic settlement on the north coast of Sicily, near the mouth of the river of the same name that runs north from the Madonie mountains into the sea. Diodorus Siculus records it as being founded in the seventh century BCE, a

Fig. 13 Carthaginian silver tetradrachm with Punic legend

place that pushed the Greek city-states' expansion on the north coast of the island to its westernmost point. Himera was a marker, founded as a border town or boundary by inhabitants who moved there from Zancle (Messina/Messana), some 150km to the east, and from Syracuse along with further settlers who came from Euboea in Greece proper, in circa 648 BCE. The foundation of Himera was a significant movement of Greeks into the western sphere of Sicily and the placement of a strategic location of Greek colonial citizens. It lies, as the crow flies, just 27km from the west Phoenician town of Soluntum and also controls one of the main trans-island passes, where the modern motorway cuts inland and crosses Sicily towards Catania and Syracuse from the north coast. This pivotal location was the focus of clashes between all sides in the period. The west Phoenician and Elymian alliance against the expanding presence of some Greek city-states, along with inter-Hellene violence and territorial reach, all culminated in a battle at Himera in circa 480 BCE.

The tale of Himera has passed down to us through claim and counterclaim over the centuries.[8] The news cycle of ancient history reflected the shifting alliances across this zone, but the eventual destruction of Carthage means there has been a reductive impact and loss of perspective – we only have one very skewed side of the story. Now, with the help of new archaeological evidence, the story can be nuanced beyond the historical sources and their deep biases against Carthage. The events at Himera revolved around a Greek tyrant named Terillus, who had been expelled from the city by Theron, the son of the ruler of Akragas (Roman Agrigentum, now Agrigento) on the south coast. The word 'tyrant' appears very often in this phase of Sicily's history, and it is useful to realise it does not mean a 'bad guy' but was an actual title held by rulers in Greek city-states; the word derives from *tyrannos*, a Greek term that reflected a person whose rule was autocratic. In this period not all tyrants were necessarily bad, which is quite different from how the word is employed today.

The tyrant Terillus attempted to reclaim his rule at Himera and this action provoked a war. Herodotus tells us that Terillus persuaded the Carthaginians to come to his aide and it was through his personal connections with their 'king' (probably *sufet*) named Hamilcar that he was able to do this.[9] Terillus was a 'guest friend' of the Carthaginian commander and linked to the ruler of Rhegium, the Greek city on the very tip of the boot of Italy. Even more interesting is Herodotus' description of Hamilcar as Carthaginian on his father's side and Syracusan on his mother's side, and that he had become leader at Carthage on 'merit'. Hamilcar brought an army to Himera that was made up of Phoenicians, Libyans, Ligyes (Ligurians), Elisyci (Iberians), Sardinians and Cyrnians (Corsicans). The 'Greek' forces fighting on the side of Himera included, among others, large armies brought by the leaders of Akragas and Syracuse. Himera is not a simple tale of Greek vs Carthaginian but reflects the relationship of alliances between elites that existed both within city-states and between families and individuals.

So, what started as a squabble between Greek city-states and tyrants became part of a much larger narrative, and the battle for power and control over a significant boundary location on the north coast of Sicily acquired huge significance. The details are remarkably muddled and scarce but, as told, Hamilcar sailed with a large army and fleet from Carthage to Sicily.[10] The claim that he had a 300,000-strong force, with 200 warships and even more supply and cargo vessels, seems wildly exaggerated, but tells us it was a big force. The crossing proved problematic and much of his cavalry was lost at sea. Hamilcar's infantry and navy were largely preserved, and the army first landed at allied Panormus (Palermo) where they resupplied and took stock. They then moved 43km east towards Himera where Hamilcar landed his army on the beach. He pulled his ships up on shore and set up camp in a defended area. The Carthaginian army proceeded to lay siege to the city and waited for their Sicilian allies to join them, namely forces from Selinus (Selinunte). The detailed story of the landing seems suspicious in its similarity to the Greeks in the Trojan War, and there may be some fanciful and creative story-making in the work of the author, Diodorus Siculus, who is the best ancient source for the events. Diodorus may have used the example of the Trojan War stories, which everyone would have known, to plump up a tale whose details were not clearly preserved.

The armies set on defending Himera were led by Theron and the tyrant of Syracuse, Gelon. The army from Syracuse was reported to include some 50,000 infantry and 50,000 cavalry. This force and their commander appeared on the field before Himera, coming to the aid of their allies and setting up camp near the Carthaginians. The arrival of Syracusan troops under Gelon first meant that there was a stalemate outside the town. The tale of the battle itself is muddled but success relied on a ruse played out by Gelon, who was able to trick Hamilcar. Gelon had his own cavalry sneak into the Carthaginian camp under the guise of being the expected reinforcements from the allied city of Selinus. The Greek army then tricked the Carthaginian commander, who is depicted as distracted by religious rituals and celebrations, and wreaked havoc. In one version of the story, the Syracusan soldiers killed Hamilcar and set fire to the ships. A fierce battle ensued that lasted all through the day with chaos and slaughter on both sides. Eventually, those of the Carthaginian army who could, fled. It was a catastrophic loss for the Carthaginians. Their defeat was so complete and total, according to Diodorus, that only a lone ship sailed back into the port of Carthage and the walls of the city were draped in black cloth in mourning for all the lives lost. We hear nothing more of Hamilcar; he disappears from the story, completely and miraculously in some cases. There are versions of the tale that claim he was murdered in the ambush, that he committed suicide rather than return defeated to Carthage, and that he hurled himself on to a funeral pyre in shame.[11]

This was a war provoked by Sicilian Greeks fighting among themselves. It was manned by a multi-allied force gathered by the Carthaginians, engaging in warfare in Sicily on the part of their allies and neighbours. That the two sides met in a battle that took place 'around the same time' as the famous invasion of Greece by the Achaemenid Xerxes dates the battle of Himera to circa 480 BCE. As a result, the events around the battle fought at Himera have been conflated in the ancient sources with the Persian wars and the sack of Athens. Herodotus claimed it happened on exactly the same day that the Greeks vanquished the Persians at Salamis. Other sources (for example, Diodorus Siculus) have linked the battle of Himera with the Persian invasion of Greece as a concerted and joined-up effort.[12] Diodorus, who wrote centuries after the events, implies that the Carthaginians in the west and the Persians in the east were acting as a unified force of the enemy, against Greeks. This later view, for which there is no proof, only tells of how the story and myths of this battle, which became so defining for Syracuse, had been passed on and became part of the common parlance, with Syracusans equating their own battles with Carthage as a part of a greater Greek struggle. It is certainly clear from the statement in Herodotus, who was almost contemporary to the events, that the initiative for this battle did not come from Carthage but from Himera and Rhegium and the family of the ousted tyrant there. But Syracusan memories used by Gelon to solidify his hold on power in the city equated their great struggles with those of the homeland Greeks, and these views have prevailed. The victory at the battle at Himera was commemorated with a monument at the sanctuary of Apollo at Delphi in Greece, and Gelon also funded the construction of a victory temple at Himera and, possibly, the construction of the great temple of Athena at Syracuse.[13]

Carthage had lost this battle in dramatic fashion and for decades the Carthaginians disappeared from Sicily. They seemed less than enthusiastic about engaging in Sicilian affairs for a long time afterwards. Although the Carthaginians continued to be allied to cities in the west of Sicily, the ascendancy on the island was all on Syracuse's side, with the city becoming the dominant force across much of Sicily for the next decades. It would be another 70 years (as far as we know) before the Carthaginians were back fighting in Sicily, such was the state of Carthage after their defeat at Himera. The realities of interstate relations of the time meant there would have been a treaty, an agreement on the spheres of operation and influence in effect, but we are ignorant of any of these details.

New science has recently changed details of this old conflict. Results from excavations at Himera help to shift the reductive effect of later historians who retold the tales based on the propaganda of the winners. The recent discovery of two separate mass graves of soldiers at the site of Himera have been illuminating. They contained bodies from the battles of 480 BCE and that of a battle seven decades later, in 409 BCE. The excavation has uncovered a large rectangular trench with the bodies of dead soldiers laid out beside each other, and the skeletal remains are believed to be those of the slain mercenary soldiers of the Greek armies that fought at Himera. It is an unprecedented glimpse into the aftermath of a battle and shows us how the Greek armies dealt with their dead. The non-citizen soldiers fighting for the Greeks, who had died far from home, were the ones buried together in mass graves, while citizen soldiers had individual inhumations.

These graves provide extraordinary insight into the realities of ancient warfare on Sicily, and the way that a soldier for hire in the ancient world could move vast distances for work. Most previous histories of Carthage like to explain that Carthaginian armies were, as often described by the ancient sources, 'mercenary armies', with the subtext being that they were inferior to the Greek citizen 'hoplites'. The mass graves, however, clearly indicate that there was a significant mercenary make-up of the Greek troops. This is implied in the ancient histories of the period but has often been overlooked. Not only were quite a number of the soldiers not local, but they came from much further afield than Sicily or even Greece. Strontium isotope analysis of the teeth of the slain can tell us about where an individual lived as a child, because strontium isotopes are absorbed into the teeth as they are created – they are like a snapshot of a person's childhood. From the recent excavations we now understand that some of the soldiers buried at Himera grew up in the far north of Europe at the edge of the Baltic Sea, in the Asian Steppe and in the Caucasus. This surprising evidence has completely shifted ideas of human mobility in the period – where a man from Siberia could end up buried in a mass grave on Sicily fighting for a Syracusan army against Carthage in the fifth century BCE.[14]

Just as interesting for our understanding of the population of Sicily – and we can assume that of Carthage too – are the ways that the surviving mercenary soldiers were integrated into the city-states. Diodorus tells us that after the war of 480 BCE, 7,000 of the surviving foreign soldiers in the Syracusans' employ were granted citizenship by the tyrant Gelon.[15] Previously it had been assumed that the recruitment and employ of mercenary soldiers were broadly Mediterranean focused. Soldiers of fortune, pursuing a career of choice for men across the ancient world, were paid well. Those younger sons and poorer men from a vast range of communities had little choice but to seek a livelihood in fighting. These men of war and soldiering would be the agents of great change in the Mediterranean in the coming centuries, and the beginning of their impact can be viewed here in these mass graves on Sicily. It is also clear from the evidence that the genetic make-up of those we consider to be Greek or Carthaginian was not what made them citizens.

Carthage's focus after Himera shifted elsewhere, we assume, perhaps to Sardinia or along the coast of Africa as we have seen with Hanno's voyage. There are oblique references to Carthaginian successes on Sardinia in the fifth century BCE, and we get descriptions of some generals who are active in the field there, although it is often only in defeat that a battle is clearly outlined by later writers. There is much more interest in remembering Carthaginian defeats than victories, so it is difficult to get a clear picture.[16] The archaeology indicates that some Phoenician sites on Sardinia in the same period were abandoned, possibly due to a regional shift in power. Carthage was now in the centre of a joined-up nexus of west Phoenician urban foundations and allied settlement that formed an integral part of its wealth. How political power functioned in relationship to these allied states, and whether it was directed through alliance and tribute payments, is not clear. The absence of Carthage for much of the fifth century BCE from the historical sources on Sicily may well show that Carthage adhered to a peace treaty signed after the defeat at Himera and sought its growth elsewhere.

When the Carthaginians finally did return to Sicily it was the late fifth century BCE and they came with a very different outlook. Whereas the earlier iterations of Carthaginian intervention in Sicily seem to stem from networks and alliances with other west Phoenician settlements this time Carthage was much more directly involved in power on the island. Although we know little about Carthaginian government and the organisation of their influence in other regions, the late fifth-century struggle was an aggressive statement of their control. It was a brutal time, with cities fighting among themselves and calling in bigger and bigger allies to battle for them. The broader context in the Mediterranean was that the Athenians were in the midst of fighting Sparta in the long-drawn-out Peloponnesian War (431–404 BCE) when they sailed to fight on behalf of the Elymi Segestans against Syracuse in the years 415–412 BCE. This was the context of their visit to the temple of Aphrodite at Eryx, mentioned earlier in the chapter. The Athenian defeat and their humiliation in the harbours of Syracuse only added to an atmosphere of suffering and loss on the island. The insertion of Athens into the already frayed environment of allies and proxies on Sicily speaks of a broader escalation. The Segestans, traditional allies of the Carthaginians, were now allies of the Athenians against the power of colonial Syracuse. Athens had reached out to Carthage in alliance, to bolster its forces against Syracuse, while Syracuse also reached out to Carthage in this moment.[17] We don't know which side the Carthaginians chose, if any, but certainly Thucydides considered Carthage a potential ally for Athens, a trading partner with no direct imperial interest in the island. Later evidence from Diodorus Siculus presents a more nuanced picture, indicating that Carthage had its own interests in the war in Sicily. Nathan Pilkington, whose research looks specifically at the archaeology of Carthaginian imperialism, suggests that the Syracusan preoccupation with the Peloponnesian War, where it had sent troops, and then the Athenian invasion, created the perfect conditions for Carthage to re-enter the fray in Sicily.[18]

After Syracuse had been unchallenged in its dominance of Sicily for 70 years, the Carthaginians' comeback must have involved a very concerted effort to build their hegemony on the island and support their allies. When the Carthaginians returned to Sicily with a military force, they came back to the place of their great defeat seven decades prior: Himera. The ancient sources tell us that Carthage returned to revenge that defeat and that it was a personal, family quest. In command this time was a general named Hannibal (a very common Carthaginian name and not the later famous general of the elephants), thought to be related to the defeated Hamilcar from the 480s BCE, perhaps a grandson.

As a brief aside, the Carthaginian names in their long history repeated through generations, and it was traditional for first-born boys to be named for their grandfather (and perhaps girls for their grandmothers but there is less evidence for this). Also, names like Hannibal and Hamilcar are theophoric, which means they were formed from the known names of a deity in the pantheon of Carthage. So, Hamilcar reads in the Punic language as 'servant of Melqart' and Hannibal means 'he who is favoured by Ba'al'. The confusing array of Hannibals and Hasdrubals and Hamilcars across Carthaginian history were most likely differentiated within Carthaginian society by who their fathers were, that is, Hannibal son of Hamilcar, or nicknames and epithets that people used – most of which are not available to us and probably were not known to the Roman sources. Occasionally there were people whose geographic origins seem to be added to the name, so in Chapter 5 we will meet Hamilcar Rhodanus (the Rhodian) and can assume he was a man who had ancestry from the island of Rhodes.

Hannibal fought a battle in 409 BCE at Himera, but this time the city stood alone, unsupported by larger allies. The results were definitive: the town was taken, destroyed and the population moved nearby to a new settlement, called Therma. The Carthaginian army did not just attack Himera; Hannibal attacked Agrigentum and Selinunte, both on the south coast of Sicily. This gave Carthaginian forces possession of ports with direct strategic access across the sea to Africa. At the ruins of Selinunte, which sit on a bluff looking out to the sea, you can still visit a city fortification that dates to this period. Parts of the land gate still stand intact and as I wandered through this complex system of outer and inner walls with moats and ditches, I could only marvel at the intricacy of the gates and angles, and the investment in infrastructure. The walls were constructed to deter any attempt at taking the city from the land side, and the fact that control of the place nevertheless shifted back and forth across these years tells of the value it held for those trying to control this corner of Sicily.

At Selinunte there are neighbourhoods of Punic-style housing that appear in this period as well. When Agrigentum was captured by an army led by a man named Himilco, the invading force then proceeded to lay siege to Gela, further east along the coast. A new tyrant ruler at Syracuse, Dionysius I, had come to power in 405 BCE (we discussed him in Chapter 3 for his raid and sack of the Etruscan port of Pyrgi). He raised a new army at this moment to support neighbouring Gela and try to relieve the siege. Himilco's army defeated the Syracusans again, whose military strength seemed weakened in this period. The new leader of Syracuse was almost killed by his own soldiers, and was only saved, according to Diodorus, by his mercenary troops who served as a personal bodyguard. When a plague attacked the Carthaginian army, both sides acknowledged a treaty. Carthage's hegemony in western Sicily was affirmed and there was a brief respite in the hostilities.

This peace was not a long one, but more of a stopgap because of the ravaging impact of this sudden plague on the island, which seems to have impacted the Carthaginians more severely. It is difficult to know what disease it was. It could have been a range of epidemic outbreaks, causing death during a hot summer, but a plague had also ravaged Athens during the Peloponnesian War a decade or so earlier. Disease was rampant, and intense fighting in a period of pandemic and its aftermath might well reflect the struggle for resources and population decline across the western Mediterranean. From this late fifth-century BCE date, a more direct imperial perspective emanated from Carthage itself. Control and the movement of people into the newly conquered territory are visible in the cities taken during these campaigns.

The city of Selinunte was refounded as a Carthaginian city; that it was possibly called Rosh Melqart comes from the Punic word *Ršmlqrt* that appears as a mint mark on some coins from the period. Also visible on the island of Sardinia are the older west Phoenician sites that had been abandoned for close to a century before being reoccupied. The full material and cultural impact of Carthage can be seen more clearly in the evidence of ceramics and coinage at many different places across the central zone in this period. Carthage had suffered economic and military setbacks, especially earlier in the fifth century BCE, but its recovery can be witnessed if we overlay the stories in later sources with the evidence of decline and then renewal at sites around the western Mediterranean.[19]

Carthage's new incursions in Sicily created a strong reaction from Syracuse. The Syracusan leader Dionysius recruited widely, with new soldiers coming from central and southern Italy and northern parts of Sicily, to raise a force to attack the Carthaginians. By the year 398 BCE Dionysius had laid siege to the island city of Motya on the west coast of Sicily with an alliance of city-states. Motya, the island city we discussed earlier in the chapter, was Carthage's key base on the west of Sicily by this time, and the Syracusans prepared an elaborate attack. Diodorus Siculus portrays Motya as a wealthy and sophisticated city that was 'embellished artistically' with fine houses built through the prosperity of the inhabitants. As Dionysius approached with warships and hundreds of merchant ships mounted with engines of war, the citizens of Motya breached their own causeway to the mainland to prepare for the defence of their homes. A fierce battle ensued, with fleets against each other in the bay, but the Carthaginian relief force was bombarded by a kind of improvised artillery by the Syracusans who had 'catapults that shot sharp-pointed missiles' from the land side. All of the fighting and preparation took place in the narrow and shallow bay between Sicily and the island state, and would have been watched by those who lived on the island and along its shore (see page 102).[20]

Motya fell and much of the elegant city was destroyed, but the Carthaginian commander Himilco returned the following year and with a new effort retook Motya, and then turned east again to confront the Syracusans. Much of the population of Sicily joined Himilco against the unpopular Dionysius, and the city of Syracuse was lain under siege in the winter of 397/396 BCE. Once again, a deadly plague that attacked the Carthaginian army meant they had to withdraw, but the war continued back and forth over the next years until both sides were spent. Finally, in 392 BCE a new peace treaty was signed between Carthage and Syracuse. The inland cities of Sicily retained their independence and the practical separation of the coastal zone of the island into the east and west was maintained.

The demise of Motya led to the creation of a new city on the west coast of Sicily that may well have been a direct colony of Carthage, rather than an allied city, for the first time (see page 102).[21] This new city was called Lilybaeum (modern Marsala) and it became the centre of Carthaginian life on Sicily from this point forward. Founded as a modern Mediterranean city, Lilybaeum grew easily and quickly into a thriving port with up-to-date facilities and easy access to Carthage south across the sea. Lilybaeum was founded on the location of a sacred spring where a sybil, a wise woman with oracular insights, provided advice to pilgrims. To consult the sybil at Lilybaeum a penitent would come to the cave where the spring water bubbled up from the ground and the oracle would project prophecy.[22] The place would have been sacred before the Carthaginians established their colony there and became much renowned afterwards. The venerable island city of Motya lost most of its significance once Lilybaeum was established. It was never completely abandoned, and the religious sanctuary of Ba'al with its sacred pool and the Tophet area were still in use for another century, but the defeat had diminished the power that the place had held. The harbour of Motya fell into disuse, the walls crumbled and the focus of commerce and the centre of trade moved south to Lilybaeum. Today you can wander through the ancient remains of the old Phoenician city on Motya, one of the few places in the Mediterranean where Phoenician/Carthaginian culture can be most fully appreciated. The island of paved streets and elegant sanctuary buildings, the sacred child-sacrifice site and the sophisticated defensive walls sits in the salt pans off the coast of Sicily, preserving the urban life of this lost west-Phoenician town.

As we have explored here, the stories and the archaeology of Sicily from the late fifth century BCE show us that it was a period of transition for Carthage. After catastrophic defeat early in the century, Carthage came back stronger and with a new attitude. This is perhaps the first clear moment when we can articulate a Carthaginian Empire in its own right. We no longer see Carthage only arriving to support allies and secure its interests in trade and foreign markets; it was interested in more direct control. It is a period where Syracuse and Carthage threw their weight around depending on who felt more inclined to aggressive imperialism at the time, and the status quo was maintained through much of the period between the two city-states. But the coming fourth century BCE would shift the dynamic and bring a whole new breed of military commander whose ambition, abilities and sheer force of will created a new kind of total war in the region. The rise of the warlords altered the history of the Mediterranean and much of the wider ancient world. These men shook the very foundations of the old order and one man in particular, the Syracusan Agathocles, presented Carthage with challenges that it had never before imagined.

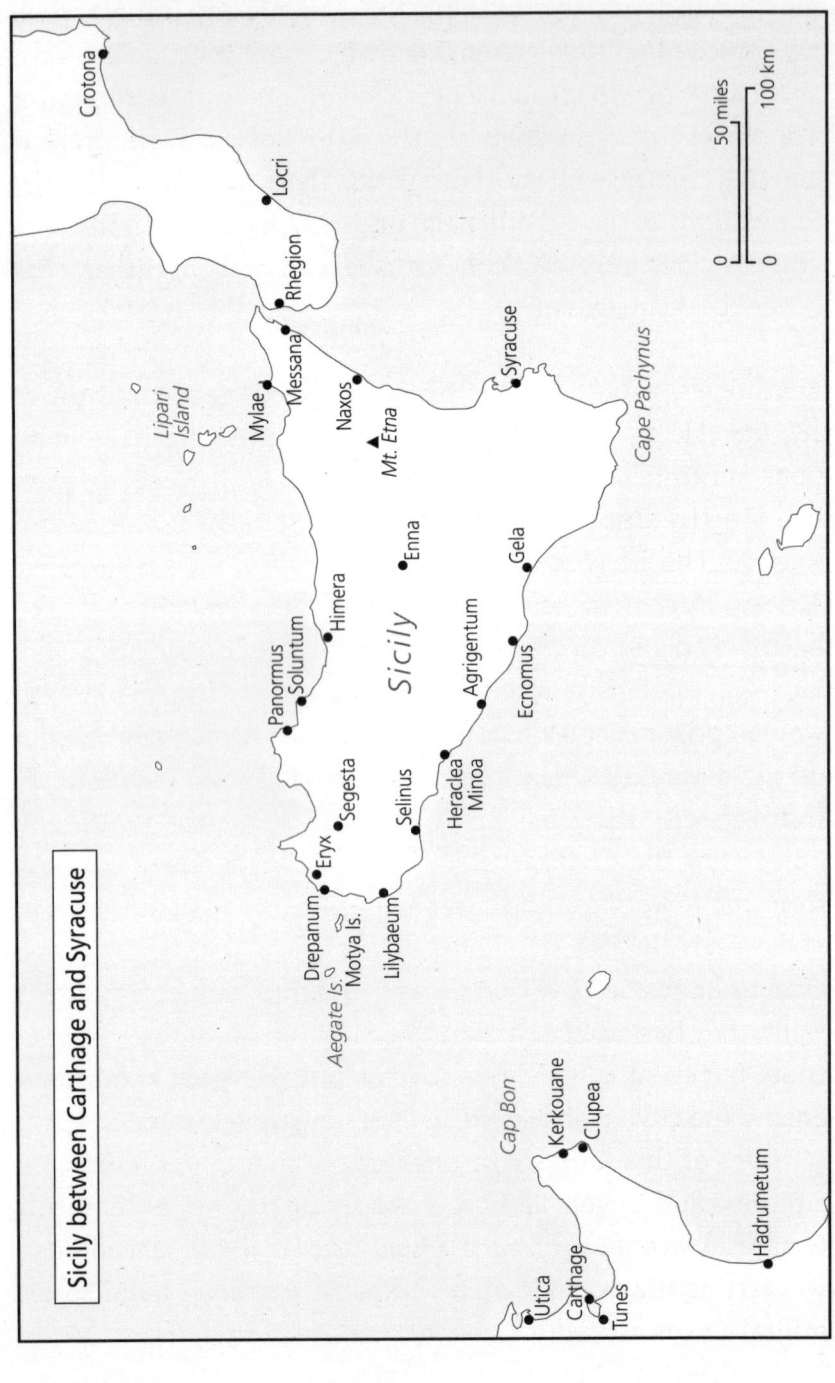

Sicily between Carthage and Syracuse

CHAPTER 5

The Age of Warlords

Agathocles, tyrant-king of Syracuse, lived from circa 361 to 289 BCE. He proved to be terrifying and unrelenting in his ambitions, very much a man of his time who was both a Sicilian tyrant in a long tradition and a new-styled conqueror for an expansive age. The grisly scene that played out during his siege of the African city of Utica sums up his methods. In a preliminary strike, he attacked and captured any citizens found outside the city's impressive defensive walls. Agathocles mounted these men and women prisoners on a massive siege engine and slowly rolled it up to the walls of Utica, moving the hulking beast inch by inch. Inside the city, the defenders on the walls preparing to withstand a siege saw their fellow citizens and family members dangling from the towering machine. The Uticans were then forced to make a terrible choice – defend their city by killing their own citizens or give in to the tyrant and lose their homes. Inside the walls, they hesitated at first, not wanting to harm their compatriots, but eventually they chose to mount a defence, killing both enemy and citizen alike with arrows, slings and catapults.

Tales of this kind shape our understanding of Agathocles, a pitiless and hugely ambitious leader operating in the Mediterranean world at the time when Alexander the Macedonian was setting the example of how expansive conquest and heroic military exploits were a route to eternal fame and fortune.[1]

Alexander's conquests would shift perspectives of power and warfare and empire across the old and new cities in the Mediterranean. That Agathocles fascinates historians and social commentators, past and present, is a measure of his importance. The Roman historian Justin called him 'a superlative illustration of unprincipled behaviour', while the Renaissance philosopher Niccolò Machiavelli marvelled at his brutality and political flexibility. Agathocles was the ultimate Machiavellian hero. He was a man who operated in the fierce political and military worlds of Syracuse and Carthage in the fourth and third centuries BCE. He took huge risks and was merciless in his approach to power and politics both on Sicily and in the wider Mediterranean, and his ambition would leave a defining mark on Carthage.[2]

On another level, Agathocles' life is the story of social mobility and opportunity in a multicultural Hellenistic Mediterranean in the Greek east, at Carthage and especially in a place like Sicily, in the colonial west. I use the word 'Hellenistic' here because it is what we conventionally call the period after the death of Alexander the Macedonian (323 BCE) to the rise of Octavian (31 BCE), soon to become the first Roman emperor Augustus. In this age of conquest and warfare the dominant idea was of a 'spear-won land' where the warlords and warrior kings who succeeded Alexander in the east would have an impact on the west of the Mediterranean. This concept reflects the dominant ethos in which to view military leadership in the next phases of the story of Carthage, and the history of its conflicts with Syracuse under Agathocles.

Agathocles' family history is worth exploring as a snapshot of the time. His father, named Carcinus, had been exiled from Rhegium at the very tip of Italy and went to live in new Therma (ancient Himera) on the north coast of Sicily. He was a potter, a solid profession in the ancient Mediterranean, where there was always work to be had making ceramics in the marketplaces of ancient cities. Carcinus met a woman from Therma and they went on to have a family. Agathocles' mother (not named) was described as a 'native of the town', which means she could have been so many things, an indigenous Siculian, a Carthaginian or fellow Greek, and likely a mix of the three. The town of Therma at this moment was under Carthaginian control; it had been occupied by those who had survived from nearby Himera, the site of the two great fifth-century battles between Greeks and Carthaginians discussed in the previous chapter. It sat at the boundary between spheres of influence, and it would have held deep memory and resonance for the people there. Therma also reflected the realities of many Sicilian cities in this period, where a constant to and fro of armies competing for territorial control and influence dominates the narrative while most of the population got on with trying to thrive and survive. The later writer Plutarch describes the social environment of Sicily at this time as 'most of the cities being occupied by peoples of mixed races and soldiers out of employment'.[3] Again, this was a simplification of complexity that Agathocles' contemporaries might have found difficult to recognise. In these years, the middle fourth century BCE, Carthage had come to terms with Timoleon, the Corinthian ruler of Syracuse, and a much-needed peace treaty had been signed. The previous decades of civil strife and brutal warfare between Syracuse and Carthage had devastated the population of Syracuse and so, to repopulate the land and territory, Timoleon offered grants of citizenship to free Greek peoples across a wide area. Agathocles and his whole family, including his parents and brother, took up this offer and moved to the big city when he was in his early twenties (c. 342 BCE).

In the Syracusan environment Agathocles showed great promise. As a child, so the later stories about his upbringing tell us, his future greatness was prophesied, which made his father wary of him, so that Agathocles was essentially brought up by his uncle. His mother gave him his name and his father taught him his trade, but the skills of a potter did not interest the young man for long. Once in Syracuse, the lure of the soldier's life beckoned for both Agathocles and his brother, Antander. The fourth-century Mediterranean was a world of personal armies, and for men of Agathocles' background the route through to success and wealth was war, loot and fighting. There is clear evidence of an increasingly high pay for professional soldiers, and it was steady and lucrative work. The Greek writer of comedy Menander describes, in his play *Aspis*, a soldier collecting 600 gold staters for his service.[4] Although its value is much debated, a gold stater was as much as a year's salary for a well-paid soldier and the play goes on to emphasise the man's fortune as he 'showed off his drinking cups and captives for sale'.

The war captives, who could be sold, loot and wages all contributed to the appeal of the soldiering profession. Diodorus includes a story about Athens where the assembly became dominated by 'those who preferred war and made their living from military service'.[5] There was an increasingly warmongering political atmosphere in the fourth century, and we can sense the later historian Diodorus' disapproval of it. This reflects the hindsight of centuries as a Mediterranean economy increasingly driven by war and personal gains led to a breakdown in order by his time. The contemporary environment glorified the warrior lifestyle and it became a world where too many men's livelihoods depended on conflict: 'war was peace and peace was war.'[6] Real and practical considerations of the economic impact on city-states and the need to raise huge sums to pay for soldiers drove conquest and economic growth equally. In the western Mediterranean, Carthage, Syracuse and eventually Rome too had the resources to compete in this environment and would do so freely.

In Syracuse, Agathocles was recruited as a soldier into the service of a man named Damas who became his patron, lover and sponsor. When Damas died, Agathocles married his widow around the year 333 BCE. Hers was an elite family with great wealth, and this gave the young Agathocles access to influential people in Syracuse. With elite family support and a close connection to the military, Agathocles came naturally to political ambition. Syracuse was ruled by an oligarchy of 600 men, but the legacy of decades of extreme political dysfunction prevailed. Agathocles was involved in a coup, an ambitious attempt to overthrow the oligarchs, which resulted in his banishment. In exile from Syracuse, he spent time in the cities of southern Italy, especially Crotona and Tarentum, where he lived as a soldier for hire. He must have had something special about him, because soon he had gathered a following of like-minded men. When the army of the Syracusan oligarchy laid siege to Rhegium, Agathocles flexed his muscles and brought his personally recruited force to relieve the siege. Impressed by this victory, the people in Syracuse then called for Agathocles to be allowed to return to the city. A populist by nature, he nurtured support beyond the elites, which allowed him to relate to the ordinary citizens of the city.

Soon after his return, the oligarchs were reinstated in power and Agathocles was banished once more. The influence of Carthage was ever present during these dramatic years of civil strife at Syracuse, and it made itself a key player in military engagements and political battles when supporting one side against another. This approach to inter-state policy is easy for us to understand from a modern perspective; the idea of intervening or even encouraging your enemy's internal strife as a method of weakening them still prevails. At first, the Carthaginian army in Sicily was allied through treaty with the oligarchy, but then Hamilcar, the Carthaginian commander, switched sides and mediated Agathocles' return to Syracuse. The result was that Agathocles was given overall military command (as *strategos*) of the Greek cities of Sicily by circa 319 BCE, and through a military coup he took control of Syracuse around 317 BCE. Once in power, he wrought bloody revenge on his political opponents. Stories tell of up to 10,000 banished or murdered, including any oligarchs who had opposed him. By ruthless and persistent violence, and with the help of Carthage, Agathocles had made himself tyrant of Syracuse.

For Carthage, helping Agathocles return to power in Syracuse might be seen as politically expedient, supporting a populist against the traditional oligarchy, but the result was a shift in the relationship between city and military on Sicily. This shift was not something that the Carthaginians would have expected or predicted. As we saw in the previous chapter, for almost a century there had been a kind of status quo, as witnessed by the ebb and flow of almost constant war and conquest, like a wave spreading across the island, with the influence of one or the other's powers growing with victory and receding with defeat.[7]

But the stories of Alexander's conquests were filtering across the Mediterranean, creating a new model for power in the ancient world. At Carthage, the reality of Alexander's exploits would have been brought home when the city of Tyre was sacked in 333 BCE. An envoy from Carthage was in Tyre at the time of the siege. His name was Hamilcar Rhodanus (Hamilcar the Rhodian) and he had been sent to meet with the young Macedonian as an ambassador on behalf of the Carthaginian state. Hamilcar is said to have tricked his way into a meeting with the great conqueror by befriending his entourage and pretending to seek refuge with the Macedonian army, claiming to abandon Carthage. As the story goes, it was all a ruse and Hamilcar used his access to send reports back to Carthage, informing it of Alexander's plans using hidden texts, written on wooden tablets and then covered with wax.[8] Even though the persistent stereotype of the 'wily Carthaginian' permeates this story, it also contains intriguing details of the practical spy craft of the ancient Mediterranean and how official embassies and diplomatic relations at the time were essentially information-gathering expeditions. Even today there is a long-held link between spying and diplomacy, and this reaches back well into antiquity. The republic of Carthage needed to be informed of Alexander's plans and had embedded an agent in his army. Carthage could not have been the only city-state to do so, and agents and diplomats from across the Mediterranean would have been keeping pace with the Macedonian conquests.

That Carthage was concerned about Alexander and the implications of his conquest for its own sphere of power was credible, especially once his new city in Egypt began construction (c. 332–330 BCE). Alexandria, on the Mediterranean coast of Egypt, would become the base for a powerful new kingdom and posed a serious issue for Carthage. Up to this point, Carthage had been the most powerful of the cities along the north coast of Africa but now it would have competition. The Macedonian king proved himself more willing to conquer than compete for trade routes and may have been thinking about encroaching on territory allied to Carthage in North Africa. The prosperous cities known as the emporia (Lepcis Magna, Sabratha and Oea, as discussed in Chapter 3) were renowned and we have seen how access was protected by the Carthaginians in their treaties with Rome. Some of our sources even report the rumour that Alexander intended to make Carthage his next great conquest once he returned to the Mediterranean after the Persian victories, but these plans were cut short by his premature death in 323 BCE in Babylon.[9]

As rumours flew from place to place, information would have come with refugees from Tyre arriving in Carthage after the destruction of their city. While more official representations of Carthage and its relationship with Tyre continued, both increasing connectivity and a knock-on impact of cultural shifts and political change would be felt across the sea. Stories such as that of Hamilcar, the ambassador/spy who had embedded in the Macedonian army, seem convincing. For this representative, however, pledges of loyalty to Alexander and his cause seemed to have convinced everyone at home as well, and when Hamilcar returned to Carthage after Alexander's death, he was executed for treason 'on the grounds that he had tried to sell Carthage to the [Macedonian] king'.[10] The end of the episode suggests that Hamilcar might have played the role of a double agent, but also resounds with Greek and Roman cliché about Carthaginians – that they were untrustworthy and duplicitous enemies. Embedded somewhere is a real man who had to negotiate the realities of the threat posed to Carthage by the limitless ambition of Alexander and his army.

Only a few years later, Agathocles' reign of absolute power in Syracuse had taken hold and he began to push for the same level of authority over neighbouring Greek cities on the island of Sicily and further afield as well. A Carthaginian army, under the command of another Hamilcar, defended Messina from Agathocles' reach, and again had to come to the defence of Akragas (Agrigentum) in 313 BCE. Some kind of status quo ensued where the Carthaginians were granted control over the Greek cities in the west of Sicily and recognised Agathocles and Syracuse as hegemon over the cities of the east. It is worth noting that this arrangement is depicted as having taken place without the consent of the other cities involved and reflected the division of Sicily into two spheres. The reality was certainly more nuanced, but the later sources prefer a simpler dichotomy.

When Hamilcar returned to Carthage from Sicily in 312 BCE, Agathocles seized Messina. Why Hamilcar had left Sicily is unknown, although there was the suspicion among the Cartha-ginian senators that his agreements with Agathocles may have not been in the best interests of Carthage. Once Agathocles had acted against Messina, the Carthaginians sent another army under yet another Hamilcar to engage with the protection of Akragas on the south coast. A hostile force in Messina, lying near to the Car-thaginian navy base of Lipara (Lipari) on the Aeolian Islands, was a huge disruption to operations and control of the seas off the north of Sicily. Agathocles then moved into the west of Sicily where he raided and pillaged through the Carthaginian-allied cities. The new Hamilcar responded by first defeating Agatho-cles in battle at Gela and then chasing him back to Syracuse and laying siege to the city.

Agathocles, in a brilliant and desperate manoeuvre, left his brother Antander in charge in Syracuse and took a small force, including his two grown-up sons, and sailed to Africa. This extra-ordinary feat of daring is dated specifically thanks to a solar eclipse that occurred the next day. It took place on 14 August in the year 310 BCE. As the later writer Justin recorded, 'the sun had been eclipsed during their voyage' and this was considered a bad omen by the Greek soldiers.[11] Slipping past the Carthagin-ian fleet and sailing across the sea to Africa, Agathocles landed at Cap Bon (see Map 102), the closest point to Sicily. Once there, the army of the Syracusan tyrant disembarked on the shore and burned the boats they had sailed across the sea on – failure, it seems, was not going to be an option. Agathocles turned his ambition towards Carthage. The surprise and impact of this attack cannot be underestimated and speaks volumes about how secure the Carthaginians had felt at home up until this point. While Carthaginian armies had operated for up to two centuries in Sicily and in Sardinia, their African homeland had remained relatively untouched by the wars. As Agathocles moved across the landscape, the agricultural lands on the Cap Bon peninsula were pillaged and looted as they went, the soldiers encountering a tantalising landscape 'full of gardens, of orchards watered by streams. The country houses followed one on the other, built with luxury . . . everywhere a picture of wealth in the estates of the Punic aristocracy'.[12]

With the main body of the army distracted by their long siege in Sicily, the Carthaginians at home in their city were completely unprepared for this surprise attack. They quickly pulled together a haphazard army of citizens, allies and anyone they could get their hands on, and at short notice set out to meet the invaders. This force seems woefully unprepared but is nevertheless described as large in number. Their opponents in the field were a small, extremely well-paid, motivated and battle-hardened force of a now infamous Greek tyrant. As is usual with ancient battles, the details are sketchy, but reports confirm that the subsequent defeat inflicted on the Carthaginian army was stunning. The source for this event is Justin, and he retained particularly vivid details. The Carthaginian army was led by a commander named Hanno and had 30,000 soldiers in the field. The meeting resulted in mass slaughter with only 3,000 Carthaginians, including their commander, left standing. Agathocles took advantage of his early successes and raged on across the landscape, storming towns and forts and capturing 'a vast quantity of plunder and killing many thousands'.

When he pitched his camp just 8km from Carthage, Agathocles is reported to have reasoned that, in this way, the citizens inside the walls might watch while their land was devastated and the countryside around them burned. It was not an easy thing to take Carthage itself, as the city was defended by state-of-the-art walls and sat on a narrow peninsula surrounded on three sides by water. Remember that Agathocles had burned his ships upon landing, leaving his army to rely on their capabilities on land but not by sea. Inside Carthage, rumours swirled about the destruction of the army and capture of the other cities. Citizens mourned the loss of their family members and as the news spread across the countryside, and through 'all of Africa' according to Justin, there was astonishment and wonder how so 'sudden a war could have surprised so great an empire'. In the heartland of North Africa, from where Carthage's allies and soldiers were recruited, the wonder gradually changed into a kind of suspicion of the Carthaginians. Believing that Agathocles was going to end up the winner, and in a sense of self-preservation, Carthage's neighbours had to think long and hard about whose side they would choose to come down on. At stake were large amounts of income and food supplies that both sides were now in desperate need of.[13]

Carthage itself was now under siege and, with many of the Carthaginian elite dead on the field of battle, the city was vulnerable to attack. Even more significantly for Carthage, the presence of a victorious Greek army led to a serious revolt among allies in Africa. Diodorus claims that in this extreme state of panic, the city undefended and at the mercy of Agathocles, Carthaginians believed they had been abandoned by their gods. They took all kinds of measures to appease those they deemed they had offended; they sent mass tribute from their own temples to that of Melqart at Tyre and a mass sacrifice of children ensued.[14] Diodorus describes how 200 of the noblest children were selected and one by one placed in the sloping arms of a giant bronze image of the god Ba'al. From the arms of the god, they then rolled into a gaping fire pit, watched by their parents and the whole community; it is an extraordinary scene. In fact, Diodorus' description was so influential that it was embraced by many who sought to describe the ancient city, including Gustave

Flaubert in his nineteenth-century novel *Salammbô* and in the early twentieth-century Italian film *Cabiria*, directed by Giovanni Pastrone. From a practical consideration, following modern excavation of the site called the Tophet at Carthage, we know this act of mass sacrifice never appears in any of the physical evidence discovered to date – the infant cremations there are individual burials, not mass graves. The story in Diodorus was an imagined scene by a hostile ancient source and the numbers presented here are outlandish and belie everything we understand about the way children were dedicated at Carthage. This kind of mass sacrifice would also have caused a massive rupture in natural population growth that would have ultimately destroyed the city. Underlying this story, however, is the reality of the huge distress that the inhabitants of Carthage were put under during the terror that Agathocles inflicted on the city itself and its neighbours. That they turned to their gods in times of strife was certain.

What is also certain is that Carthage had not reacted effectively to Agathocles' expedition. There was a succession of fiercely fought battles that challenged the city's position in Africa for the very first time. The opening scene of this chapter describes how the key Phoenician-allied city of Utica was placed under siege and the close alliances were frayed. The tenuous nature of Carthaginian control over the wider communities of the prosperous and agriculturally rich lands of North Africa had also been exposed. Perhaps even more dangerous for the Carthaginians was that Agathocles attempted to make an alliance with the Ptolemaic ruler of Cyrene, Ophellas. This alliance would have challenged the long-held and respected spheres of influence between Carthage and Cyrene along the north coastal strip of Africa but in these heady years of conquest that followed in the aftermath of Alexander all norms ceased to apply. An alliance between

Agathocles and Cyrene could have ended in total disaster for Carthage in Africa.

Ophellas was the governor of Cyrene and was related to the Hellenistic king of Egypt, Ptolemy I. The events that took place are nowhere properly explained and only alluded to as if our sources don't really understand what happened either. The alliance was attempted but failed to materialise, and the only reasonable conclusions are that some kind of betrayal led Agathocles to attack and kill his erstwhile ally Ophellas. He then incorporated the soldiers of Cyrenaica into his own army.

Carthage remained isolated and increasingly cut off from its traditional allies in Africa, but its enemies were cannibalising each other. When the Syracusan forces finally took the cities of Utica and Hippo Acra to the north of Carthage and the African allied states flocked to the side of Agathocles it had all looked dire, but by 307 BCE, after four eventful years, Carthage still stood despite all the odds. Then Agathocles very suddenly changed his tactics, upped sticks and returned to try to save his own power base in Syracuse, which had been undermined by his absence. What is even more extraordinary is that he left his army, including his own sons, in Africa. He essentially abandoned the army that had proved so loyal to him and left them to their fate. Carthage eventually won back all the territory it had lost and even seems to have incorporated some of the army of Agathocles into its own society, providing a glimpse into the possibilities of social mobility in the state and the flexibility of a soldier's professional life. Despite its ultimate failure, Agathocles' bold adventure in Africa had exposed how vulnerable Carthage was to invasion and illustrated this to the wider world.[15]

Agathocles' invasion of Africa shifted the boundaries of engagement. For the better part of a century, Carthage and Syracuse had fought wars of attrition on Sicily. With one failed but bold surprise attack, Agathocles changed that. Certainly, inspired by the limitless approach to conquest, the Hellenistic Age had come to the central and western Mediterranean. Conquest became the norm for kings and tyrants like Agathocles or the generals of the Carthaginian republic who fought against him and remembered these events. Individual military commanders expanded their horizons for conquest beyond the traditional zones of conflict. It was no longer just about battling over the resources and sanctuaries of Sicily and defending allies against incursions from one or the other side. Larger and far more geographically expansive power was now possible, and this opened the door to a constant threat of an invasion of Africa, which would become Carthage's greatest vulnerability.

In hindsight, the shift Agathocles created in the battle for Sicily altered the trajectory of the wars to come. His significance should not be underestimated. He created the playbook that became the standard for warring against Carthage and, as we will discover in the following chapters, this was a strategy emulated by the Romans in the First and Second Punic Wars. Agathocles showed the world that Carthage was vulnerable at home and that its allies could be prized away without too much effort, a lesson Carthage itself would take a long time to learn. Agathocles also linked southern Italy with North Africa, raiding equally in Campania and on the south shore of the Mediterranean, transferring populations around the island of Sicily and using the whole of the central Mediterranean zone as his chessboard.

The memory of Agathocles was still fresh in the minds of many of the main players when the next of the Hellenistic warlords to buffer Carthage arrived on the scene. This was king Pyrrhus (319–272 BCE), of the Greek Adriatic state of Epirus that lay across the Adriatic from southern Italy (see page 80). He had married one of Agathocles' daughters, Lanassa, in 295 BCE.

She was sent to live in Epirus and brought the gift of the island of Corcyra (Corfu) as her dowry to the king. Lanassa was an influential woman in her own right and not particularly keen on her husband Pyrrhus' habit of taking other wives. The Macedonian Hellenistic kings tended towards polygamy, so although the couple had two children together, Lanassa eventually left Pyrrhus and went to Corfu to live. On Corfu she naturally would have needed support from another hegemon and found one in another of the Hellenistic kings of the moment, Demetrius Poliorcetes. Demetrius then married Lanassa and took the island of Corcyra for himself.[16]

The story of Lanassa, along with a rare glimpse into the agency of women in the era, shows how Pyrrhus was driven to conquer neighbouring kingdoms and used intermarriage with powerful neighbours as a way to build alliances and grow his power and wealth. Being from Epirus, he would have seen his sphere of influence naturally extending to Greece, to southern Italy and into Sicily. There is a striking portrait of Pyrrhus written by the Roman historian Plutarch that is worth looking at in detail for the way it constructs leadership in the period. Plutarch wrote that Pyrrhus was such a man that even in the aftermath of a military victory, the soldiers he defeated did not loathe but admired him:

> The conflict left a lasting impression on all those involved, sparking endless discussions and admiration for Pyrrhus' bravery among both participants and observers. They couldn't help but draw parallels between Pyrrhus and Alexander the Great, noting similarities in appearance, speed, and vigor on the battlefield. Many perceived in Pyrrhus a reflection of Alexander's fiery and impetuous nature, further fueling their awe and reverence for his military prowess. (*Life of Pyrrhus* 8)

Pyrrhus is written about here as a great hero of the age and celebrated by an ancient writer for his bold tactics and bravery. This is the man whose arrival in southern Italy set in motion a chain of events that would bring the Romans directly into the Carthaginians' traditional sphere of influence. When Pyrrhus of Epirus clattered into southern Italy in circa 281 BCE he did so because he had been invited. The southern Italian Greek city-state of Tarentum (Taras, a colony of Sparta in origin) had turned to its neighbour across the Adriatic, and the Epirot kings had a long history of coming to the aid of Greek cities in the south of Italy. The reasons for intervention had previously rested on one Greek city-state fighting against another, so the rulers of Tarentum would call in an army against the neighbouring towns of Locri or Crotona, or Metapontum, and had been doing so since about 350 BCE (see page 124).[17]

The arrival of Pyrrhus and his invasion of southern Italy was different because it was a new enemy, the Romans, who had been the catalyst for the invitation by the Tarentines. The entrance of Rome into the southern Italian scene shifted the dynamics between the Greeks and the Carthaginians in both the Italian peninsula and Sicily. This is an important moment in the history of the region because, for the first time, it saw a king and army from the post-Alexander Greek kingdoms on the Italian mainland fighting the Romans and resulted in the entanglement between Rome, Sicily, Carthage and the wider Mediterranean world that would dominate the next century of warfare in the region.

Perhaps most famously, it was about elephants too. In Pyrrhus' exemplary 'Hellenistic' military force that arrived in Italy were 20 war elephants to be used in battle. These were the 'strange monsters of the Macedonians', and the elephants of Pyrrhus were first deployed in Italy and then Sicily on this expedition.[18] It is often claimed that this event was the first military encounter the Romans and Carthaginians had with 'the civilised core of the Mediterranean world', although the history of the previous century in Sicily illustrates that, for the Carthaginians at least, this was untrue. The elephants obviously struck a chord with some of the Carthaginian military, however, and it was not long after this period that Carthage first used elephants in its own forces. Indeed, the elephant would become one of the most important and iconic symbols of Carthage, used by the third-century Barcid generals of the city to great effect in their future conquests in the Iberian Peninsula. Pyrrhus' army most likely brought the Asian species of elephant with it to Italy, perhaps acquired from the Seleucid Macedonian kingdom that bred its elephants in the city of Apamea in Syria (according to the Roman geographer Strabo).[19] They were prestige animals, used for shock and awe to unnerve enemy troops, but were also hugely expensive to support and maintain.

There is, as yet, no general consensus on the kind of elephants used by Carthage for its own military exploits. The animals were employed to have the impact of tanks on the field but brought with them some of the drawbacks too: they were not easily man-oeuvrable, although impressive as a scare and intimidation tactic. The city of Carthage developed a whole system to care for and train its elephants. The city walls, the state-of-the-art casemate construction that surrounded the land and sea of Carthage, had areas built between two courses where elephants were housed along with weapons, stores and soldiers' barracks. These animals, and their specialised trainers and riders, became a frequent image in Carthaginian life after the encounter with Pyrrhus. Whether Carthage used the species of Asian elephants thought to be employed by the post-Alexander kings in their armies, or the southern African elephants we are more familiar with today, is a matter of debate and conjecture, and will remain so until the archaeological research produces enough convincing evidence to allow for specific DNA analysis. There is, now, a general agreement that it may not have been just one species, and that different kinds of elephants were used in different scenarios. The African elephants, the extinct North African wood elephants and Asian elephants are all present in the archaeological evidence from the ancient Mediterranean, so a more multi-faceted approach to their deployment is likely (see Fig 14).

The invasion of Pyrrhus had been precipitated by the Roman Republic's expansion into the south of Italy. The prosperous Greek cities of southern Italy had grown nervous of Roman influence in Italy over the fourth and early third centuries BCE. When Rome's final victory in the three Samnite Wars took place in 290 BCE, the Greek cities saw the removal of the strong buffer state between Rome and the region known as Magna Graecia, or Greater Greece. Pyrrhus crossed with his army to Italy in 281 BCE and won two hard-fought battles against Roman forces, the first at Heraclea in 280 BCE and the second at Ausculum in 279 BCE (there are two Auscula in Italy – this one, modern-day Ascoli Satriano in Apulia, and one further north, Ascoli Piceno in Le Marche). The intensity of these battles still lives on with us today. Justin describes the victory of Pyrrhus as 'not bloodless; for he himself was severely wounded, and a great number of his soldiers killed; and he had more glory from his victory than pleasure.' Pyrrhus did win both battles but had sustained such heavy losses

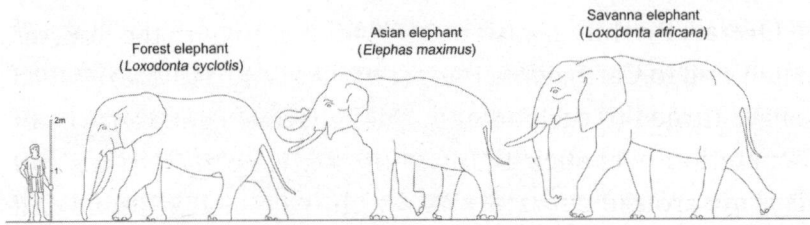

Fig. 14 Variant elephant species with relative sizes

that it gave rise to the term 'a Pyrrhic victory' and cemented his immortal reputation.[20] From this date onwards it became more common to use 'Pyrrhic victory' rather than the term 'Cadmean victory' for a battle that is won but at such a heavy price it's akin to a loss, such as because of the death of so many soldiers.

In the year 278 BCE Pyrrhus accepted an invitation from the city of Syracuse, which saw the opportunity to use the travelling Epirot army against their old enemies, the Carthaginians. Syracuse offered Pyrrhus control of important cities in Sicily such as Agrigentum, Leontini and Syracuse itself, in return. The presence of Pyrrhus and his army was too good an opportunity for the Syracusans to pass up. Pyrrhus even pursued a claim to power at Syracuse through his marriage to Agathocles' daughter Lanassa, with the familial ties linking Greece and Sicily even closer in this age. The Carthaginian army on Sicily proved to be no match for Pyrrhus and suffered a heavy defeat. Pyrrhus went on to storm the fortified stronghold of the Carthaginians at Eryx, the fort that sat near the sacred shrine of the goddess and dominated the landscape above Drepanum (modern Trapani) in western Sicily. The defeat pushed Carthaginian influence back to the very southwestern tip of Sicily, where the forces were held up at Lilybaeum and isolated there. This was something Carthage's old enemies the Syracusans had never achieved. Pyrrhus, though, without a navy in support, could not take Lilybaeum so was not really capable of completing the task, and the Carthaginian presence in Sicily held on.

Overall, Pyrrhus' invasion posed a threat to both the Romans in Italy and to Carthaginians in Sicily. The two cities are believed to have turned to each other at this time and signed a treaty of cooperation over their mutual hostility towards Pyrrhus and his army around 279/278 BCE. Pyrrhus presented Rome and Carthage with a common enemy and the two old allies renewed this alliance in the face of a common threat. The existence of this treaty, referred to as the 'treaty of Philinus', is one of the hotly contested issues debated by academics today. The treaty named as 'of Philinus' is so-called because of the name of the author of a lost history of the period who was a Sicilian Greek named Philinus. The Greek author Polybius had access to this history, but we cannot read it for ourselves. Philinus was a profoundly anti-Roman historian from the Sicilian city of Agrigentum who told the tale of the First Punic War. Polybius claimed that Philinus invented this treaty, but it should equally be considered that it was an inconvenient document for the Romans and has been written out of history. The treaty of Philinus, if it existed, claimed that the Romans and the Carthaginians had renewed their long-standing treaties in this period of the Pyrrhic Wars and agreed to their respective spheres of influence, Sicily being Carthaginian and southern Italy being in the Roman sphere. The coming wars between the two powerful city-states would see the terms of this treaty violated. It may be that Polybius was not aware of the treaty. Equally, it is possible that the treaty did exist and had been destroyed and denied. The debate rests upon whose feet we lie the responsibility for the epic Punic Wars, and we'll learn more of this in the coming chapters.

When Pyrrhus returned home to quell unrest in his own kingdom of Epirus, the Carthaginians almost immediately retook all their lost territories and pushed even further than before. This was true also of the Romans, who extended their control in Italy right to the tip of the southernmost point of the peninsula – the tip of the boot of Italy. Only the narrow straits of Messina separated Roman and Carthaginian interests now. The two sides remembered Pyrrhus as the catalyst for change in their long relationship. Up until Pyrrhus and throughout the period of his threat, Rome and Carthage had maintained the good relations of previous centuries, adhering to their respected treaties, as far as we know. Once Pyrrhus had withdrawn from Sicily, the two most powerful cities of the western Mediterranean would come face to face over the island and meet there in hostile contact. History records that even Pyrrhus was aware of this new dynamic, and he is alleged to have left these final words as he sailed off back home: 'what a battlefield we are leaving to the Carthaginians and the Romans' (Plutarch, *Pyrrhus* 23).

Central Mediterranean in the Punic Wars

Placentia

R. Po

Genoa

Lucca

Arminium

Arretium
Crotona

ETRURIA

Adriatic Sea

Alaria

Corsica

Caere
Pyrgi
Rome

Casilinum
Luceria
Arpi
Salapia
Canusia
Capua
Nola
Ausculum
Compsa
Brundisium
Napoli
Grumentum
Venusia
Tarentum
Metapontum
Heraclea

LUCANIA

Tharros

Sardinia

Carales

Consentia

Sulcis
Nora

Lipari

Crotona

BRUTTIUM

Panormus
Mylae
Drepanum
Eryx
Soluntum
Messana
Locri
Aegate Is.
Lilybaeum
Rhegion

Hippacra
Cap Farina
Heraclea
Agrigentum
Minoa
Ecnomus
Utica
Cap Bon
Kerkouane
Thrabaca
Carthage
Clupea
Sicily
Syracuse

Cirta
R. Bagradas
Cape Pachynus

Naraggara
Sicca
Malta

Theveste
Hadrumentum
Thapsus
Acholla
Thaenae

Gabes

0   200 miles

0   300 km

CHAPTER 6

The Boxing Match

The spark that ignited the prophecy told by Pyrrhus begins with a group of mercenary soldiers. The Mamertines were a powerful armed group who originated from central Italy and who had been left over in Sicily from the days of Agathocles. The word 'Mamertines' comes from the 'sons of Mamers', who was the Oscan god of war they worshipped. Mamers is better known in the Latin version as the god Mars. Oscan was a key language of Italy spoken widely in the middle and south of the peninsula in the period up to the Roman conquests of the fourth and third centuries BCE, after which Latin gradually became the common tongue. In the time of Pyrrhus and the aftermath, Oscan was still more prevalent than Latin in the central and southern regions of Italy. When Agathocles died in 289 BCE, these Oscan men of war were left unemployed and unchecked. Relatively young, wealthy and well-armed, they took the opportunity to seize the city of Messina as a base from which to operate. At Messina, a kind of soldier state formed. They drew others to them and generally wreaked havoc in the region. They exerted a powerful influence on life in the northeast corner of Sicily, especially since the soldier's life was such a draw. Their numbers dramatically increased in the decades after Agathocles. The ever-increasing warfare of the period needed manpower. These men had relative autonomy, due to how highly valued soldiers were.

The high pay of mercenary soldiers and the lure of the life-style come up in some of the contemporary writers like Theocritus, a Greek poet born in Sicily around 300 BCE. Theocritus lived in Alexandria in Egypt and wrote poetry under the patronage of the Ptolemaic king there. He presents an imagined conversation where two men discuss going off to fight. The young man 'determined to clasp the warrior's cloak' about himself is told to go to Egypt where Ptolemy is the 'best paymaster a man can have'. Carthage too was renowned for paying high wages to soldiers. While calculating the amount some states would have to lay out for military expenditure is difficult and has to be speculative, there is evidence to show that a very significant proportion of the public purse was spent on arming and supporting men for fighting.[1] The very production of coinage in Sicily by the Carthaginians was geared towards supporting military interventions and life 'in the camp' as discussed in Chapter 4.

At the northeast tip of Sicily, the Mamertines were just a few kilometres away from the tip of the toe of the boot at the southern end of the Italian peninsula (see page 124). The Strait of Messina, the narrow gap between Sicily and Italy, was guarded by the city of the same name. This waterway was the gateway to Sicily and the west coast of Italy, a place of great strategic importance that controlled the shipping through these waters. From Messina the soldiers could pillage far and wide, kidnap women and destroy crops, and then hold towns and cities to ransom. They pirated on the sea and looted the land around Messina, protected by the harbour and substantial walls around the town. At its most narrow, the Strait of Messina is less than 4km wide, and the city of Messina was just 12km across the water from the ancient city of Rhegium (Reggio Calabria). Rhegium had only recently been seized by the Romans, who had ousted another group of mercenary soldiers there.

Around the mid-260s BCE, though the exact timing is uncertain, the Mamertines suffered a decisive defeat at the hands of Syracuse. The Syracusans were led by the newly appointed and dynamic general Hiero II, who had ascended to rule as king. Hiero was determined to crush the Mamertines, and by approximately 265 BCE their leaders were captured. Faced with imminent destruction, some of the Mamertines sought assistance from neighbouring powers to counter the Syracusan threat. As recounted by the historian Polybius, a faction of the men of Mamers approached Carthage, offering to surrender their citadel, while others dispatched an embassy to Rome, seeking support from the Italians as 'kindred' people. Both Carthage and Rome had strategic interests in controlling the city: Carthage maintained a naval presence on the nearby island of Lipari, while Rome's influence extended to the southern tip of the Italian peninsula. Both powers seized upon the opportunity presented by the Mamertines' plea for aid. Polybius, in his account of Rome's rise, begins his first book by acknowledging the significance of this pivotal event involving the Mamertines, capturing the moment that the Romans took their first steps outside Italy: 'I shall take as my starting point the first occasion on which the Romans crossed the sea from Italy.'[2]

This one event, a cry for help from mercenary proxies, was the catalyst that first pitched the Carthaginians against the Romans in war. The details are confused but the scenario, from what we can glean from the ancient sources, played out as follows. The Carthaginian commander of the fleet at Lipari sailed to Messina and took it, with the support of one faction of the Mamertines. The Romans sent their consul, named Appius Claudius, who aided another faction of the Mamertines and then ousted the Carthaginians from the citadel of the city. Then the Syracusans showed up in support of their old enemy Carthage and the two cities allied against the Romans. Appius Claudius was victorious against the Syracusans, and now held Messina for Rome. The Carthaginian commander, whose name we don't know, was reportedly crucified by his own troops for his cowardice in giving up the citadel. The Romans had, by then, battled the Carthaginians, pillaged the countryside and moved south. They set up camp and began to lay siege to Syracuse.

In Rome, the dominant Italian city-state that had steadily risen to prominence throughout the fourth century BCE, a moment of decision arrived. Years of relentless military campaigns had brought it to this juncture, and the triumph of Appius Claudius spurred the Roman senate to dispatch its next two elected consuls, Manius Otacilius and Manius Valerius, to Sicily. As noted by Polybius, they deployed 'their whole armed force and both commanders' to the conflict.[3] The consular duo arrived with an estimated army of 40,000 soldiers, representing the full might of the formidable Roman military apparatus converging on Sicily. This Roman expeditionary force, comprising both citizen soldiers and allied auxiliaries, dwarfed any available forces at the disposal of Carthage or Syracuse at that time. In the midst of these developments, Hiero of Syracuse, reassessing his strategy, renounced his alliance with Carthage and negotiated terms with Rome. This shift left Carthage and its allies in Sicily confronting a unified threat: the combined military and naval power of Syracuse, now allied with a massive Roman army. With a solid foothold established in Sicily, the Romans gained control over the entire eastern coastal region, significantly altering the strategic landscape of the conflict in a few short years.

This marks the beginning of an epic saga known to the Romans as the First Punic War, and presumably to the Carthaginians as the First Roman War. We have seen how, for more than two centuries, Sicily had been a battleground between Greek and

Carthaginian forces. When the Romans embarked on their initial expedition beyond the Italian peninsula to seize control of Sicily, they did so in earnest, viewing the island as a natural progression in their southward expansion. According to Roman accounts, both Carthage and Rome entered the conflict by responding to the call for assistance from the minor mercenaries. However, the deployment of a substantial Roman military force in Sicily from the outset suggests a deeper, more calculated strategy to assert control over the island, despite attempts to downplay this in historical narratives. The ensuing conflict spanned 23 years, exacting a heavy toll in lives lost and resources depleted, nearly bankrupting both Carthage and Rome. It stands as a testament to the unforeseen repercussions of actions taken, and forever shaped the history of the central Mediterranean.

In the Roman narrative of the First Punic War, Carthage and Rome were two equal powers whose dispute was over the 'empire of the world'.[4] It may have seemed that way, but evidence suggests that Carthage was not quite as powerful as Rome when they first encountered the other in the mid-260s BCE. This matters because the study of this war has dominated the narrative of both Carthage and Rome since it was fought and right up to today. Pyrrhus had soundly defeated Carthage but had barely defeated Rome in the previous decades, while the Roman-friendly sources like to play up the wealth and prosperity of Carthage. One way that we like to try to understand the relative strengths of the two powers in the third century is to look at manpower resources and these tell us that Rome and Carthage had a similar total population size. The big difference between the two was that the Roman system was more amenable to accessing greater manpower resources through the way they made their alliances. Estimating population sizes in the ancient world is notoriously difficult and there is much more data available about

Roman than Carthaginian manpower in this period.[5] Nonetheless, they were the two most powerful city-states in the region, but with Rome in alliance with Syracuse, its resources dwarfed those of Carthage.

The First Punic War took place in stages.[6] There were the opening gambits around Messina and Syracuse, and then the fighting moved south and around the island westward. The action played out on land and at sea with periods of intense fighting between the combatants. The two sides built and lost fleets at great effort and expense, and then there were periods of stalemate with little action, giving the combatants a chance to recuperate. We are almost entirely reliant on how Polybius, the Greek who wrote Rome's history, tells the story – it is the only history that focuses on the First Punic War that we have. His narrative gives a sense that the Romans were relentless in their efforts during these years, while the Carthaginians generally come across as ineffective and not entirely sure what to do. The pro-Carthaginian (or at least anti-Roman) sources that were discussed by Polybius have disappeared except for brief fragments. There once existed a much broader perspective on the events of the war and many of the historians were Sicilians, but they have long been silenced.

The powerful alliance of Rome and Syracuse meant that Roman army numbers on Sicily could be reduced, with Syracusans supplementing their troops. This combined army moved next to take the city of Agrigentum (Greek Akragas) in the year 262 BCE (see page 124). Boasting a population of 50,000 Agrigentum, the most important city on the south coast of Sicily, was originally founded in circa 580 BCE by the people of the city of Gela (to the east of it) who were in turn Rhodian and Cretan in origin.[7] The Greek city of Agrigentum had been controlled by Carthage from the fourth century BCE. The Romans and their Syracusan allies intended to gather food and disrupt the Carthaginians from doing so themselves, breaking their supply chain along the coast. The Carthaginians had used Agrigentum as a strategic base from which to defend the southwest corner of Sicily but had only a garrison there. The garrison in the city was now vastly overwhelmed and they had to send to Carthage for reinforcement. A new army of 'Ligurians, Celts, and still more Iberians' was dispatched to Sicily under the command of Hanno. They had been sent to defend Agrigentum from an impending Roman attack but by the time they arrived a siege was already in place.[8] The newly arrived Carthaginian army encircled the besieging army.

The Romans used a strategy of starvation to force surrender. The besieging army disrupted the harvest, leaving the citizens of Agrigentum with nothing to eat. Soon, famine pursued those within the city walls. In an attempt to alleviate the suffering, Hanno led his army in a pitched battle against the Romans, aiming to break through and provide relief to the populace. The intense clash unfolded outside the city walls, witnessed by the starving population peering down from above. Despite the fierce resistance, the Romans emerged victorious, securing the day. At this moment, after a five-month siege, the Carthaginian garrison inside the city escaped, perhaps under orders to save themselves from the Romans. The result left the citizens of Agrigentum completely unprotected from the Roman onslaught. Details in our sources describe the mayhem and slaughter as the Roman soldiers stormed into the city and plundered everything and everyone they could find. Huge quantities of loot and enslaved people were moved out of Agrigentum, with one source recording that the whole population, all 50,000, were taken to Rome to be sold in the markets.[9]

In Rome, the people were excited by the victory, in the words of Polybius:

> when the news of what had happened at Agrigentum reached the Roman Senate, in their joy and elation they no longer kept to their original designs . . . but hoped that it would be possible to drive the Carthaginians entirely out of the island.[10]

The statues and gold of the treasury of Agrigentum were displayed to the people of Rome, paraded in a grand triumph, and had the populace clamouring for more. The appetite for conquest only grew. This change of intention inspired by the sack of a wealthy city in the culturally Greek part of Sicily portrays Polybius' disapproval of politics led by the masses, of populism, which becomes a persistent theme in his history. It is difficult to attribute any truth to the story and the Carthaginian reaction to the loss of Agrigentum is not recorded, except that the army regrouped and was reinforced. For a long time, the leadership at Carthage and in Sicily had been involved in a war of attrition fought for an increased share of the island, but they slowly began to realise that this situation was different: they were engaged in all-out conquest.

The initial years of the war unfolded primarily on land, yet simultaneous naval engagements were also underway. While the siege of Agrigentum was ongoing and leading up to the first open battle at sea, the Carthaginians had not been entirely idle elsewhere. They had embarked on a strategy of harassing the Romans and raiding along the coast of Italy, using their maritime skill to try to disrupt Roman transports.[11] There is a Punic ship on display in the archaeological museum of Marsala (former Lilybaeum) that was found off the coast in the early 1970s along with another ship of a similar form. It is an example of the ships that the Carthaginians might have been using on their raids. This is a liburna, a small galley ship used for raiding and patrols. The details are fascinating;

the wooden planks of the ship, which have been preserved, were made from pine and Mediterranean maple species. On planks that comprise the curved keel of the ship are letters for each piece, indicating that it was easily constructed – the individual pieces were labelled to enable quick and efficient shipbuilding, perhaps even on an industrial and mobile scale (see Fig. 15).[12]

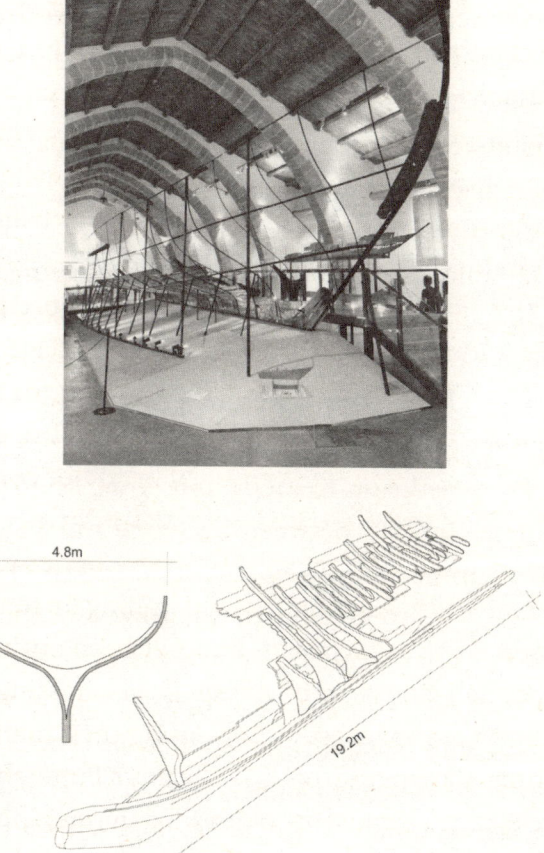

Fig. 15 Photo of Punic ship as displayed in the museum at Marsala with schematic rendering of the size and remains

The inaugural naval confrontation occurred around 260 BCE off the northern coast, west of Messina near the Mylae (Milazzo) promontory. The location was strategic, just adjacent to the Carthaginian naval stronghold on Lipari Island. As we saw in Chapter 3, Carthaginians had long wielded maritime dominance in the central Mediterranean and we can assume they believed themselves unrivalled in naval prowess and influence. However, the inner workings of their naval structure within the state remain somewhat obscure. Many captains, along with their recruited crews, traversed Carthaginian-allied ports, undertaking various responsibilities akin to a merchant navy. Rather than solely projecting aggression, Carthaginian naval forces boasted versatility, deploying a diverse array of ships and engaging in multifaceted actions. Sailors were renowned for their ability to navigate open waters, a testament to their rigorous training and meticulous ship maintenance, evident in the advanced port facilities of Carthage and its allied cities.[13]

Roman naval capabilities present a contrasting view. Polybius tells us that the Romans had no prior experience in naval warfare before their expedition to Sicily, but some scepticism is warranted. These conflicts between Carthage and Rome were fundamentally conflicts between alliances, and the Romans were able to effectively leverage the naval prowess of their numerous skilled allies. They availed themselves of penteconters and triremes from allies such as the Tarentines, Locrians, Eleans and the people of Neapolis, not to mention the whole Syracusan navy. Polybius has been criticised for downplaying Roman naval experience for rhetorical effect, and scholars note significant evidence of Roman maritime interests in the centuries leading up to the war. This discrepancy likely reflects a deliberate construction by the ancient author to make the Roman successes seem even more remarkable by emphasising the Romans' adaptability and resourcefulness. We always have to remember who Polybius was writing for – he was explaining Roman success to Greek audiences.[14]

During this period, the Romans also committed themselves to developing a navy capable of rivalling that of the Carthaginians, drawing upon a broad recruitment base from their maritime allies. Polybius again provides the insight into their efforts, noting the construction of 'a hundred quinqueremes [fives] and twenty triremes'. Remarkably, the larger quinqueremes were modelled after a captured Carthaginian vessel, with the Romans introducing a notable innovation known as the *corvus* (or *corax*, Latin for crow).[15] This was a boarding bridge, affixed to the prow of Roman warships, and used to significantly enhance the efficiency of grappling and boarding enemy vessels. In the naval tactics of the third century BCE, ramming was predominantly relied upon, with fleets aiming to sink adversaries by using solid-bronze rams mounted on their ships' fronts (see Fig. 17 on page 155). This tactic favoured the Carthaginians, renowned for their superior skill and manoeuvrability at sea. Carthaginian sailors excelled in outmanoeuvring opponents. However, the incorporation of the corvus into Roman ships disrupted the seamanship of their adversaries, enabling the Romans firmly to engage and board enemy vessels when in close proximity.

The first naval battle at Mylae played out to dramatic effect. When the Carthaginian fleet put out from their base at Lipari they had Hannibal in command, the same man who had led the relief force at Agrigentum. Here is evidence for a military commander from Carthage interchangeably taking charge in both sea and land battles. The Carthaginian fleet had 130 ships and the commander led out his fleet in a large ship described as a luxury vessel that was a 'seven-banked galley formerly belonging to King Pyrrhus'.[16] The Roman fleet met them with 120 ships

(100 quinqueremes and 20 triremes). Considering the number of rowers needed for each of these ships – for example a quinquereme would carry 300 rowers (not to mention the hundreds of marine fighters) – these are enormous numbers and we are well familiar by now with the idea that the ancient sources meant to impress us by exaggerating these estimates. The Carthaginian fleet did not know about the new Roman corvus and the records describe the dismay when their ships were grappled and held by Roman vessels. The corvus was a great success and the Carthaginians saw 30 of their ships captured with all their crews and another 50 ships were completely sunk. The capture and reuse of ships was extremely important: if you could take an enemy vessel rather than sink it, then your own navy was augmented in the process – such was the advantage of the corvus over the ram.

Mylae was a total disaster and shook the Carthaginian command to its core. More losses followed on quickly around other vital locations such as southern Sardinia. Even if we factor in gross exaggeration of the losses in our sources, the fact that the Carthaginians were so ineffectual at sea battles in this moment and unable to adapt to new strategies speaks of some complacency and dysfunction in the system of command. Were they incompetent or do our sources repeat a narrative of their failure to undermine their leadership? We can't really know but, at this moment, the Romans were buoyed by their successes and, while certainly being advised by their Syracusan allies, they reimagined their whole strategy. Carthage was in disarray and on the back foot on land and sea. The Romans were feeling confident enough to plan a massive invasion of Africa to lay siege to Carthage. The ghost of Agathocles came back again to haunt the Carthaginians as the Romans reasoned that Sicily would surely fall quickly if Carthage itself was placed under a blockade.

In the summer of the year 256 BCE the Romans gathered an invasion force on the south coast of Sicily where they prepared to sail across to Africa. The Carthaginians were determined to prevent the crossing at all costs. The result was a massive naval engagement at Cape Ecnomus just off the coast to the east of Agrigentum (see page 124). The Carthaginians had sailed across from Africa to Lilybaeum and then rounded the south corner of the island to their base at Heraclea Minoa. They had a fleet of 350 decked ships and the Romans had around 320 (plus ships carrying horses and supplies for invasion). Again, the numbers are so enormous that modern naval scholars and those who study ancient seafaring have revised them downwards to 230 ships for the Romans and 200 for the Carthaginians. There is no solid factual base for these revisions either, and although it is probable that our guide to the story, Polybius, exaggerated his numbers to emphasise his point, it is difficult to contest them with any proof. The precise detail offered by Polybius suggests he had a very good source for his numbers, maybe an eyewitness. If the ancient estimates are followed, the Roman forces totalled roughly 140,000 men and the Carthaginians close to 150,000. Polybius notes his own surprise at the numbers, and emphasises that 'these figures are bound to strike not only an eye-witness but even the reader with amazement at the vast scale of the encounter and the enormous outlay and resources of the opposing states.' Even using the lower estimate, with as many as 200,000 rowers and marines on the sea alone, this would make Ecnomus one of the largest sea battle ever fought in terms of numbers.[17]

The Roman fleet must have made an impressive sight, commanded by both the consuls, Marcus Atilius Regulus and Lucius Manlius, sailing side by side in flagship hexaremes (sixes) at the head of the convoy of ships. They left port making for Cap Bon on the northernmost tip of Africa, hoping to sail westwards up the coast of Sicily to the closest point of crossing, where the distance is about 175km. The Carthaginians lined up with Sicily on their left and their ships extending along into the open sea to the south. Their tactics were to break through the Roman lines, sailing straight into the enemy ships at pace and disrupting their formation. They relied on the ability to outmanoeuvre their enemy and isolate ships into smaller groups so they would be easier to attack.

The massive battle raged close to land, the Carthaginians successfully breaking up the Roman line, meaning that there were three different engagements happening across the sea. It was a very close match; Polybius claimed that the Roman corvus adaptation was the difference between the two sides. The Carthaginians were hesitant to get too close to the Roman ships, fearing the corvus, so they hedged the Romans ships in but kept their distance. In the end, 64 Carthaginian ships were captured and 30 lost, while the Romans lost 24. The Romans carried the day and were able to regroup and sail on towards the tip of Africa, their invasion force largely intact.

As we have seen, the tradition at Carthage was to drape the walls of the city in black cloth when a naval disaster occurred, so closely tied were the citizens to their navy.[18] The city must have presented their deep mourning to the world, and the human price of a naval disaster. After Ecnomus it must have seemed especially poignant. Two of our ancient sources even claim that Carthage sued for peace after the battle and that one of the Carthaginian leaders sent an envoy to the Romans with a 'peace proposal at this time'. There is some dispute over the validity of this claim because our main source, Polybius, makes no mention of it.[19]

In the face of the defeat and loss at Ecnomus, Carthage had to regroup. The leaders in the city had more ships built and dispatched a mission to Greece to recruit more troops, seeking both soldiers and military advisors to help it turn the tide of the war that for almost a decade had been unrelenting. The resolve and resources of Carthage, when confronted again by invasion of its territory, were profound. Protecting Carthage was paramount and remembering how easy it had been for Agathocles meant that the Carthaginians would be more prepared for round two.

The Romans landed and set up base at the city of Clupea (Polybius calls it Aspis, modern Kelibia in Tunisia), which has one of the few natural ports on the east side of the promontory (see page 124). The Romans plundered the countryside of this prosperous and fertile region, and there are descriptions of the 'handsome and luxuriously furnished houses' that presented tempting targets. The properties were 'ransacked, livestock confiscated and thousands captured by the Roman forces who were unchallenged'.[20] There is a distinct similarity in the sources' descriptions of this invasion to that of Agathocles over 50 years earlier and we should be a little bit suspicious about this use of 'wealthy landscapes' as a way of describing the prosperity of a place that makes it worth invading – is it a real description or just a stock phrase?

On orders from Rome, one consul, Regulus, was left on African soil and the other, Manlius Vulso, returned to Sicily with the fleet. Vulso then carried on to Rome the plunder and prisoners the Romans had captured so far, which Polybius lists as 20,000 enslaved people. Regulus had 40 ships at his disposal and 15,000 foot soldiers along with 500 cavalry to carry on with the invasion.[21] These modest numbers indicate that perhaps the Romans were not expecting much of a fight from Carthage and hoped to persuade the Carthaginian allied cities in Africa to come over to their side.

There is a city along this coast that was abandoned as a result of the invasion and the existing archaeological site still preserves enough to allow an exceptionally rare glimpse into the lifestyle of the people in the countryside of this heartland region of Carthage. Between the very north of Cap Bon and Roman base at Clupea sat the small town of Kerkouane (ancient name unknown). It was in an agriculturally rich and fertile area where the population of the city was involved in the production of the purple dye extracted from murex shells that was much coveted across the ancient world. The urban plan of the town reflects a high standard of living for the period with small but well-built houses, each containing mosaic floors and interior plumbing. When I visited the ruins of this peaceful small town set out on the very tip of Africa in a landscape of cultivated fields up against rolling seas, there was still a sense of the cohesive and closely knit urban community that had built the town and thrived there. The population lived off agriculture and fishing, along with the dye production, and lived well. Hints of the trouble they faced in this period are still visible on the walls of the houses where there is evidence of replastering and repair that tells us that the people of Kerkouane had only just put their homes back together after some previous destruction – perhaps Agathocles had passed by. So the invasion of Regulus was the final straw and led to the abandonment of the city. The ancient descriptions of 20,000 captives being taken back to Rome at this stage probably included many who lived here. The remaining population abandoned the city, moving away from a site so exposed to repeated invasion.

Regulus moved out west towards Carthage in the spring of 255 BCE. The Carthaginian forces moved towards him and the two sides met near the town of Adyn (modern Uthina, just south of Tunis). The commanders Bostar and Hasdrubal led the Carthaginian army against Regulus' small and well-trained force. The Romans won that encounter and moved north through the hills, making their way around the Gulf of Tunis and heading north again up towards Carthage. Tunes (modern Tunis) fell and now the Romans controlled the city sitting just 12km south of Carthage. They were poised to attack (see page 148).[22]

At the same time defections among Carthage's allied cities began to take place. The Libyan and Numidian forces who made up much of the essential cavalry and infantry in the Carthaginian army abandoned Carthage, switching over to the side that looked more likely to win. The countryside around Carthage was devastated, and inside the city the population was under a great deal of pressure. A group from the senate at Carthage entered into negotiations with Regulus but they failed to come to an agreement. Polybius reported Regulus' demands were so extreme that the Carthaginian senators, deeply offended, rejected them out of hand.[23]

Just when it looked to the Carthaginians as if they were doomed, their recruiting expedition returned from Greece. There were new soldiers to fill the ranks, accompanied by a Spartan commander named Xanthippus. The Carthaginian senate gave Xanthippus full authority in the way the war would be fought, trusting in his experience and knowledge of battle. The Spartan general reorganised the battle lines and employed the Carthaginians' many elephants to a maximum advantage. With a newly structured army and Xanthippus in command, the Carthaginian army set out to engage with Regulus' Roman troops on open ground. The Romans were feeling confident, having won engagement after engagement over the previous years, and perhaps unaware of the changes in Carthaginian command. The battle ended with a complete rout and the Romans defeated. The consul Regulus was captured and it was a total victory for Carthage and validation of Xanthippus' skills. He had saved the city.[24]

Now the fates of the two sides were in the balance. With Carthage holding the Roman consul prisoner, the momentum of the war shifted. The Carthaginians' former allies presumably returned to the fold with this change in their prospects. The remaining Roman army withdrew to its base at Clupea and a new Roman fleet was raised to sail back to Africa to pick up the survivors. The Roman relief force that collected the soldiers was massive, reportedly numbering over 350 ships. A terrible storm gathered while the Roman fleet was sailing along the south coast of Sicily towards Syracuse and a majority of the ships were destroyed; only 80 of the 350 Roman ships remained intact. If true, then the loss of life would have numbered almost 100,000 men and, while these may be inflated numbers, the losses were surely in the tens of thousands. There is one theory frequently mentioned in discussions about this huge disaster – that it was the Roman corvus that made their ships less stable when threatened by rough seas and may have exacerbated the losses.[25]

The hero of Carthage, Xanthippus, departed from the city in search of new battles to fight, but drowned on the way back to Greece. There is even some suggestion that his death was not an accident, and that some factions within Carthage had intentionally sabotaged his return, feeling envious about the Spartan's influence in the city.

The focus of the war returned to Sicily, where the Romans came back again with a new fleet and army. They had recovered so quickly it was 'not easy to believe', as Polybius comments.[26] The fortunes of the Carthaginians fluctuated. They attacked and tried to retake Agrigentum in 254 BCE and reportedly succeeded in razing it to the ground, but in the same year the Romans took the Carthaginian allied city of Panormus (Palermo). Palermo was a famous port with a deep natural harbour, set on the mountainous northwest corner of Sicily, that had been founded by Phoenician-speaking peoples in the eighth/seventh centuries BCE. With its loss, most of the territory along the north coast of Sicily was now out of reach and the interests of Carthage were limited to the west coast cities of Drepanum (Trapani) and Lilybaeum.

Roman failures and political infighting during this period of the war had not slowed their successes. Again, the Carthaginians sued for peace, and this time they sent the captured consul Regulus to Rome to negotiate. The story of Regulus and the humiliation of the consul who was returned to Rome 'clad as a prisoner in Punic garments' was burned into the memory of the Romans. It is repeated often and turns up in many different sources and genres for centuries later. The story highlights the Roman outrage that the Carthaginians would dare to send their own consul back to them. The story of Regulus implies that Carthage believed sending the ex-consul to negotiate a peace treaty or perhaps a prisoner exchange would be effective – this would have been a normal way to dialogue in times of war. But when Regulus appeared before the senate in Rome, he described a desperate financial situation at Carthage. He told the Romans to never accept peace, and that they could fight on and destroy Carthage. Regulus returned voluntarily to Carthage, as he had promised to do, and there he disappears from our story, either executed or dying in captivity – Polybius makes no further mention of it. Later Roman authors embellish the tale further, revealing gruesome details about the way Regulus died, all of them designed to emphasise how barbarous the Carthaginians had been. One particularly popular version is that his captors shut him into a box where he had to stand with iron spikes sticking into his sides and was left to die a slow and cruel death. That underneath the narrative of battles much cruelty took place is emphasised by a story by Diodorus, who claims that Regulus' widow in Rome had been accused of the torture and murder of two Carthaginian prisoners-of-war in retaliation for her husband's death. The brutal realities of this war and the impact on families on both sides rarely become the focus but the accusation at Rome was serious enough that the family of Regulus was almost prosecuted in the Roman courts.[27]

The financial impact of the war and successive losses on Carthage becomes very clear in these years through an analysis of its silver coinage. With no written record of what the people were experiencing, we can read their economic woes in the data. At the beginning of the third century BCE, Carthage began to mint silver coinage based on the shekel standard (the Tyrian shekel is a unit of weight – 7.6 grams). A classic example is a half-shekel with the head of the female deity on the obverse and a horse looking backwards on the reverse (see Fig. 16). The shekels were used as currency in Africa, and after the war had gone on for ten years or so there was a significant debasement in the silver quantity of the Carthaginian shekels. The Carthaginians were running out of silver and inflation must have been rampant in the city. The debasement of the coinage continued until there was less than 10 per cent silver in the Carthaginian shekels and half-shekels at the end of the First Punic War, so we can see the economic toll

Fig. 16 Silver Carthaginian half-shekel from First Punic War

the war had on Carthage. The Carthaginian coinage used in Sicily continued to have a higher silver quantity than the coinage in circulation at Carthage during these years, with all the funds going towards paying for the war. The resources and wealth of the city were being poured into the military effort.

With the rejection of its peace offer, Carthage was facing a blockade of its allied cities on the west coast of Sicily. Stories of individual effort provide insight into the way that Carthage operated its navy. Although there was a standing navy at Carthage, some evidence suggests that privately funded ships or even fleets supplemented this. For a specific mission we are told that individual citizens could finance the building, equipment and manning of ships. In 250 BCE a tight Roman blockade around Lilybaeum was evaded by a Carthaginian admiral named Hannibal the Rhodian and his skilled crew who were celebrated for their daring across Sicily and at Carthage. The sources describe how the Rhodian had fitted out the ships himself and slipped in and out of the port with relative ease. The information about the Rhodian's exploits also provides some insight into the pressure from Rome on the Carthaginian allied cities. More practically, it implies there was a kind of incentive behind the culture of naval warfare at Carthage; not surprisingly this gave increased status to an individual in command of a skilful fleet. The rewards taken for these great risks must have been substantial.[28]

By the year 249 BCE, Rome and Syracuse were basically in control of the whole of Sicily when another dramatic naval battle took place. Off the city of Drepanum on the west coast of Sicily, a Carthaginian fleet under the command of Adherbal faced a Roman fleet with the consul Appius Claudius Pulcher in charge. The tale of the naval battle opens in a scene of ritual and sacrifice. The Roman consul was offering sacrifices and reading the auspices, as would have been traditional for both sides before any military engagement, to ensure the gods were on his side. As the Roman orator Cicero later remembered, the consul, who was from an old elite family in Rome and renowned for his arrogance, was irritated that the sacred chickens used to decipher the will of the gods would not eat according to the specified rules. Appius Claudius Pulcher is reported to have famously noted, 'if they will not eat then let them drink', before throwing the sacred chickens overboard in a fit of anger. For us today, this is a wry, humorous story as we visualise the chickens being hurled into the sea, but as told in Cicero it is an example of consular arrogance in the Roman state. Ignoring the auspices was considered an extreme affront to the gods and that decided the outcome of the battle. In so offending the gods, Appius Claudius Pulcher was abandoned by the fates and lost this sea battle in dramatic fashion. Two-thirds of his ships were sunk with all hands. The Roman defeat at Drepanum gave Carthage some breathing room. The consul was prosecuted after the battle and charged for his violation of the auspices.

It would be the turn of the Roman citizens to suffer as they scrambled for more manpower and financing to raise yet another fleet by drafting the enslaved into their forces and using loans from private citizens to build more ships. Despite the huge Roman losses and the financial desperation at Carthage, the First Punic War was not yet over and Carthage and Rome at this moment were like boxers going round for round, teetering on the brink of collapse as they continued to pummel each other.[29]

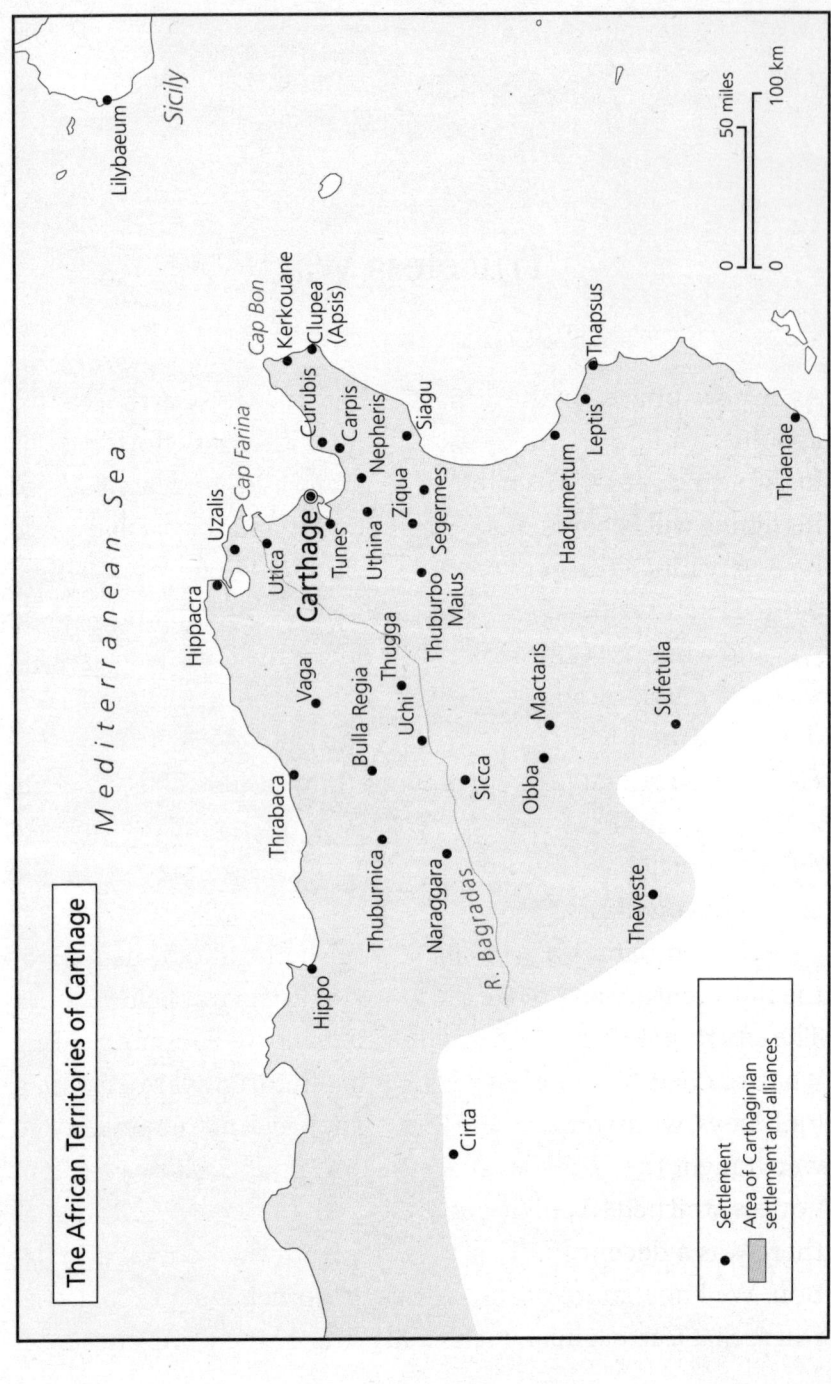

The African Territories of Carthage

Sicily

Lilybaeum

Mediterranean Sea

Cap Farina

Uzalis

Hippacra

Utica
Tunes
Carthage

Cap Bon

Kerkouane
Clupea
(Apsis)
Curubis
Carpis
Nepheris
Uthina
Ziqua
Siagu
Segermes

Thapsus

Leptis

Hadrumetum

Thaenae

Thuburbo
Maius
Thugga
Uchi
Bulla Regia
Vaga

Sicca
Obba
Mactaris

Sufetula

Thrabaca

Thuburnica
Naraggara

R. Bagradas

Theveste

Hippo

Cirta

50 miles
100 km

Settlement

Area of Carthaginian
settlement and alliances

CHAPTER 7

Truceless War

As a new phase in the long war began, the Carthaginians appointed a new leader to take charge of the war effort in Sicily in the year 247 BCE. His name was Hamilcar Barca. Hamilcar and his family will become so important in the story of Carthage, and he is very much the hero of the history of Polybius over the next decade, that we need to take a moment to understand who he was and where he came from. He is one of the few Carthaginians we know anything about, and Hamilcar and his Barcid family will dominate the policies of Carthage for the next half a century. Here it is worth taking a moment to think about society and life at Carthage in these years to get a sense of Hamilcar's early life and what may have motivated him through the coming years of crisis and conquest.

Hamilcar Barca grew up in Carthage in the middle decades of the third century BCE while the war with Rome was being fought. The city he grew up in had grown and prospered despite fighting what seemed like endless battles. Its children were educated (only boys, we assume) in the Punic language and numeracy, and were taught the Greek language and religious cults too. Written notices attached to public buildings in the city may indicate that there was a decent level of literacy within the general population. We know more of the men than women and are told elsewhere that Carthaginian males had pierced ears, wore long tunics and were probably circumcised. The wealthier houses had mosaic floors and private bathrooms, and cisterns filled with fresh water. Less is known about the housing of the poor, but there were public bathrooms and washing areas in the city as well, which might reflect communal use. The ritual of bathing and washing seems to have been an important part of the interchange between private and public lives for Carthaginians. This is assumed from the location of baths and bathrooms near the entrance of the few houses we have from the Punic period, like those at Kerkouane mentioned in the previous chapter.[1] Carthaginians were derogatorily called 'porridge eaters' by some non-Carthaginian sources, probably because their diet included a wheat or barley porridge; the Roman Cato even included a recipe for a savoury 'Punic porridge' in his treatise on agriculture.[2] The hearty porridge was made from soaked spelt groats with eggs and curd added, along with lots of honey. Fish was another constant in the diet of Carthaginians and meat was something reserved for special functions, religious festivals and sacrifices.

Carthage was a city of beautiful public spaces, with elaborate defensive walls that stabled horses and elephants and housed soldiers. The population worshipped within the city at temples dedicated to an array of local and Mediterranean gods and goddesses. The elites who governed the city had rural estates to which they could retreat, and also had homes in town as to travel back and forth would have been time consuming and difficult. Wealthy estates and agricultural production were integral to the prosperity of the city. The estates of the wealthy were likely manned by enslaved people; although the evidence for this is much less apparent than in contemporary Roman society, we can assume the Carthaginians also used slavery across their industries. By the early 250s BCE, a whole generation of young men from these elite families would have been lost to the war. Hamilcar belonged to a new generation – young men born and raised with the idea of war against Rome as a constant in their lives.

The family of Hamilcar Barca would become the most famous of all the Carthaginian elites. The meaning of their surname, Barca, is debated. It may have been an epithet, meaning something like 'lightning', but one intriguing theory argued by scholars is that the Barcids originally came from Barce, a city founded by Greeks whose population was a mix of Greek, Phoenician and Libyan ethnicity. It is possible that an ancestor of Hamilcar may even have joined the expedition of Agathocles against Carthage a century earlier.[3] Our historical sources tell us that many soldiers in Agathocles' army – those he abandoned when he returned to Sicily – were absorbed into the Carthaginian military. Perhaps in this we can see the rise of a line of talented generals to the very pinnacle of Carthaginian society, and a portrait of a time of great fluidity in social mobility. The Carthaginian tendency was to use geographical surnames as a way of distinguishing one Hamilcar from another or one Hannibal from another. We discussed Hannibal the Rhodian in Chapter 5 but also know of a Hanno the Bruttian and a Hasdrubal the Samnite, so the very name Hamilcar Barca may be telling us about the origins of the family, of the Barcid ethnic roots.

For the 40 years following on from 247 BCE, the Barcids and their intentions dominate the story of Carthage and fascinate those who wrote the history of Carthage in the ancient world. In that year, the young commander Hamilcar took charge of the Carthaginian fight in Sicily, heading up a squadron of what Polybius refers to as *mixhellenes*. From the name this was clearly a group of mixed Greeks, so an elite force of North African fighters perhaps reflecting their commander's identity as a Phoenician, Greek and Libyan. Hamilcar was probably in his thirties by this time, was married with three daughters and in that year celebrated the birth of his first son. That firstborn son was named Hannibal after his grandfather, and Hamilcar would go on to father two more boys, whose names were Hasdrubal and Mago. We do not know about their mother at all; she may have been Carthaginian, Numidian or Greek, but the family estates were in the Sahel region (perhaps near modern Sousse), rich in olive-oil production, so their link to that part of Africa may have come through their mother. Hamilcar was relatively young and dedicated to taking the fight to Rome. His command shifted the narrative of a war that had so often seen Carthage on the defensive.

The Carthaginian naval victory at Drepanum in 249 BCE, two years earlier, meant that Rome had largely abandoned control of the sea along the west of Sicily, so once again supplies and ships could cross back and forth from Africa unimpeded. Hamilcar set out to disrupt the Roman presence on the west part of Sicily and to dislodge them from their seemingly comfortable hold on Palermo and the northwest corner of the island. He did not engage with the Roman standing army head on, but took out patrols, harassing them and making their lives as difficult as possible. Bit by bit, the tactics began to restore Carthaginian morale and helped to bolster the confidence of their Sicilian allies.

Hamilcar focused on recapturing the hilltops in the northwest corner of Sicily and especially the mountaintop site of Eryx, that place of significant strategic importance that was sacred to the cult of the goddess Astarte/Aphrodite. The Romans had sought to dominate the landscape above the west coast of Sicily and attack from there. We have seen that Eryx was a place of significance to all the peoples of the island and the worship of the goddess on this spot was syncretised across cultures. The Romans too sought to claim this legacy, linking the sanctuary to their legendary Trojan origins, to Aeneas and his divine mother Venus (the Roman iteration of Aphrodite). War in this period was fought both on the ground and through divine favour. The fight over Eryx underlines that religions and beliefs were essential for control over the landscape. The favour of the goddess was intertwined with military success and a holy place like Eryx was contested by all sides. With commanding views to the west and north, the sacred enclosure of the goddess at Eryx directly overlooked the Carthaginian allied port of Drepanum. When Hamilcar and his *mixhellenes* took the town of Eryx from the Romans, they did not manage to capture the enclosure of the goddess and her temple – these remained in the hand of a Roman garrison. Hamilcar could now easily cut off Roman supplies and communication lines but had put his own forces in a precarious position. A kind of stalemate ensued as both sides battled for control of this holy site (see page 102).[4]

Hamilcar's small victories and his successes on the hilltops of the west of the island had a positive and lasting effect on his reputation. It must have restored some faith on the Carthaginian side that they might hold on to their homes after more than a decade of humiliating defeats. Every family in Carthage, at all layers of society, and those living in its allied territories, would have been touched by the war. The loss of citizens, property, land and livelihoods would have generated tens of thousands of refugees, not counting the many thousands who had died or been captured and sold into slavery. The war had taken a deep economic and psychological toll and it is no wonder that Hamilcar received great acclaim for this command. As his popularity grew, it spread across the Mediterranean. This also gave him increasing influence in the senate at Carthage.

We have seen how, across at least a decade, Carthage and Rome stretched their economic resources to the very limits in an exhausting war. The Roman historians emphasise this and repeat it over and over. For example, Appian, writing about the events in the year 252 BCE, commented that 'both the Romans

and Carthaginians were destitute of money', and yet the war continued for another decade.[5] The Carthaginians were in desperate
financial straits to the extent that they had applied for a loan of
2,000 talents from the Egyptian king Ptolemy II (1 talent = 26kg).
Ptolemy, an ally of Rome, failed to support Carthage. Polybius
emphasised this issue when he commented that both sides were
paralysed and had exhausted their resources, repeatedly pushing
their populations and stretching them to the limit through
'protracted taxation and expense'. The Roman state turned to
private finance, pushing individual citizens to raise funds for the
construction of one more new fleet during the final phases of
the war.[6]

Things came to a head early in the year 241 BCE. We can
imagine that from his command on the heights of Eryx, Hamilcar
might even have watched as the final naval battle of the First
Punic War played out. It was March, the beginning of the navigation season, so the Carthaginians had put together another
fleet to resupply Hamilcar at his base up on the mountains above
Trapani. The Carthaginian fleet came up from the south and
rounded the Aegates Islands, heading for the port of Bonagia,
north of Trapani, that Hamilcar used for resupply. The heavily
laden Carthaginian ships were caught by surprise by a newly
raised Roman fleet: the Romans pounced on the Carthaginians near the northernmost island of the Aegates, now known as
Levanzo. The seafloor off the island of Levanzo is littered with
the detritus of the battle. There are bronze helmets and ships'
rams, amphorae and other containers, and lead anchors from
the ships that clashed there. Underwater archaeologists have
been able to uncover the details of the ships and their crews, the
armour and the tangible remnants of this historic battle. The
battle scene is spread across a wide area. At least 15 of the heavy
bronze rams used to crash into enemy ships have been collected

from the seabed, each one weighing 125kg (see Fig. 17). Some of the rams carry inscriptions in the Punic language, while others have Latin letters. The rams came from ships made by both sides, one of the Punic ones carrying a prayer to Reshep, their god of war, and the Roman rams the more prosaic name of the consul under whose orders they were made.

Roman maritime efforts had been severely restricted after the chaotic defeat off Drepanum eight years previously. Since that point, the Carthaginians had operated unchallenged at sea, as far as we know, and were perhaps a bit complacent. Polybius wrote expressly that Carthage 'never expected the Romans to dispute the sea with them again'. So when Carthage suffered a loss of fifty ships and 'seventy more captured with all their crews', they could fight no more. The ships and their crews that survived the encounter fled back home across the sea, but the loss was final.[7]

When the returning ships brought news of the defeat to Carthage, the army in Sicily was ordered to sue for a settlement. The Roman consul Lutatius had sailed on to reach the Carthaginian capital on Sicily, Lilybaeum. There, as the historian Appian

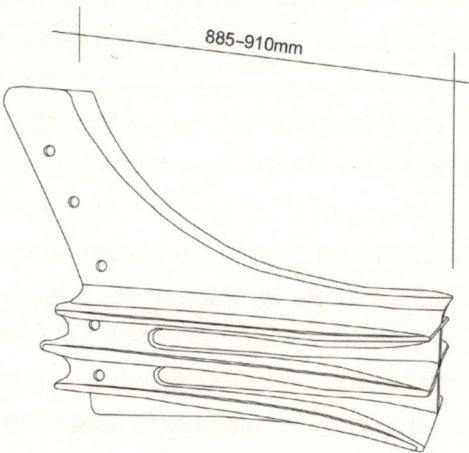

885–910mm

Fig. 17 Schematic drawing of a ram from a Carthaginian or Roman ship of the First Punic War

noted, 'already short of money, ships and men, the Carthaginians sought an armistice from Lutatius'.[8] Although this was not as dramatic a defeat for Carthage as some of the previous battles, it was the last straw for Carthage and for the garrison at Eryx. The peace of Lutatius was punitive for Carthage in terms of land and finances. The text of the treaty reads:

> there shall be friendship between the Carthaginians and the Romans on the following terms . . . The Carthaginians shall evacuate the whole of Sicily and the islands between Italy and Africa [i.e. the Aeolian Islands, Pantelleria and Lampedusa]; they shall not make war upon Hiero, nor bear arms against the Syracusans nor their allies. The Carthaginians shall give up to the Romans all prisoners without ransom. The Carthaginians shall pay the Romans 2,200 Euboean talents of silver over a period of twenty years. (Polybius 3.27.1–6)

The First Punic War had ended. Carthage had lost Sicily and the islands between Italy and Africa, constituting an enormous territorial loss. Its central zone of operation had been, for centuries, the ports and seaways that linked each of these islands. Carthage had always, in the existing written record, been connected to Sicily, to the people and cities there, to the deities worshipped in the sanctuaries. The treaty took this all away. The peace agreed was deeply restrictive and would have hampered the normal functioning of the city. Carthage was broke, suffering high inflation with a debased coinage and food shortages at home. Little could the Carthaginians have realised that this was only the beginning of their problems.

In that summer of 241 BCE after the end of the war, the city of Carthage was teeming with soldiers of all nationalities. There were Greeks and Ligurians, Italians, Libyans, Iberians and Egyptians, and they had all been evacuated there from Sicily after the peace treaty with Rome. There was mayhem in the city as a result. On conclusion of the treaty Hamilcar had 'transferred his soldiers from Eryx to Lilybaeum and immediately resigned his command'.[9] He departed for Carthage, perhaps feeling that he could have fought on, perhaps disagreeing with the orders to make peace. The responsibility for the demobilisation fell to Gisgo, the commander of Lilybaeum. Gisgo organised for the troops to be sent back to Carthage in detachments. Polybius records that Gisgo wanted to demobilise the Sicilian army in stages with each group being paid as they arrived in Carthage and then disbanded. His plan went awry when the civilian government at Carthage allowed the soldiers to flood back into the city and did not pay them right away. They hoped, Polybius tells us, to negotiate with the soldiers.

The soldiers were owed money and, it seems, could not be paid in full. The evidence of low-quantity silver coinage at Carthage at the end of the war backs up this assertion. There was financial turmoil and political unrest in the city. The governing magistrates and senate were at odds about what to do. The civil magistrates of the city (the *sufetes*) and the military command (the *rabbim*) also disagreed on policy in this moment of crisis, leading to social and military turmoil. It was the height of summer and in the warm nights thousands of restless men were now thronging the streets of the city and clamouring to be paid. Things went quickly from bad to worse. Violence among the soldiers escalated until the war-weary Carthaginians had a full-scale rebellion on their hands, only months after the end of their epic war with Rome.

The city became unruly with idle, unpaid men of war and we can imagine the upheaval they caused. Polybius recounts that the men committed 'frequent offences there both by night and by day'. They were drinking and carousing in the streets, acting violent and feeling aggrieved, attacking men and women and causing mayhem. In the mix were Numidian horsemen, who made up the cavalry, and Libyan foot soldiers from neighbouring kingdoms and territories in Africa. Some of the men came from the wider area of the Mediterranean; some, such as the slingers from the Balearic Islands, were connected through shared origins and others had no relationship to Carthage but were hired from regions famous for producing soldiers. These were men from the Greek east, from Liguria in the northern Italian peninsula or Lusitania (part of Portugal) and perhaps even further afield. Polybius makes a specific mention of 'Iberians, some Celts, some Ligurians and some from the Balearic Islands' among the angry soldiers at Carthage that summer.[10]

The men suspected Carthage was trying to avoid paying them altogether and the situation was explosive. The magistrates at Carthage asked the commanders of the various detachments to withdraw from the city to await pay. Each of the different ethnic groups would have had their own command structure so the idea was to get the soldiers out of the city where they could be better supplied (and controlled). The restless commanders of the soldiers agreed to withdraw, suggesting they had not yet decided to rebel. The mercenary army was then sent southwest from Carthage to the town of Sicca, in the agricultural heartland of Carthage about 170km away (see page 148). Sicca was a Libyphoenician town, which means that the population there was a heterogeneous mix of the indigenous and Carthaginian/Phoenician peoples.[11] It could well be that the destination was chosen because many of the unpaid soldiers were from this part of the world. The Carthaginians provided each soldier with a gold stater to cover the cost of the journey. This was worth about four days' wages for the men. It would not have just been soldiers who made this journey, but the people who travelled with them too – women and their children, born on campaign, and various other hangers-on also made the trek to Sicca. Polybius disparagingly called this the soldiers' 'baggage' but this was a reality of war that we often don't consider today – there were whole communities of people who travelled with the soldiers and whose lives were lived in the service of the camp.[12]

Removing the soldiers to Sicca was not a strategically sound decision. The men had little to do but think about the money they were owed, and the promises that Carthage had made to them. It was not an atmosphere in which to engender sympathy for Carthage and they were now residing in the lands that had been heavily exploited by the Carthaginians to raise funds and support for the war. The war in Sicily had meant that for 23 years the region had suffered exploitation, high taxation and conscription. The local population and the newly arrived soldiers shared a mutual hostility for Carthage at that moment, and this led to a rapidly growing fury that spread across the region. It was not long before the soldiers were vocally expressing discontent, so that when a Carthaginian commander named Hanno arrived in Sicca he was met with a clamour of new demands. That Carthage could barely afford what was already due did not seem to matter to the soldiers. They felt betrayed and did not trust this man Hanno. As a general, Hanno had been overseeing the domestic policies of Carthage over the last years of the war while Hamilcar had operated in Sicily. The soldiers could not understand where the commanders who had made promises to them in the field – the likes of Hamilcar and Gisgo – were. They were certainly nowhere to be seen at this moment.

It is worth considering the whereabouts of Hamilcar in earnest. He disappeared from the story after resigning his command and did not reappear until after the insurgency was well under way. Where had he been? Polybius argued that because Hamilcar had commanded the mutinous soldiers in Sicily and his promises had not been met, he was not a popular choice to placate them. There may be some truth in this, but equally Hamilcar was the general most respected among the soldiers. Conflict between civil magistrates and the generals may lie at the heart of the absence; if the popularity of a general like Hamilcar was put into contrast with the actions of the senate at Carthage, there may have been elements of competition and hostility at play. The historian Appian mentions that Hamilcar was prosecuted for his actions in the running of the war in Sicily, which would be in line with what we understand about the accountability of generals who fought wars for the Carthaginian state. Diodorus Siculus' explanation was that the Carthaginians, in times of war,

> advance their leading men to commands, taking it for granted that these should be the first to brave the danger for the whole state; but when they gain peace, they plague these same men with suits, bring false charges against them through envy, and load them down with penalties. (20.10.2–5)

The reality may have been that Hamilcar was fighting against legal proceedings, which was why he was not given command at the beginning of the subsequent insurgency.[13]

Hanno was unable to placate the army at Sicca, with the result that 20,000 soldiers left and marched back to Carthage. They camped 12km southwest of the city at the town of Tunes (modern Tunis). There, a very large contingent of Libyans, along with a mix of soldiers of many different ethnicities – Iberians, Celts, Ligurians and 'a mixture' of Greeks – could count on local support. The senate at Carthage sent out negotiators to meet the rebels in their camp and caved in to all their demands. The Carthaginians seemed intimidated by the soldiers and the army forming at

Tunes was increasing in number every day; Carthage was without resources and at the mercy of its mercenaries.[14]

Eventually Gisgo, who had commanded at Lilybaeum, was called upon to engage with the rebellious soldiers. Two leaders emerged on the side of the mercenary army, a Campanian named Spendius and a Libyan named Mathos. Both men were powerful voices with personal reasons for rebellion, and neither was inclined to come to a settlement with the Carthaginians. Spendius was an ex-Roman slave who had deserted from the Roman army and wanted to avoid being repatriated to the Roman state, where his fate would be execution. Mathos, as a Libyan, represented local concerns and the African perspective on their cause. He was the voice who spoke of the harsh conditions that had been imposed on the Libyan homeland during war with Rome. Along with the other Libyans and Numidians fighting in the rebellion, his became the voice of an independence movement against Carthage. These were the people who had taken on the economic brunt of Carthage's expansion into Africa and were key to fighting its wars. This was also an important moment in the shaping of the cultural and historical identity of the Numidian peoples as they start to be written about for the first time in detail when they rebel against Carthage's power and exploitation.

Gisgo's overtures were rejected, and the result was turmoil. He was seized by the rebels and held in chains, an act of open rebellion that marked the beginning of an all-out war between Carthage and its mercenary soldiers that would become known as the Truceless War. The Libyan and Numidian soldiers sent out envoys across Carthaginian territory to gather support and to urge others to join the fight. This was a serious blow to Carthage, with towns declaring their support for the rebels. Polybius claims the impact was decisive and the Carthaginians were 'deprived of all their resources at one blow'. This was the region from which

Carthage took its best soldiers, the land where its taxation income and surplus food supplies originated. The rebellion extended through the lands that Carthage claimed direct control over – all the way to Tebessa (the Roman Theveste and in Greek Hecatompylus), now in modern Algeria (see page 148).[15]

Our sources write that the Libyan leader Mathos had 70,000 soldiers fighting with him. He launched a well-thought-through and multi-pronged attack in the spring of 240 BCE. The rebel commanders were well-seasoned fighters and capable military practitioners who had been 'schooled in the daring tactics' of none other than Hamilcar Barca.[16] They cut Carthage off from the rest of the countryside with a land blockade of the peninsula and placed the Carthaginian-allied cities to the north, Utica and Hippo Acra (modern Bizerte), under siege. Trapped behind their city walls, the Carthaginians could still be supplied by sea but found very few supporters out there in the countryside. Hanno was sent out to relieve the siege and proved no match for the rebels.

The people of Carthage began to call for a change of leadership and it is not hard to imagine that questions about Hamilcar's whereabouts rang through the senate. Polybius completely destroys Hanno's reputation and his military capability in a passage that describes how he clearly 'had no idea how to avail himself of opportunities and generally showed an entire lack of experience and energy'. Described as 'heedless and lacking judgement' and without any creativity, Hanno's manoeuvres were limited to employing his elephants to charge the enemy camp. Even more criticism focuses on his lack of ability to capitalise on any success. The hero of this narrative was Hamilcar Barca, and eventually the inevitable occurred and he appeared again in the story, commanding an army.[17]

The new army that Hamilcar led did not replace Hanno's, but instead operated with him in the field, so Carthage had mobilised two armies to face the serious threat. Hamilcar had been given 'seventy elephants, all the additional mercenaries they had been able to collect and the deserters from the enemy, besides their citizen forces, horse and foot, so that in all he had about 10,000 men'. A quick success, where he lured the mercenary army into an ambush, 'restored some confidence and courage' among the Carthaginians. It was not going to be that easy, however, and the rebel army did not retreat. They regrouped and managed to encircle Hamilcar's army while he had camped on a plateau. The situation looked dire for Hamilcar when Naravas, a Numidian prince of the Massyli people, arrived with a force of 2,000 cavalry to join him, giving Hamilcar the upper hand.[18]

The Numidian people of North Africa were grouped into kingdoms known as the Massyli, the Masaesyli and the Mauri, and they lived in the regions south and west from Carthage. This area includes much of modern Algeria and Morocco today. In the third century BCE these were distinct kingdoms ruled autonomously. The situation was complex and shifted often; one kingdom might be allied with Carthage or at war with another. The family of prince Naravas and the Massyli people were traditional allies of Carthage. Naravas had appeared on the scene in support of Hamilcar personally, which suggests close ties between their two families, along with broader alliances from the past. Hamilcar gave his daughter in marriage to Naravas, sealing the bond between the two men. That all of Hamilcar's daughters were married off in order to secure political alliances gives a brief view into the lives of elite women and their importance in the political landscape of the time. Hamilcar was able to operate on a personal level within this landscape, using his family and ties to cement alliances, which may well reflect how elite families at Carthage operated with autonomy within the system of the city-state. The alliances between Numidians and the Barcid family would maintain Hamilcar's reputation and prestige, and play a crucial role in his military conquests.

From the first move, Naravas and his cavalry were impressive and key to a victory in battle that saw a reported 10,000 rebel soldiers killed. While we know to be suspicious of the numbers, the impact of the victory here is designed to impress the readers of the ancient texts. It was a stunning win for Hamilcar and his Numidian allies. Under Hamilcar, slowly, the Carthaginians regained some authority in the region and lessened the impact of the rebellion as those watching realised that, perhaps, for Carthage all was not lost. Hamilcar treated his captive enemies with leniency and wooed them over to his side where possible. Captives were offered a place in Hamilcar's army or granted their freedom as long as they swore an oath not to take up arms against Carthage. It was an intelligent and expansive policy that began to restore some credibility in the heartland of Carthage. The realities of the neglected rural regions seem to have been recognised but it would be a long battle before all was calm in the Carthaginian countryside.[19]

Nor was it easy, and the rebel army did not give up its aims and aspirations quickly. The Libyan rebel army was determined, powerful and well organised. Polybius' dismissal of them as 'brigands and uncivilised barbarians' who were only fighting to overthrow the 'civilised' forces of Carthage is based in his own loathing of mercenaries. What appears in this story was an idea, the beginning of an African independence movement that seems to have been embraced broadly across the territory. It was not the first time that the local population had risen to support an army against Carthage. Remember, back in around 310 BCE when

Agathocles invaded he anticipated the support of 'the Libyan allies of the Carthaginians, who had for a long time resented their exactions'. Agathocles understood that they 'would grasp an opportunity for revolt'.[20]

The colonial intentions of the Carthaginians and the extreme pressure put on the indigenous peoples of North Africa in the fight against the Romans was a catalyst for the emergence of these key players in this last century of Carthaginian existence. The minting of coins by the rebel armies during the war provides the clearest perspective. The legend used on the coins, many of them overstruck on Carthaginian coins, was LIBYA written beneath a figure of a lion, a strong symbol of defiance (see Fig. 18). This brings focus and emphasis to the idea that it was a distinct identity that the soldiers were claiming in opposition to Carthage.

The rebellion spread through Carthaginian territory and a further revolt broke out on Sardinia during the mercenary war. The garrisons there joined the rebellion, emulating the revolt in Libya. It is not hard to imagine that the soldiers stationed

Fig. 18 Copper alloy coin of the mercenary army with head of Melqart on obverse and lion on reverse, LIBYA legend below

in Sardinia, where there were many long-established Phoenician cities linked to Carthage, had also gone unpaid given the extremes of the situation. The Carthaginian command sent Hanno (different to the one fighting in Africa) with a newly raised army to regarrison the island. The situation only grew worse when, on arrival, these new troops promptly joined the rebels. The Carthaginian commander was crucified by his own troops and the rebellious army set about murdering and torturing all the Carthaginians on the island. Carthage was powerless to respond.[21]

Again, Carthage found itself very close to defeat on all fronts. The reality of this can best be grasped from the reactions of its former enemies, Syracuse and Rome. Carthage was cut off by land from all its resources so supplies had to arrive by sea. The city was forced to 'resort to an appeal to the states in treaty alliance'.[22] This means that Carthage reached out to Syracuse for support against the rebellion, and King Hiero responded quickly and immediately, giving us a clear idea of how dire things seemed to be. He promptly met requests for aid, sending, we can imagine, soldiers and food supplies to the beleaguered Carthage. This would have been very much in his own interest, for Hiero understood that the demise of Carthage would only favour Roman hegemony. Syracuse had to be wary of Rome and its play for dominance in the region. It is easy to forget, in hindsight, how much the balance of power was still at play in the central Mediterranean.

Rome's reaction to the plight of Carthage was much more ambiguous. The Romans had an obligation to help the Carthaginians, as stated in the terms of the treaty they had just signed. The capture at sea of 'traders coming from Italy to Libya with supplies for the enemy' shows how the Romans were actually backing the rebels, breaking the treaty terms and may well have been more involved in the rebellion than we know. The Carthaginians captured 500 prisoners from the Roman allied fleets and used these to negotiate further concessions including the return of all the captives who had remained with the Romans from the first war.[23] The Romans returned 2,743 captives in exchange for those 500 captured trying to supply the rebels. This is a significant number, reflecting the depth of the Roman interference in the Carthaginian civil war. After this, Rome's merchant ships began to support Carthage, in accordance with the treaty. It is nonetheless clear that Rome's first instinct was to help the rebellious soldiers, an action that betrayed Roman intentions towards Carthage and their readiness to exploit an opportunity to destroy their enemy, despite the terms of the treaty.

The rebels were finally defeated in 238 BCE. The war had lasted three years and four months, as Polybius described.[24] In a final bitter note, at the very end of the war the Romans seized Sardinia from Carthage. Rome had, at first, refused to get involved in Sardinia since it was recognised as Carthaginian territory in accordance with the treaty of Lutatius. Subsequently, the Romans changed their policy towards Sardinia, and in the same year (238/237 BCE) accepted an invitation from the rebels on the island to intervene, just as Carthage was preparing to take back its rebellious territory. Carthage objected, claiming its sovereignty over Sardinia had been agreed in the peace treaty, but the Romans chose to push Carthage on this matter, knowing they could not really put up a fight. The Romans used the pretext of Carthaginian preparations against Sardinia to declare war. They claimed, falsely as far as we can tell, that Carthage was planning to attack Rome, and not Sardinia. Our guide Polybius himself chastised the Roman audacity and deceit. Even the Roman Livy – never one to criticise his own people – says, 'the Romans tricked the Carthaginians into the loss of Sardinia.'[25] Polybius claimed that the seizure of Sardinia by Rome was the catalyst for the start of the Second Punic War. The Carthaginians were left with a bitter taste of betrayal but were in no condition to take on Rome in another war and were left with no choice but to yield to the new demands. Carthage even agreed to pay a further financial penalty to Rome, another 12,000 talents on top of the payments agreed in the peace treaty, to avoid a conflict.

The difficult lessons learned by Carthage from their defeat in the First Punic War and the Mercenary War were significant for the generation who would confront the next war. Hamilcar Barca's son Hannibal, who was only six years old in 241 BCE, would have just begun his education, and have been starting to gain a sense of awareness of the city he lived in and the world around him. For Hannibal's generation of Carthaginians, raised to be proud of Carthage's long history and noble past, the loss of Sicily would have had a profound impact. The shadow of the war with Rome loomed large over young boys like Hannibal and his cohort, who were accustomed to sharing tales of great sea victories and heroic commanders from their history. The staggering loss of life in the naval battles likely created a generation of heroic dead and a deep-seated animosity towards the Romans among those who lived through the events. While the next generation of Carthaginians likely blamed the Romans for the First Punic War, it also became evident that many of the Carthaginian commanders – apart from notable exceptions like Hamilcar Barca and Xanthippus the Spartan – had not been prepared for the challenge.

The last passage of this chapter relies on Polybius' own words, because he explained why he had spent so much effort and detail describing the Mercenary War. One of the reasons is practical; he felt that mercenary soldiers were dangerous, and rebellion and upheaval can only lead to mayhem. There was, in Polybius' words, a 'great difference of character between a confused herd of barbarians and men who have been brought up in an educated, law-abiding and civilized community'. In the story of the Mercenary War, this educated and civilised community was Carthage. Polybius went on to explain how 'one can see very clearly from all that took place what kind of dangers those who employ mercenary forces should foresee and take early precautions to avert'. The ideas were also very much in line with the story as Polybius wanted it told, but the most important thing for him 'was that from the events of that period one can get an idea of the causes of the Hannibalic war between the Romans and the Carthaginians'. Polybius admitted that what happened in the war that followed, even in his time, 'was still a matter of dispute, not only among historians, but also among the combatants'. This was a period of such deeply contested history that Polybius felt the need to narrate the events as he saw it, to lay down his version of these seminal years.[26] These words lead us on from rebellion in Africa to war across the western Mediterranean. The wheels were already in motion for the epic battles to come.

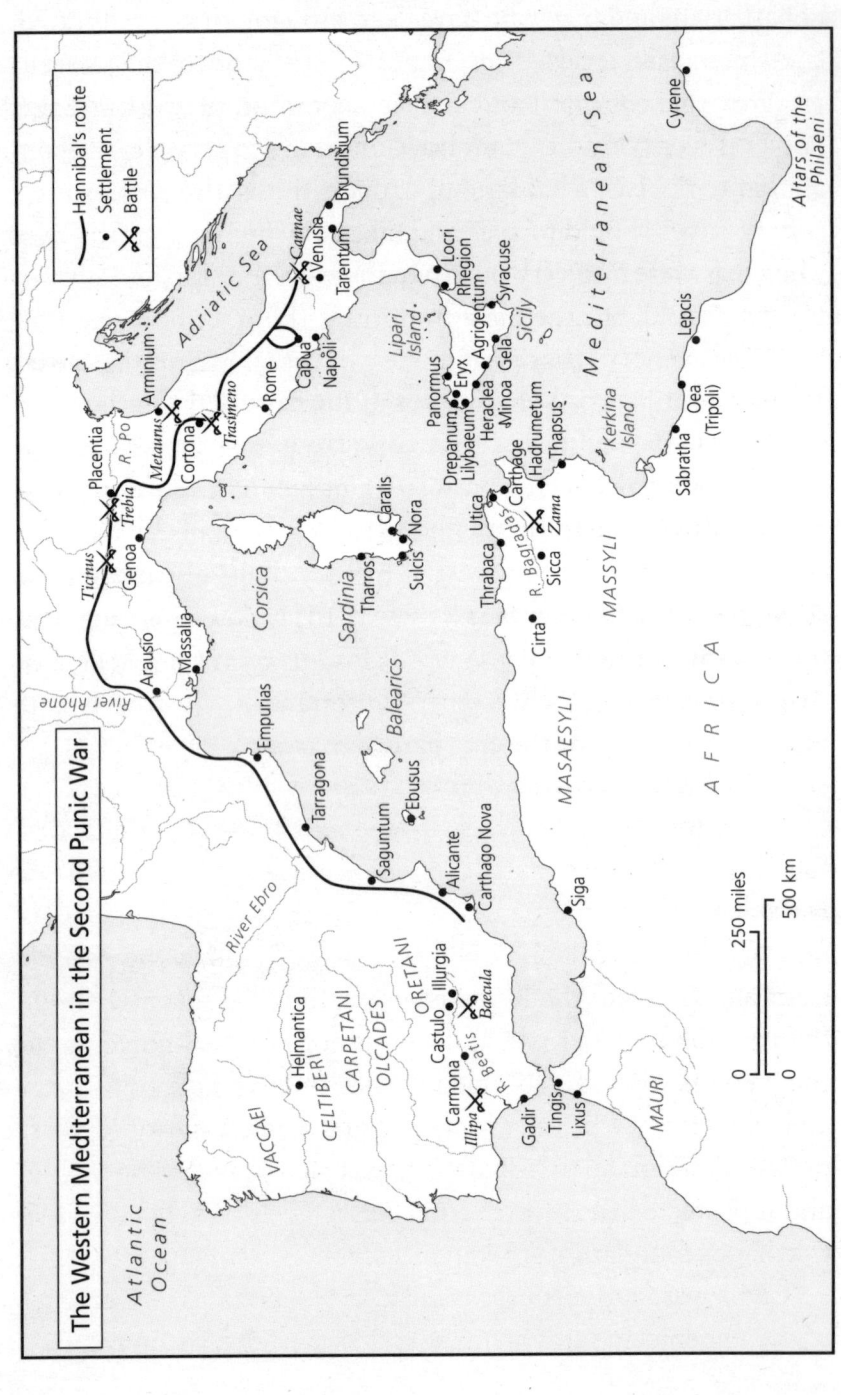

The Western Mediterranean in the Second Punic War

Hannibal's route
• Settlement
✗ Battle

Atlantic Ocean

River Rhone

Arausio
Massalia
Genoa
Ticinus ✗
Trebia ✗
Placentia
R. Po
Arminium
Cortona ✗
Trasimeno
Trasimeno ✗
Metaurus ✗
Rome
Capua
Napoli

Adriatic Sea

Cannae ✗
Venusia
Tarentum
Brundisium
Locri
Rhegion
Syracuse
Agrigentum
Gela
Minoa
Sicily
Eryx
Heraclea
Panormus
Drepanum
Lilybaeum

Lipari Island

Mediterranean Sea

Cyrene
Altars of the Philaeni

Lepcis
Oea (Tripoli)
Sabratha

Kerkina Island

Carthage
Utica
Thrabaca
R. Bagradas
Sicca
Zama ✗
Thapsus
Hadrumetum
Cirta

MASSYLI
MASAESYLI

A F R I C A

Siga
Tingis
Lixus
MAURI

Gadir
Carmona
Illipa
R. Baetis
Castulo
Illurgia
Baecula ✗
ORETANI
OLCADES
CARPETANI
CELTIBERI
Helmantica
VACCAEI

River Ebro

Carthago Nova
Alicante
Ebusus
Saguntum
Tarragona
Empurias

Balearics

Sardinia
Caralis
Nora
Sulcis
Tharros

Corsica

0   250 miles
0   500 km

CHAPTER 8

Implacable Enemy of Rome

To witness the next three decades of the history of Carthage we must move with the action to a new location – to the Iberian Peninsula (modern Spain and Portugal). This is where Hamilcar Barca and his army focused their efforts from the end of the Mercenary War (c. 238 BCE) onwards. It is worth understanding more about the connections and settlements that linked Carthage to the southern regions of Iberia, where there were coastal cities with long-standing Phoenician roots. This will help us perceive what may have motivated Hamilcar Barca to seek his remedies there, and why Carthage was so willing to support him in his quest.

Sometime around 1000 BCE, an ancient oracle commanded the people of Tyre to establish a city outside of the 'Pillars of Herakles' on the Atlantic Ocean, on the far side of the Mediterranean.[1] We call that city Cádiz, which was Gadir to the Phoenicians and Gades to the Romans. It was founded in a place more than 3,000km from Tyre, and to this edge of the known world the Tyrians took sacred objects from their temple of Melqart and established a brother temple there. The temple of Melqart of Cádiz was linked to its patron temple in the mother city Tyre, and it protected the settlers and their new city – very much like Carthage's foundation story in its essence.

Cádiz was, so our sources tell us, the location of the very first of the Phoenician settlements in the west of the Mediterranean.

Across the whole width of the sea, the god Melqart travelled with the Tyrians and other Phoenician speakers in their ships, acting as their protector and deity that supported their endeavours, and creating cultural synergies and ideas that moved back and forth across the sea. Sitting outside the Mediterranean just off the Atlantic coast of the Iberian Peninsula, Cádiz was founded on a long narrow island, placed near to the mouth of the Baetis (Guadalquivir) River, which travels inland to some of the richest ore and metal deposits in the whole region. The oracle had guided the Tyrians to a strategic and prosperous part of the world, the pragmatic and sacred aspects of the colonial voyage coming together in the locations and spaces of the colonies themselves.

The temple came to dominate the religious landscape in this far western zone for over a millennium. Melqart was a travelling deity, brought from place to place and mixed with local myths and stories. In his origins the god was likely aniconic, so worshipped in a place but without an image. As the worship and identity of the people who lived in Cádiz evolved, so too did the identity of the god, and a place that was first dedicated to Melqart shifted into one place where the Graeco/Roman Herakles, a version of the same deity, would be honoured for centuries afterwards.[2] At Cádiz, every spring, there was a festival to Melqart, who was reborn through the ritual of fire on an annual basis. It became a place of pilgrimage where worshippers would attend from all over the Mediterranean. The Roman geographer Strabo tells of the great temple with huge bronze pillars inside that described the story of the construction of the building.[3] These pillars, according to Strabo, are what gave the name to the whole geographical region that was the western entrance to the Mediterranean Sea from the Atlantic: the Pillars of Herakles (as Melqart was known in the Greek). Sailors from far and wide came to worship there and offer votives to the god. The temple of Melqart at Cádiz became so famous that it was believed to mark the end of the world, the termination of the land and the sea.

By the third century BCE, Cádiz was already centuries old, and its people expressed their heritage and their origins with their coinage, for example one showing Melqart on one side and a large tuna fish on the other (see Fig. 19). The imagery on the currency combines the figure of the patron deity and the rich seagoing traditions of the Atlantic. The god and the tuna fish give us insight into how the citizens identified themselves in these years: they came from a place with a renowned religious shrine and wealth from the gifts of the sea. A connection to music was another part of their identity. Cádiz in later Roman times was celebrated across the Mediterranean most of all for its *puellae gaditanae* ('girls from Gades'), its dancing girls. One story recalls an expedition to circumnavigate Africa as a route to India by a certain Eudoxus (this in Strabo via Posidonius, *c.* second century BCE). Posidonius claimed that Eudoxus prepared a large ship at Cádiz and among the cargo included 'the enslaved who were trained in music', linking the traditions of music and dance back much further than our imperial Roman sources. Not unrelated, perhaps, are beautiful terracotta figurines from the Punic period of occupation on the island of Ibiza that show women playing a variety of musical instruments. These figurines are often associated with funerary rituals and confirm the link between gender and music in the broader western Phoenician world. It is difficult to know what the figurines meant to their owners, but they show strong links to traditions of music and dance, which perhaps originated in religious rituals and evolved into exotic dancing girls and more prosaic entertainments after the city's capture by the Romans.[4]

This old city, almost 1,500km from Carthage to the west, was prized along with its links to the sea, especially to the Atlantic, and was part of the wider Phoenician diaspora. The relationship

Fig. 19 Copper alloy coin from Cádiz, third century BCE. Head of Melqart (obv.) and two fish (rev.)

between Cádiz and Carthage was long held, and one source even calls the Gaditanians, as they were later known, 'kin' of the Carthaginians.[5] This assumption of a blood relationship was widely known and appreciated, linking the two cities closely.[6] The Roman historian Justin remembered a moment, early in its history, when Cádiz was threatened by an inland Iberian army and the Carthaginians came to its aid by providing military support. There is no evidence that indicates when this happened, but the fifth century BCE is a good bet given what we know about Carthage's history. The better documented evidence, as we have seen, has Carthage providing support and military aid for the Phoenician-speaking diaspora of Sicily and Sardinia, and likely applied to Cádiz too.

The choices made by Carthage and her leaders in the face of the betrayal by the Romans in 238 BCE over Sardinia saw the city reorient towards the west. This drew the city of Cadiz even closer to Carthage than before, and there was a concerted effort to expand more direct control west along the coast of Africa and across into southern Iberia by the year 237 BCE. Hamilcar Barca and his army travelled there once the Mercenary War in Africa was over. There is some uncertainty over whether Hamilcar was welcomed or imposed his presence on Cádiz, and it is not clear whether he went as an allied friend or conqueror. Some evidence points to Hamilcar taking Cádiz by force, although Cádiz may well have willingly joined the cause of the Barcids.[7] In either scenario, the arrival of the Carthaginian forces in Iberia led to a monumental shift in the history of both regions and the fortunes of the family of the Barcids.

Hamilcar had a personal relationship to the god worshipped in Cádiz, Melqart, who was like a patron and protector deity to him. As he set out to reinvigorate Carthage's wealth and establish its prominence in the western Mediterranean, Hamilcar was acting much like the conquering warlords of the previous century we have already seen, especially Alexander, who also claimed to have divine patronage. Hamilcar began by sweeping up many of the old Phoenician cities that were culturally linked to Carthage. Starting out among the allied cities of coastal Iberia where he could raise troops and support, Hamilcar planned to extend Carthage's influence into new territory. The allied cities then would have broader choices to make in view of a complex geopolitical reality in the third-century BCE Mediterranean – support Carthage and their new commander or face destruction. Hamilcar and Carthage had decided to move to the west to extend their control because this was viewed as territory ripe for conquest, a place where they could make up for the military losses they had suffered in Sicily and Sardinia.

The commander acted in the ways his position as *rab* (general) and commander of the military would have demanded. Hamilcar prepared to set out on an expedition from which he might never return. He gathered his forces in Carthage in the spring of 237 BCE to depart for this new venture and took his family with him. He had built a network of support and looked now to the gods for an auspicious departure. As Hamilcar geared up to leave Carthage, financial support in the form of silver and gold was collected, and the elephants prepared. We have already seen how, in all ancient societies, military success was closely linked to ritual, and a religious offering would have been made to the gods before any action. This was to ensure the essential deities remained onside and continued to support the commander, all the soldiers and the city; the population needed to believe they were favoured. In Hamilcar's case there may even have been a sense of renewal, for among the citizens of Carthage there was an awareness of the new frontiers to be explored and a new beginning after the disastrous decades of recent memory. This is the context for an often-told scene at Carthage where a moment of sacrifice and religious offering before Hamilcar's departure was described in some detail by two of our ancient sources.

The Roman historian Livy begins his account of the Second Punic War at this very moment of departure, describing how Hamilcar solemnly sacrificed to a deity at an altar while watched by the dignitaries of the city and by his whole family. This was also the moment when Hamilcar's eldest son entered the historical record. The nine-year-old Hannibal watched his father perform the rituals, all the while begging and pleading to be allowed to accompany him, excited by the prospect. It was a serious and sombre scene when Hamilcar stood at an altar and offered libations to the god Ba'al at the start of his expedition. 'Hamilcar poured a libation to the gods and performed all the customary rites', and then, 'the omens being favourable', he called on his nine-year-old son to approach the altar, which was covered with the remains of the sacrifice of a large animal. With the smell of incense and smoke and blood filling the air, Hamilcar turned to Hannibal and asked him if he wanted to join the expedition. When the boy accepted his father's words with 'delight', Hamilcar took Hannibal by the hand and led him forward to the slaughtered animal on the altar. There, the father laid the hand of the son on the sacrificial victim and asked the young boy to vow that he would never befriend the Romans, that he would remain an implacable enemy to Rome (see Fig. 20 in plate section).[8]

The Roman writers of their later empire, looking back on the history of the Punic Wars, would make this the moment that the new war began, and turn it into a personal vendetta of the Barcid family. This has the result of reducing Mediterranean-wide geopolitics to the story of one family. One historian from the first century CE remembered another scene where Hamilcar sat watching while his three sons played roughly together, like boys do. Hamilcar, the story went, looked at the boys and then declared 'these are the lion cubs I am rearing for the destruction of Rome.'[9] The lion cubs evoked the powerful symbol of a warrior and of place, of Africa and the origins of the Carthaginians, but these are much later apocryphal tales of the Barcid generals and their aims to 'destroy Rome'. The Roman myths emphasised that Hamilcar Barca hated Rome and all his actions were driven only by this hatred, in some ways justifying the eventual actions of the Romans against Carthage. The reality, as we have seen, is far more complex when viewed from Carthage. Hamilcar's generation could not have trusted the Romans after the previous decade of war and betrayal, but the very idea that his whole motivation was driven by Rome is a reductive and much later retelling of the tale.

Hamilcar arrived in Cádiz and set about consolidating a power base in the Iberian Peninsula with a multicultural army. He employed the full playbook of conquest strategy, using hard and soft power, military force and negotiation, intermarriage and alliance. Like most Carthaginian citizens Hamilcar was educated and multilingual, and there would have been a range of advisors and allies around him who helped to strategise and plan. These were likely from across the Mediterranean and may have included Tyrians, Carthaginians, Greeks, Numidians, Sicilians and people from allied cities like Cádiz and friendly Iberian tribes as well. A broad coalition would be the only way to succeed in a hostile land and this was the way imperial powers operated. The successes that Hamilcar had in Iberia were summed up by Roman writers like Cornelius Nepos more succinctly. Nepos wrote that Hamilcar 'did great deeds through the favour of fortune', that his military successes were celebrated in his conquests of 'mighty and warlike nations' and that the result was his enrichment of 'all of Africa with abundant horses, arms, men and money'. Essentially Hamilcar was able to carve a power base out of the southern hinterland of the Iberian Peninsula. In the way that success breeds success, his original army that may have numbered 20,000 on arrival became, with conquest and consolidation, a force that had more than doubled in size, to 56,000 by the early 220s BCE (see page 170).[10]

These conquests had been hard fought. Hamilcar's soldiers were well trained and organised but fighting took place against one fortified hilltop city and its hinterland after another. Iberians had a reputation as fierce warriors but were not unified under a single power structure. Each region was ruled by local kings and chieftains who had often warred against each other and their coastal neighbours. Each region or town had to be dealt with individually, and given a chance to join the Carthaginian cause or resist. Then when defeated, the local power base was absorbed and reorganised. A few specific examples were reported in various sources. Diodorus Siculus tells how Hamilcar made war on Iberian and Celtic tribes (including Tartessians) and was successful in each battle, then 'he took over and enrolled the three thousand survivors in his own army.' Another story speaks of an

Iberian king named Indortes who had raised an army to resist Hamilcar but was captured, tortured and crucified. Hamilcar in turn released Indortes' army and incorporated his soldiers into his own force. The policy of conquest was repeated, again and again, across the region.[11]

Conquest and consolidation also meant securing the regions with garrisons, treaties and founding cities. Diodorus Siculus records that 'after bringing many cities throughout Iberia under his dominion, he founded an important city . . . named Acra Leuka.'[12] The name means 'white fort' or 'white cape' in Greek and some scholars argue that it was located at modern Alicante. Others put it to the west in Portugal (Castelo Branco reflects the same meaning), while more recent research has made a convincing case for the site of Carmona along the River Baetis.[13] As a strategic centre for controlling and coordinating newly conquered territory in nearby key regions, Carmona seems the practical choice.

The city may have acted as a garrison in the strategic zone of the river valley and the heartland of the silver mines that were so valuable to the Carthaginians. Control over the silver mines in the region resulted in some of the most compelling evidence from the period in the form of the coinage. The most famous of these was a double shekel, minted in Iberia on the Tyrian shekel standard, thought to be in circulation from circa 230 to 220 BCE (see Fig. 21 in plate section). On the face of the coin is a bearded man with a distinguished profile carrying a club on the right shoulder. This was meant to represent Melqart, patron of the Barcid family and of the Iberian territories they had created for Carthage. Some people believe that this coin was a portrait of Hamilcar Barca, the face of the man himself, but the reality is more subtle. The profile head on the coin was not meant to represent a living man and was clearly the image of the Melqart/ Herakles figure because of the club on his shoulder. The soldiers operating in the region – for these coins were minted to pay them – would have recognised the imagery and identified with it. The depiction of the god as an older, bearded man may implicitly have echoed Barcid rule and their conquests for the soldier audience, and may even have been meant to symbolise Hamilcar and his devotion to Melqart. But it would not have been intended to *be* Hamilcar.

The most celebrated aspect of the coin is the elephant on the other side. It is a beautifully crafted image of the iconic animal, possibly an African elephant rather than the customary Asian species. It is a bold statement of power. The elephant became a symbol of the Barcids and their years of conquest. The animal and the aged, bearded hero on the obverse combined these two concepts of the Carthaginian/Barcid authority to rule, the might of the Barcids and the deity who guided their path. Local tribes looked to the Barcid family as leaders and there would have been many who held a personal loyalty towards them. This coinage was intended to show off the status of the family as the local ruling power.

After six years in Iberia and ten years after the end of the First Punic War, in 231 BCE, a Roman embassy arrived in Iberia. The stories of Carthaginian successes and great conquest in Iberia had made their way across the Mediterranean, and when Hamilcar met this Roman delegation, he explained his motives and plan. Carthage had, he claimed, been forced into the region by Rome, for they had come to acquire new territory to pay off their old war debt.[14] The Romans were driven to be curious about the state of things in Iberia by the interests of their allies in Gaul, the Massalians (from what became modern Marseille). They took the opportunity to stir up as much hostility to the Carthaginians among the Iberians as possible while also negotiating with them on their own terms – connecting to tribes further north.

Hamilcar's successes in Iberia had also led to his growing influence in Carthage, which became even more apparent when a rebellion broke out in North Africa among the Numidian allies and Hamilcar sent Hasdrubal, his son-in-law, from Iberia back to Africa to deal with the revolt. Military and political policy at Carthage was being influenced in terms of financial, diplomatic and military support by Barcid Iberia.[15]

Just two years after the embassy from Rome, in the winter of 229/228 BCE, Hamilcar died in battle. Many ancient authors recorded his death, among them Livy, who refers to Hamilcar's 'timely death', but there are various versions of the event. Perhaps the most romantic is Diodorus' explanation that recounts how Hamilcar was laying siege to a city called Helice when he was ambushed by a local king. This king had at first pretended to be an ally, and then launched an attack. The heroic Hamilcar, with his army routed, single-handedly diverted the hostile troops away from his own army by plunging into a deep river while still on the back of his horse. He had done so to save two of his sons, Hannibal the eldest and Hasdrubal the second, who had been on campaign that winter with their father. In this version, Hamilcar 'perished in the flood under his steed but his sons were saved' while Polybius tells us only that death came 'bravely in a battle against one of the most warlike and powerful tribes'. In still another version 'he fell in battle fighting against the Vettones', a tribe located in the vicinity of modern Toledo.[16]

These stories of the heroic and noble death of a Carthaginian conqueror take us to the root of so many of the issues in writing a story of a lost people and history. Hamilcar, implacable enemy of the Romans, was remembered as a heroic warrior and commander by his most dreaded foes. The assumption is that the original sources used by the later surviving histories, now lost to us, included positive, pro-Carthaginian accounts of his life in which he was a figure of legend and drama. What else can we learn? That Hamilcar was a towering influence and heroic figure in the later third-century BCE Mediterranean and that he was a role model for his sons. The eldest, Hannibal, would have been 18 or 19 at the time of his father's death and Hasdrubal a few years younger at 16 or 17. The sons would have learned at their father's side, fighting with him, watching and understanding the politics and strategic approach as he set out to subdue Iberia. This was truly an apprenticeship, as one great scholar of the period has called it, and reflected the harsh reality that the Barcid brothers were brought up to live in.[17] The two elder boys had witnessed the death of their heroic father on campaign, betrayed by an erstwhile ally, while Mago the youngest had remained back at camp. These three teenage boys were left with a gaping hole in their lives and a legendary father to whom they would always be compared.[18]

Hamilcar's successor and son-in-law was also named Hasdrubal. As an important ally in the political sphere and a member of the Barcid family by his marriage, Hasdrubal succeeded Hamilcar to command the armies in Iberia. Hannibal, Hamilcar's eldest son, was considered still too young to take on his father's role. Hasdrubal's character, as well as his tenure in power, are only briefly mentioned by the sources and he received mixed reviews. He operated across the western Mediterranean with some impunity, as a kind of fixer. He could be found in many places, in the senate at Carthage, in Africa campaigning or undertaking discussions with local allies, and in Iberia as the right hand of Hamilcar. There were many accusations against Hasdrubal, including that he purchased his political power at Carthage through bribes and used his influence in the popular assembly to sway events. This brief observation gives us a view into the political power of the popular assembly at Carthage, a behind-the-scenes perspective as Hasdrubal relied on the support of the people's assembly to pass Barcid policies through the senate. Livy even claimed that Hasdrubal was made the leader in Iberia solely on behalf of the popular assembly and against 'the wishes of the Carthaginian elite'. This presents another view and alludes to conflict in the republic between the senate and the assembly, although the question remains as to whether Livy was reflecting more on the issues in the Roman system rather than the realities of the Carthaginian one. Livy went even further in his aspersions and undermined Hasdrubal's masculinity and therefore his integrity – the sources certainly did not like him.[19]

By far the longest-lasting imprint of the Carthaginians in the Iberian Peninsula took place under the command of Hasdrubal when he founded a new city on the southeastern coast. The place was called 'the new city' (again *Qart Hadasht*) after the original version of Carthage in Africa and became known as Carthago Nova in the later Latin version, or Cartagena in the modern region of Murcia in Spain. New Carthage was established in 229 BCE and quickly thrived; it was the foundation of a city at the location of one of the great natural ports of the western Mediterranean, and continues to be the home of the Spanish navy today. This gave the Barcids and the Carthaginians a showpiece city in their new territory, a centre for their power with easy access by ship back to Carthage. The visible remains at Cartagena today are mostly later Roman buildings but a visitor can still get a glimpse of the original city walls built by the Barcids. These were magnificent examples of casemate defensive architecture, standing 10m high and encompassing a dramatic landscape with the two hills of the town dominating the views. The walls would have been alive with activity, living quarters for soldiers and animals, filled with weapons and surrounded by forges. New Carthage was established with all the modern conveniences of a sophisticated third-century BCE city, and people flocked there from across the western Mediterranean, making it a cosmopolitan place with a multicultural population. After visiting Cartagena and its museums and ruins, and reading Polybius' description, I had the sense of a place that must have felt like a colonial boom town, with ships coming and going through the deep harbour, busy with construction projects, artisans, merchants and miners, and full of soldiers for hire who would have gathered to drink in the taverns and take their chances with the new power.

On his father's death at the age of 18 or 19, Hannibal Barca had taken on a more active role as lieutenant to his brother-in-law and in command of his own unit of cavalry. In a now famous description of the young man, the Roman Livy described how the older soldiers saw the father in the son's look and actions: 'they saw that same dynamism in his expression, the same forcefulness in his eyes, the same facial expression and features.' Livy's romanticised portrait of the young man tells how he was able to rouse the soldiers' loyalty through the similarity to his father. Hannibal was the chosen and dashing young commander who had his brother-in-law's trust: 'there was no one whom Hasdrubal preferred to put in command when a gallant or enterprising feat was called for, while there was no other officer under whom the rank and file had more confidence and enterprise.'[20]

As Hannibal led his unit on attacks to the north of Iberia, deep into the territory of the Celtiberians, he was feted for behaving just like any one of the lads, for working hard with no time for rest or the luxuries of his position. He was a man's man and through his comradery and diligence gained the loyalty of his fellow soldiers. Hannibal would lie 'wrapped in a soldier's cloak' to take a short sleep, was described as skilled and brave 'on horse or foot' and was always 'the first to enter the battle and the last to leave'. There is little specific information or detail on the life led by the Barcid brothers in these years other than curated tales for later narratives. Livy's description conjures up a young, vigorous Hannibal riding into battle and in turn teaching his younger brothers the arts of war.[21]

Hasdrubal had an official role in Iberia, acknowledged with the title of 'general with unlimited power', and also married the daughter of an Iberian prince. This link between the Carthaginian ruling elite and the Iberian royalty outlines how fluid loyalties were in this period and how local alliances meant the difference between success and failure. We know that Hasdrubal had been married already, to Hamilcar's daughter, but there is no mention of her whereabouts or even if she was still alive. Hasdrubal may have married more than one woman, but there is so little information about the practicalities of Carthaginian custom in marriage or in command that we can only speculate. Monogamy seems to have been the tradition in Carthage, but alliances and intermarriage would have been essential in keeping control of its new territory. With the relationship between Hasdrubal and the Carthaginian senate strained he may have acted as he chose. Polybius remarked that he 'governed Iberia . . . without paying any attention to the Carthaginian Senate', which implies a shift from Hamilcar's tenure but this is not clearly stated anywhere. The military title and his marriage reflect the duality of Hasdrubal's role – he was both local hegemon among the Iberians and the governing representative of Carthage.[22]

The successes and growing independence of Barcid Iberia stirred up tensions and political unrest, both in the senate at home and among the Romans. By the year 226 BCE the Carthaginian territory in Iberia was again visited by a group of Roman senators on a diplomatic mission. Rome had been busy developing its empire and conquering in the north of Italy and across the Adriatic Sea to the east through these same years as the Barcids expanded in Iberia. The Romans had also been pacifying regions and establishing their own new colonial foundations and extending their territory. The new meeting of the old enemies took place during the late summer or perhaps early autumn of that year, and must have been a success, for it resulted in a formal agreement between the two sides called the Ebro Treaty. The Ebro River is in the northeast of the Iberian Peninsula and drains into the Mediterranean in today's region of Catalonia. The new treaty, named for the river, outlined the Ebro as the northern edge beyond which the Carthaginians agreed not to cross in conquest. Rome's motives for the treaty are clear: they sought to contain Carthaginian power inside the Iberian Peninsula. Especially at that point, because Roman conquest and settlement of northern Italy were in process, and they faced a threat from the Gauls beyond the Alps. Polybius wrote that 'for the present . . . the Romans did not venture to impose orders on Carthage or to go to war with her, because the threat of a Celtic invasion was hanging over them.' So Polybius' claim that Rome was employing a holding measure also implies that they intended to go to war with Carthage later on. In the meantime, they needed to contain any possible threat.[23]

The Carthaginian motivation for signing the Ebro Treaty is harder to ascertain, because Polybius chose to leave out the Carthaginian incentive from his history. Perhaps he didn't know what had motivated Carthage, or it was not in his interest to tell us. We can consider that the Carthaginians must have also imposed some limitations on Roman operations. They may have genuinely expected the Romans to refrain from interference in their territory south of the Ebro and were satisfied not to expand further north. Did the Carthaginians take the treaty of 226 BCE as a Roman acceptance of their domain south of the Ebro River just as they seemed to acknowledge Roman (or Roman-allied) influence north of it. It is hard to imagine that the Carthaginians could be so gullible after all they had experienced with the Romans in the previous decades, and when limitless conquest was the prevailing idea of the period. At this point in the story, it becomes difficult to know how much of Polybius' account was contrived to suit the Roman justification for the start of the coming war. The details of the Ebro agreement will be essential for Roman accusations against Carthage, whom they accused of breaking the treaty, so even though the two sides may have had very similar reasons for signing the treaty, ensuing events meant that the details have been argued over for centuries.

In the year 222/221 BCE, four years after the Ebro agreement, Hasdrubal was assassinated by a disgruntled Iberian ally. The 25-year-old Hannibal Barca, son of Hamilcar, was raised to command of the Carthaginian army. Hannibal had grown from a boy to a young man while his father conquered, and he had come of age at his brother-in-law's side. He had mastered the arts of conquest and diplomacy, along with his two younger brothers Hasdrubal and Mago. They learned how to ride and fight on horseback, had lessons in military strategy and command and had tutors to teach them more traditional skills. A Spartan named Sosylus taught Greek to the boys, and this was not just about teaching the language but the associated arts of politics, rhetoric and leadership too.[24]

Hannibal may have married an Iberian princess named Imilce before he came to power. She was the daughter of a chieftain from Castulo, the strategic capital of the Oretani people. The city was on a main artery in Carthaginian territory and closely linked to the resource-rich mines of the region (see page 170). Hannibal's marriage to Imilce would have bound the people of Castulo to the Barcids, so that the personal bonds and loyalty between the extended Barcid family and the Iberian people sealed the links with Carthage. Imilce was only named by one much later source, a Roman epic poet named Silius Italicus, whose poem, the *Punica*, puts the human touch on Hannibal by giving him a wife and son, so the truth remains elusive.

When Hannibal succeeded Hasdrubal in 221 BCE, there was no rest or consolidation but only endless conquest. Chosen by the soldiers to succeed Hasdrubal, he immediately moved north against the Olcades tribes. The story of Hannibal camped in front of the city of Althaea with his army evokes perfectly how he operated in the field. At first, he 'terrified' the city with a succession of attacks and captured the town. This happened so quickly that the neighbouring towns all 'submitted to the Carthaginians' without any further resistance. Hannibal, flushed with this success, went further and deeper into the Iberian Peninsula that campaigning season with strength and flair. He pushed his soldiers, marched them long distances across a wide region, and the results were indisputable. Only when he had imposed tribute on all the towns and acquired his payments did he take his soldiers back to New Carthage for the winter.

Hannibal's success as a commander rested on his soldiers and their loyalty to him. He was renowned for treating his men with 'great generosity, distributing a bounty to them at once and promising further payments later'. Integral to Hannibal's military reputation was this ability to grow and sustain the loyalty and belief of his soldiers. The unwavering allegiance of his army helped to create an aura of invincibility around him: his soldiers trusted his instincts and in turn he rewarded them for this devotion. Hannibal, like all great conquerors, was a risk taker. He needed

Fig. 1, page 23: A late 8th- or early 7th-century BCE Assyrian palace relief showing a Phoenician decked warship with two banks of oars known as a bireme, with marines and shields on deck, reflecting early innovation in Mediterranean seafaring

Fig. 2, page 24: Assyrian royal relief showing a tribute bearer – perhaps a Phoenician – bringing monkeys as gifts to the king

Fig. 3, page 28: Sandro Botticelli's 15th century painting *The Birth of Venus* shows the enduring legacy of the myth of Venus (Aphrodite/Astarte) arriving on Cyprus, washed up from the sea

Fig. 5, page 35: The sign
of Tanit embedded into a
mosaic floor from the
Punic city known as
Kerkouane, Tunisia
3rd century BCE

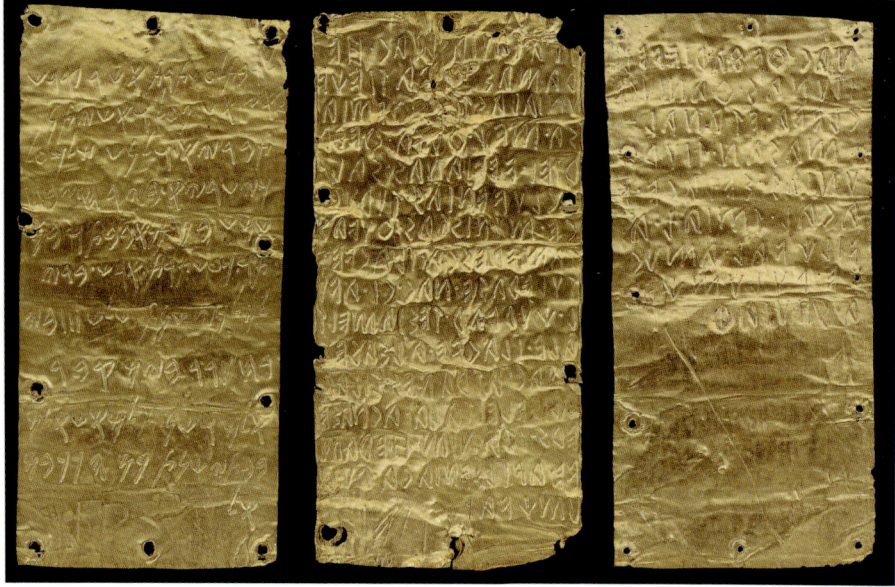

Fig. 10, page 70: Bilingual Etruscan/Phoenician incised gold tablets once hung on the doors of the Temple of Uni at Pyrgi (Italy). These reflect the close relationship between the Etruscan city states and Carthaginians and Phoenicians in the 6th/5th-century BCE Mediterranean

Fig. 20, page 177: Benjamin West, *The Oath of Hannibal*, 1770, oil on canvas. This painting imagines the famous scene of Hannibal's sworn pledge against the Romans in c. 238 BCE

Fig. 21, page 179: Silver Carthaginian double shekel with head of Melqart (obv.) and elephant and rider (rev.)

Fig. 22, page 208: The top of the Traversette pass looking towards Monte Viso where Hannibal would have passed with his forces, including elephants, in the early winter of 218 BCE

Fig. 26, page 252: A scene on a third-style Roman wall painting from
Pompeii captures the drama of 'the death of Sophonisba", *c.* 1st BCE/CE

Fig. 27, page 260: Satellite image of the area of modern Tunis with the Punic ports of ancient Carthage still clearly visible

Fig. 28, page 293: 'Marius, as he gazed upon Carthage, and Carthage as she beheld Marius, might well have offered consolation the one to the other' – John Vanderlyn's *Caius Marius and the Ruins of Carthage*, 1807, oil on canvas was based on a passage from Roman author Velleius Paterculus (2.19)

an army that would follow him anywhere, believed in his abilities and would carry out his orders to the letter. He achieved his triumphs by being bold, taking the initiative, outthinking his opponents and trusting his own skills.[25]

We know more about Hannibal than we do any other Carthaginian who ever lived. For 20 years from 221 BCE the sources focus almost exclusively on him. This tends to skew our evidence about Carthage around the life of one man and his great deeds and adventures, and somehow the broader story of the western Mediterranean in all its complexity gets lost in the appetite for daring deeds of great soldiers. This closely studied man and the boldness of his command become the focus of epic tales of courage and brilliance. We see Hannibal campaigning against the Carpetani people north of the Tagus River. While returning to New Carthage he found himself vastly outnumbered and surprised by an army that blocked his way. Hannibal, faced with an ambush, retreated to the far side of the river and drew the enemy after him. He used the water as a buffer and positioned his 40 elephants to challenge the enemy as they crossed. Polybius described how 'the Iberians tried to force a crossing at various points, [and] the greater number of them were killed as they left the water by the elephants.' The confusion sown by the elephants made cover for Hannibal and his army to cross back over to the other side of the river and attack the attackers from behind. The surely exaggerated claim is that Hannibal was able to scatter a 'force of more than one hundred thousand' of his enemies.[26]

The first years of his command continued with expanding territory and tales of great deeds, securing Hannibal's reputation. In 220 BCE he returned to New Carthage after this highly successful season of campaigning and there he found an embassy of Romans waiting for him. The diplomatic envoys were very high-level delegates from the Roman senate. New Carthage would have been busy and bustling, and at the end of the campaigning season the active ports and multicultural population surely impressed the Roman delegation. There, Hannibal granted an audience to the Romans. These were important men, used to carrying a great deal of authority with them, and included the ex-consul P. Valerius Flaccus and ex-praetor Q. Baebius Tamphilus. The meeting did not go smoothly from all reports – the young, confident and bold Carthaginian who had just returned from a successful campaign was indifferent towards the Romans and their formalities. It was a crucial moment in the history of Carthage, and it all revolved around a city by the name of Saguntum (see page 170).

Saguntum (now Sagunto in the province of Valencia) is a city on the east coast of the Iberian Peninsula, well south of the Ebro River. At the meeting the Roman ambassadors accused Hannibal of getting involved in the internal affairs of Saguntum. The stated intention of the ambassadors was 'to issue a formal caution to Hannibal to leave the people of Saguntum in peace as allies of the Roman people'.[27] Hannibal dismissed the Romans and did so with some scorn. He accused them of being hypocrites and, in turn, of meddling in internal Saguntine politics. Hannibal accused the Romans of interfering and causing the death of some citizens in Saguntum who had pro-Carthaginian views. Polybius' view was that the Romans might have negotiated with Hannibal if he had been willing take the opportunity and also accept Roman interference south of the Ebro River. Hannibal defended himself with the claim that a Carthaginian 'never to neglect the cause of the victims of injustice'. The Roman envoys warned Hannibal not to interfere with Saguntum and then sailed onwards to Carthage to convey the same message. Hannibal too sent word to Carthage and asked them for instructions. He reported that the Romans were interfering with Carthaginian allies in the region, south of the Ebro River. Polybius states that 'from this moment on the Romans believed that war was inevitable and that they would fight the Carthaginians in the Iberian peninsula.' It was, notably, a year after the end of the 20-year period of reparation payments that Carthage had made to Rome following the First Punic War, so by 220 BCE there were no longer any payments being made or treaty in place – beyond the Ebro Treaty – to keep the two sides apart.[28]

Sitting high on a ridge near the sea and dominating the landscape, Saguntum was an important town. A well-fortified, wealthy and independent city surrounded by a fertile plain – 250km north of New Carthage and 135km south of the Ebro River. There were few cities left in the peninsula willing to challenge the Carthaginians by this point, except for this one place. A quick look at the map will tell you that Saguntum lies well south of the Ebro River so we have to ask: how could it be protected in the treaty Carthage had just signed with Rome? The Romans, in 220 BCE, claimed Saguntum as their ally and alleged that Hannibal had interfered with them, implying the Carthaginians were the aggressors. Carthage accused Saguntum of hostility towards Carthaginian-allied peoples, those both within the city and among neighbouring tribes. The details of the story hinge on the Ebro agreement but as far as we know there was no mention of the city of Saguntum in the treaty. Nonetheless, at some point between 226 BCE, when the treaty was signed, and 220 BCE, when trouble started, a relationship formed between Rome and Saguntum, even though it clearly lay within the bounds of Carthaginian influence. A plausible scenario is that some leading citizens of Saguntum were worried about Carthaginian influence and reached out to the Romans as a counterbalance, or perhaps reached out to allies of the Romans – the Massalians.

At the heart of the matter is the question of when Rome and Saguntum first created this alliance. Polybius' vague claims that it was 'an acknowledged fact that the Saguntines placed themselves in Rome's protecting grasp a good many years before the time of Hannibal' tell us nothing.[29] A closer look at the details reveals that between 223 and 220 BCE some leading citizens from Saguntum, members of a pro-Carthaginian group, were put to death in the city and the Romans were involved. There was also another incident that involved a neighbouring pro-Carthaginian community attacked by Saguntum. These two events – one internal and one outside the city – brought Hannibal into a confrontation with the Romans. There was nothing unusual about settling a regional dispute by calling in larger powers in the third century BCE, but we can't easily piece together the run of events because the details have been so obscured by other narrative agendas.

Hannibal spent that winter in New Carthage and in the spring of 219 BCE moved to lay siege to Saguntum. He began a long and arduous assault on a town built to resist such an attack. This time in front of the walls of Saguntum taught Hannibal some very harsh lessons about being tied up in a long siege. The campaign began sometime between late March and early May and lasted until December 219/January 218 BCE. The Romans did nothing to help their allies throughout the whole period. Perhaps disagreement in the Roman senate about what to do meant they were reduced to inaction; or a more cynical view sees the Romans, feeling ready to go to war, as provoking Hannibal, using Saguntum as the bait.[30]

The Roman poet Silius Italicus paints a picture of Hannibal during the siege with 'his war-trumpets sounding' as a man eager 'for a greater war to come'. A three-pronged attack on the city involved advanced siege craft, with catapults, ballistas, platforms and assault towers. The Saguntines defended as fiercely as the Carthaginian troops attacked. A new kind of weapon, a *phalarica*, caused havoc among the Carthaginian forces. Livy describes a flaming 3-foot-long head on an iron javelin, wrapped with 'tow and smeared with pitch', so forceful that it was able to 'pass through a man's body as well as his shield'. After many months and despite their *phalaricae*, the city walls were undermined and the Saguntines were forced to retreat to their citadel. Hannibal fought at the front and was so seriously injured by a spear at one point that he had to retreat from the field. Otherwise, he was present, 'on hand in person to give encouragement' and promising great spoils of victory when the town was taken.[31] At one moment, Hannibal had to leave the siege and marched off to quell an uprising among the Oretani and Carpetani tribes but left his lieutenant Maharbal, son of Himilco, to carry on the attack. Finally, after eight long months and no help from Rome, Saguntum could hold out no longer. The city fell and was sacked. The men, women and children inside were dispersed, slaughtered or sold into slavery. It was a violent end to a city that had bravely dared to challenge the conquerors, and the story of Saguntum became an epic tale and one that was repeated and recalled over and over. Saguntum was the trigger for the war to follow.

Hannibal returned to New Carthage after Saguntum fell and then carried on to Cádiz. We think he retraced his father's first steps on the peninsula back to where it had all started when he was a boy, and visited the temple of Melqart. Hannibal formally deposited part of his spoils of victory to the god, thanking him for his patronage and support, perhaps imploring him to continue to work on his behalf. For the upcoming war, Hannibal would need to rally allies from around the Mediterranean more effectively than ever. He and his relationship to his patron god Melqart were vital in this; whether in the guise of Herakles or as the Phoenician or Iberian versions of this powerful figure of the colonial west, the clout carried by the deity would be needed by the young conqueror. At Cádiz, in the sanctuary of the temple, he must have contemplated his choices, the future war and the path he had chosen for the voyage ahead.

CHAPTER 9

On His Mauritanian Beast

Almost ten months after the sack of Saguntum, from the top of a pass that crosses the Alps and links Gaul to Italy, the 29-year-old Hannibal Barca addressed his soldiers. The men were spread out below him in a natural hollow, as if in a theatre watching a leading man stood before an audience. For two days he had waited at the top of the mountain while the tens of thousands of exhausted men, horses and elephants caught up with him, the stragglers and animals that had broken free all somehow ending up back in the camp on the top of the Alps that look down upon Italy. They had followed a long road from New Carthage to arrive there, and they looked up to their leader standing at the summit of the wild and dangerous mountains and listened to his every word. As remembered by Polybius, who claims to have spoken to eyewitnesses, Hannibal could see he needed to boost the morale of his army. He celebrated the great virtues of his men and emphasised the glory that waited for them down below in Italy. He spoke of the allies who would support them and gestured towards the south, to Rome itself. Then Hannibal turned away from the men, stepping across the top of the pass and at the head of his invading army began the long descent into Italy, towards war with Rome.

Even today there is still no agreement on the exact events that led Hannibal into the mountains and to the start of the second war between Carthage and Rome. The stories from Saguntum, from the siege and sack of the city, are so contorted and the chronology so mixed up that even our best ancient source, the Greek Polybius, expressed his frustration with his sources, describing them as 'the common gossip of a barber's shop'.[1] Still, we do know that by the end of the year 219 BCE there was a sacked city in Iberia and a young, talented and enormously charismatic Carthaginian general standing in its wake. As the trail of Hannibal moved on from place to place, his legend grew and became more exaggerated with every step. Hannibal evolved in the story from the victor at Saguntum into a supernatural hero leading an impossible army of soldiers from across the Mediterranean and a herd of 37 elephants across the Alps. It is no coincidence that these stories harked back to the labours of the hero Herakles, the Greek version of his patron god Melqart, whose support and protection Hannibal would have evoked all along the way. The more extreme the journey, the more heroic the man. Alexander the Macedonian had supposedly once urged his men on with tales of Herakles as they waited near the Indus River, noting that Herakles 'would never have earned the glory which transformed him from a man into a god, or demigod' if he had not ventured well outside his comfort zone.[2] Hannibal channelled this kind of heroic leadership in his campaigns against Rome.

The previous ten months had been frantic as the two biggest powers in the region prepared again for war. There was a mobilisation of troops and diplomatic envoys crisscrossing the western Mediterranean. When Hannibal had returned to New Carthage after visiting the temple of Melqart in Cádiz it was already spring of 218 BCE. By that time the Roman senate had chosen its consuls for the year and these men were busy raising armies for conquest in their spheres of operation (Latin *provincia*), Sicily and Iberia. The consuls were Publius Cornelius Scipio, who was given Iberia as his 'province', and Tiberius Sempronius Longus, who had

Sicily and Africa. The consuls levied six legions (4,000 infantry in each) making up troops totalling 64,000 infantry (24,000 Roman and 40,000 from 'allies') with 6,200 cavalry (1,800 Roman and 4,400 from allies) and a fleet of 220 quinqueremes.[3] Rome believed it was going to war with Carthage in Iberia and Africa and intended to capture her territory quickly.

The news of Saguntum's fall would have reached Rome when the plans to go to war were already underway. As soon as the sailing season allowed, an embassy of senior Roman senators, including the outgoing consuls of the previous year, stood in the senate at Carthage and demanded the recall of Hannibal from Iberia. Recriminations flew back and forth between the two sides, each blaming the other. The Carthaginian senators refused to act, knowing that by abandoning Iberia they would be ceding it to Rome. They also must have known that at that moment Hannibal was more powerful than Carthage itself, and they did not have the military muscle to impose their will upon him. The history is not a simple story, and there were debates on both sides of the respective senates calling for a more peaceful approach, negotiation and some kind of working arrangement, but the overwhelming feeling from the historical sources points to the inevitability of war.[4] In the third century BCE there were few mechanisms to settle a geopolitical dispute except for war: the way forward for all sides was to fight.

All these events are recorded as simultaneous, although the planning for this war must have been more drawn out on both sides. Romans knew they were sending armies to Sicily and Iberia by January 218 BCE and Hannibal too must have been preparing and planning before the actual declaration of war. Hannibal knew the Roman plan as well. He was well-informed by his vast and admiring network on the movements of the Romans and would remain so for the next few years of the war, always staying one step ahead of his rivals. For Hannibal and for Carthage, it was simply essential to stop the Roman invasion of Africa. The plan hatched at New Carthage in early spring was beyond bold. Hannibal and his armies were going to take the fight to Italy. As the later Roman historian Dio wrote, Hannibal believed it 'better to be the first to act than the first to suffer'.[5]

The land route to Italy was the only option open to the Carthaginians, with the sea between Italy and Iberia controlled by Roman or Roman-allied ships. The First Punic War had proven that the Carthaginians could not consistently defeat the Romans and their allies at sea, so instead they would move on land. A keen student of strategy and history, Hannibal's idea was to follow the advice of the Epirote king Pyrrhus and to fight in Italy and try to separate the Romans from their allies.[6] At New Carthage an army was mustered, and envoys sent out on the land route to Italy to ensure support. Hannibal likely encouraged his envoys to stir up anti-Roman feeling along the route, all the way to the Celtic peoples of the north of Italy who had so recently been fighting the conquering Roman armies.

In Iberia, Hannibal meticulously planned his attack, gathering as much information as possible through his contacts, his envoys and spies. There would have been a flow of people across the seas bringing information to him as ships travelled from Rome through Sicily to Carthage and Iberia. Ships involved in commerce were frequently suspected of espionage and indeed frequently acted as spies, selling cargo and information as they moved from port to port. Hannibal's network was more sophisticated than most and he was kept informed of the plans of the Romans by his agents embedded in Rome and perhaps even in the Roman army itself.[7] He was consistently able to surprise his enemy, which must reflect the scope of his intelligence network.

Hannibal left his younger brother Hasdrubal Barca in command of Carthaginian Iberia against an inevitable Roman attack. Supporting Hasdrubal were other Carthaginian and Numidian commanders and key Iberian allies. Hannibal also sent soldiers to Africa from Iberia (13,850 infantry, 1,200 cavalry and 870 Balearic slingers) and to Iberia from Africa to 'bind . . . the two provinces to reciprocal loyalty'. Hasdrubal was left with a fleet of almost 60 ships, with a complement of cavalry made up of 'Libyphoenicians, Libyans and Numidians' along with infantry from Africa supported by Ligurians and Balearic slingers. The specific detail provided here comes via Polybius who claimed to have read an inscription written by Hannibal himself. The now-lost inscription was in the south of Italy on the Lacinian promontory near Crotona at a famous temple dedicated to Juno Lacinia (see page 124).[8] Hannibal's careful planning and details of his actions were inscribed for posterity in this sacred place.

Hannibal's army was made up of 'Africans, Iberians, Ligurians, Celts, Phoenicians, Italians and Greeks' – not simply a hired army, but a mix of different units and types of soldiers who were carefully woven together into a cohesive force.[9] There were units who fought under their own command and others who were under the control of Carthaginian commanders, like Hannibal's youngest brother Mago, who accompanied his brother as a leading lieutenant. The individual units wore their own traditional uniforms and kept their own identity in battle. This was a paid professional army, but its heterogeneous attire perhaps made it look uncoordinated, which may be one reason why Hannibal was consistently underestimated in the early years of the war. The diverse array of soldiers had one thing in common: they were extremely loyal to their commander and committed to the cause.

Hannibal's approach to command and warfare was egalitarian, and the Roman commentators noted that he valued talent (and commitment) over status. Hannibal's army came from territories now subject to Carthaginian rule and directly linked to Carthaginian power. This included, if we believe Polybius' account, territories stretching from the Altars of the Philaeni in Libya all the way to the Atlantic coast of North Africa and much of Iberia. The military obligation of the army seems to have been first and foremost to the Barcid family, and Hannibal himself. Livy portrays Hannibal as a tough soldier who lived with his army, eschewed the luxuries of command and was brave, resourceful, intelligent and quickly able to react. He was the ideal fighting man.[10] The degree to which these descriptions are generically describing a 'great soldier' in the post-Alexander Mediterranean world or really reflecting the character of Hannibal is unclear. The specific attributes of good command and soldiery in the ancient (and, to be fair, modern) construction of leadership are all reflected here.

It was likely the end of May or even early June by the time Hannibal left New Carthage. He marched north towards the Ebro River supported by 90,000 infantry and 12,000 cavalry, 37 elephants and thousands of pack animals in his train. The army would have had to wait until the first harvest of the summer to be able to feed itself along the way. Imagine the sight as this massive force marched along the coast, and the stories and legends that followed along with it. There was an almost mythical aspect to the departure of the army. There were also those who supported Hannibal in more abstract ways whose role was to spread stories and build legends. The myth management of an ancient campaign was a key part of its success and Hannibal understood and cultivated his own mythology, linking his journey with that of the legendary Herakles whose tenth labour had placed him in the far west of the Mediterranean, stealing the cattle of Geryon, and marching across the land back towards the east. Hannibal was heading to Italy along this same heroic path, the 'way of Herakles' as it was known in antiquity. The coinage, the stories and the reports of dreams where the figure of Melqart/Herakles appeared all tied into the sophisticated presentation of the great adventure ahead.

Once across the Ebro, the army split into three columns to approach the not insignificant challenge of the Pyrenees. In this region between the Ebro River and the mountains they had to fight and faced stiff resistance. Hannibal left a rearguard of troops with his lieutenant Hanno in charge to hold the region. This was surely a place the Romans would come to take as soon as they could, so Hannibal wanted to ensure some protection. Polybius tells us that Hanno was left with 10,000 foot soldiers and 1,000 cavalry. Hannibal also sent the same number of troops home after this initial push. Was this a goodwill gesture to ensure loyalty behind him in Iberia? One source records that he saw these forces as a fallback 'if he ever had to call on them for reinforcements'. Equally, another 10,000 soldiers left the march, wanting to return home. The result was that a slimmed-down force continued on over the Pyrenees, with 50,000 foot soldiers and 9,000 cavalry heading for Italy.[11] They continued, marching steadily across the southern part of Gaul, and turned inland as they got near Massalia (Marseille), an allied-Roman city at the mouth of the Rhône River. Modern estimates of a fully loaded force like Hannibal's army put them as moving quickly, but perhaps unevenly, at a pace of around 15km a day. The fastest and slowest parts of the train would have spread out over a long distance, but the average is equivalent to the distance given in Polybius of roughly 10 Roman miles per day.[12] Nonetheless, the sources record that the Romans were surprised by the speed of their opponent's progress when reports of the army at the Rhône reached them.

Hannibal, at the edge of the mighty river, faced an epic challenge. How to get his army and elephants across quickly and safely? The Romans were four days south of Hannibal at

Massalia, and Publius Scipio sent out scouts to find the Carthaginians, hoping to fight them in Gaul. It was late summer, and the river was at its lowest depth, but it was still a fast-flowing and massive waterway. Today's Rhône is a highly managed river system, yet still impresses with its depth and width; in Hannibal's time it would have been much wider and less tamed. The details of the crossing recorded in Polybius are fascinating, with Hannibal making friends and using up every resource to buy and borrow enough river craft to make the crossing. It took him two days to gather enough resources and by that time a force of hostile Gauls had gathered on the far bank of the river, looking to harass the crossing army. The reality of a massive and well-supplied army crossing territory like this would have made them seem fearsome, yes, but a professional army also carried a huge amount of wealth with them in coinage and metal. This made them vulnerable when they had to stop, break formation and cross natural barriers. The Gauls on the opposing banks were opportunistic locals, looking to take advantage of the vulnerability of the Carthaginian army at the moment of crossing.[13]

To distract the forces on the opposite bank, Hannibal sent one of his commanders named Hanno (son of Bomilcar the *sufet*) to cross the river further north with a small force. Hanno would then circle back and approach the waiting enemy from the east bank of the Rhône. Once Hanno was in place, Hannibal began to cross with his troops. He led from the front, encouraging his men as they rowed across the river to face those opposing them. It was noisy with cheering and shouting from the Carthaginian army, racing each other across the river while war cries of the Gauls met them. In a well-orchestrated move, as the Carthaginians reached the east bank of the river, Hanno and his advance guard moved to attack the Celtic tribes from the rear. The crossing was won quite easily in the end, with the enemy falling away once they could see they were defeated. Hannibal turned now to the task of getting his elephants and animals across the river.

These elephants were important to Hannibal, a symbol of power and of the self-definition of the Barcid family. As beasts of war the elephants were very effective against less-organised opponents like the Celtic chieftains in Gaul and northern Italy or Iberian armies, but they proved less effective against the more structured forces of Rome. What cannot be underestimated, however, is their symbolic value, how the presence of the beasts added to Hannibal's aura of power. As he went further and further into the territory of the enemy, this aura was, at times, the most essential part of his survival. Whether the elephants that travelled with Hannibal were of the Asian, African or North African wood or forest species (now extinct) is a much debated and discussed topic, as we saw in Chapter 5. The Carthaginians had been deploying elephants in warfare for over 60 years by now and would have used what was most regionally available and effective, probably the African or North African wood species. However, later sources list the name of one of the last surviving of Hannibal's elephants as Suria, perhaps a play on Syria, thus linking that particular animal to the Seleucid kingdom and the Asian species of elephants.[14]

When he arrived on the east bank of the river Hannibal learned of the Roman army and consul now at Massalia. He sent off 500 of his Numidian cavalry to survey the situation while he entertained Celtic chieftains from across the Alps. These men had come to meet with Hannibal and provide encouragement for the troops, assuring them of their having allies waiting for them in Italy. When the Numidians came racing back into camp that same afternoon, chased by a Roman advance guard with whom they had skirmished, the urgency to keep moving was more keenly enforced. The Roman cavalry came right up into the camp and then swung back to report to Publius Scipio that they had found the Carthaginians. Hannibal knew his time on the banks of the Rhône was up; he could not engage with the Romans in Gaul, where they would be supported by their allies the Massalians and able to choose the field of battle. He had to press on into Italy.

The scene on the banks of the Rhône that next morning saw Hannibal send all of his cavalry south to act as a rearguard against the Romans. The heavy infantry he sent north, and they began the march ahead up the east bank of the Rhône while Hannibal remained at the crossing and waited for the elephants. This only emphasises the value Hannibal put on the elephants, and once he saw them across, the remaining army turned north and marched up the river. How the elephants crossed the Rhône is a matter of much conjecture. Some descriptions have them marched out on to pontoons that had been built on to the riverbank and then detached from shore once the elephants were onboard, so they crossed on these makeshift rafts. Using the female elephants as the guides, the mahouts led the animals out into the river on these crafts. There are many questions about how feasible this was, and the fact that elephants can swim does not seem to be taken into consideration by our ancient sources.[15] The crossing must have gathered an audience from across the region and people would have remembered the details for centuries: it is not hard to imagine that the story was twisted and turned with each telling. In the end, the elephants all made it across, although some of their guides were swept downriver. Once the beasts had reached the east bank, Hannibal turned and marched north upriver and then climbed into the mountains.

When the Roman army of Publius Scipio reached the Rhône crossing place, the Carthaginian army was at least four days gone. Publius Scipio had to turn back towards Massalia, regroup and make some tough decisions. Once back on the coast, he decided to split his army and send his brother, Gnaeus Cornelius Scipio, on to Iberia with half the consular force while he himself turned back and sailed with the other part of the army to Italy. He knew that Hannibal was heading for Italy and his plan was to return there and march up to the north. When he sent his brother Gnaeus onwards with half of the consular army he made one of the best decisions by a Roman commander over the next four years. The presence of a Roman army in the Iberian Peninsula meant that any plans the other Barcid brother, Hasdrubal, had to reinforce Hannibal and Mago were put on hold as the Carthaginians were forced to defend their Iberian territory. The war expanded to two theatres, and while all eyes remained on Hannibal in Italy, another crucial fight played out in the west.

Meanwhile, Hannibal marched for ten days up the Rhône before turning east and beginning to climb. He was helped by local chieftains who supplied the army with warm clothing and footwear needed to make the crossing. It was the autumn by now and even though the weather was still warm in the valleys, up in the high passes of the Alps, all of which are over 2000m, snow was already beginning to fall. Leaving behind the lowland and climbing up to the top of the pass took another nine days of marching. They had guides with them as they marched, but the Carthaginians were harassed and ambushed along the route by hostile locals, looking to steal all of the valuables this massive army and baggage train carried with them. It was a hard slog, and many soldiers and animals were lost. The terrain was wild and terrifying, and the Allobroges, who inhabited this region, knew every high narrow cliff or pass through which they could attack the baggage train. They made every move treacherous. Hannibal's army was exposed like a thin, vulnerable thread while they trudged up and up.

After nine long days, Hannibal reached the summit of the pass. Which pass he took is another much-contested question.

The two credible options for the crossing of the Alps are the Col du Clapier and the Col de la Traversette, both of which are rugged and wild. After years of writing, teaching and thinking about Carthage and Hannibal, when I finally had the chance to climb up to the Traversette pass myself I was astounded. Not only was the footing treacherous as we walked up from the French side in the footsteps of the Carthaginian army and then crossed the border into Italy, but the sheer magnitude of the endeavour was captured in the towering mountains dominated by the peaks of Monte Viso that loomed all around. The snow-covered mountains and swirling mists with clouds below created an otherworldly feel to the landscape (see Fig. 22 in plate section). It is no wonder that ancient societies stood in awe of Hannibal's feat, and we still do so today.

Over the past decade, very specific investigations into this location involved the excavation and scientific analysis of potential campsites used by Hannibal and his army. The results include the discovery of bacterial DNA related to horse dung and dated specifically to the third century BCE that came from a site on the ascent to the Col de la Traversette. The evidence from the excavations there indicate that a substantial force of animals did cross the pass in the period and that this may be related to Hannibal's army. Although we are only at the very beginning of scientific research in the mountains, new technologies make it feasible that one day we will know for certain. There are many people invested in proving which pass Hannibal took, and where it was exactly that he stopped and turned to encourage his exhausted troops with tales of all of Italy waiting for them below.[16]

The army reached the pass close to the time of the setting of the Pleiades, the constellation visible low in the sky in the late autumn that sets with the coming winter. The descent into

Italy proved even more treacherous for his exhausted soldiers and animals, with the way blocked by a landslide and the steep path, covered in a sheet of ice from the previous year and now topped with fresh snow, making the footing deadly. The army had to inch down the mountain, soldiers cutting a new path using fire and vinegar to split open rock across the landslide.[17] It took them four long days and nights stranded on the edge of the mountain with no rest before they finally reached a meadow where the starving animals could graze. The surviving soldiers rested for a few days before the final push to the plains of the Po River valley below.

By November 218 BCE Hannibal had arrived in the Italian peninsula. The journey from New Carthage to the Po Valley had taken the army at least 150 days. The army had crossed over 1,125 Roman miles (1,000 miles/1,600km) of all kinds of terrain and ascended into the mythical heights of the mountains.[18] The number of men who survived the journey was a shadow of those who had departed from New Carthage. In his own inscription, Hannibal recorded his forces as now numbering 20,000 infantry and 6,000 cavalry. He had lost '36,000 men and a huge number of horses and other beasts after crossing the Rhône'.[19] When Napoleon Bonaparte, a keen student of Hannibal, wrote about the crossing he remarked that the commander had 'sacrificed the half of his army for the mere acquisition of his field of battle, the mere right of fighting'.[20] This had been the goal, and Hannibal had now won the right to fight in Italy and to force the Romans back into the Italian peninsula.

Invasions of the Italian peninsula from the north are extremely rare precisely because the high and mighty Alps protect Italy, and it would be another 600 years before it happened again. Hannibal had achieved what he set out to do; he had shifted the focus of Rome's war effort and created a legend for all times. So impressive was his achievement that Polybius forcefully argued with his own sources in the text he wrote. Polybius played down Hannibal's achievements, almost mocking 'some . . . writers' for trying to impress their readers with Hannibal's supernatural abilities. Polybius claimed that by his time, some 60 years later, the story had been so blown out of proportion 'that unless some god or hero had met Hannibal and showed him the way, his whole army would have gone astray and perished utterly'.[21] Divine support for a mythical journey was what the population of Italy believed; the problem was that Hannibal's army was hardly fit for battle and extremely vulnerable that November in the Po Valley. He could not afford to lose now, and the Romans were gathering their armies to face him in the north.

The Roman consul Tiberius Sempronius Longus had been in Sicily preparing to invade Africa. The Carthaginian fleets skirmished with the Romans and raided where possible, hoping to retake their city of Lilybaeum on Sicily and stop the planned invasion. There was obviously a coordinated strategy between Hannibal and Carthage; very likely it had been devised by Hannibal himself, who had been directing military operations across the western Mediterranean and had the resources available. News of Hannibal's arrival in Italy forced a sudden recall of the consular army and they rushed back to Italy. The valley of the Po River had only just been conquered by the Romans; they had founded a new colonial city at Placentia (Piacenza) in the same year. This was a region ripe for Hannibal to exploit anti-Roman sentiment. The Romans planned for the two consuls to meet up with their armies in the Po Valley and face the Carthaginian troops. Publius Scipio was the first to arrive; landing at the port of Pisa, he marched north.

After some rest and restoration of his army and animals, Hannibal moved to take the main city of the Taurini people (probably now Turin) using similar strategies he had employed in Iberia. He offered friendship first, and when rejected he took the city by force. He then incorporated those willing into his army and kept moving on, gathering support as he did. The first encounter with a Roman army took place near a tributary of the Po River, the Ticinus. Livy recorded the words of the Roman consul before the battle as provoking.

> I want to see if this Hannibal really is, as he himself claims, on a par with Hercules on his travels, or rather has been left by his father as a mere tribute – and tax-payer, indeed a slave of the Roman people.[22]

It was late November when the sides met in more of a skirmish than a full battle. North of the Po River in heavy fog the two armies had moved towards each other, Hannibal coming from the west and Publius Scipio from the east. They camped very close and the following morning the two commanders led out their armies. At first, both sides held their own, but Hannibal's Numidian cavalry outflanked their Roman counterparts and the Romans fled, leaving the consul exposed. Publius Scipio was seriously wounded in the encounter and saved by his young son of the same name, who would eventually become Hannibal's nemesis. On that cold November day, the Romans retreated back to the safety of their colony at Placentia and Hannibal and the Carthaginians held the field. It was a first victory, small but significant, and more of the Celts in northern Italy flocked to Hannibal's cause.

Inside the colony at Placentia, the Celtic auxiliaries of the Roman army revolted, spreading terror among the Roman soldiers by killing and wounding many and decapitating the slain. The Roman consul had no choice but to escape the city and seek shelter in a camp established in the hills near the River Trebia.

With Hannibal's cavalry dominating the plains of the Po Valley, any engagement there favoured them. Injured, the Roman consul had to stall until reinforcements could arrive, granting Hannibal undisputed control over the area. Consequently, more cities and towns allied with the Carthaginians. Relief came for the Romans when the second consular army from Sicily arrived. The two commanders then put their forces together and looked to defeat the numerically inferior Carthaginians. It was deepest winter by now, getting close to the solstice, and the Roman system meant that the consuls were only in office for a matter of weeks more until new consuls were chosen. This seemed to pressure them into battle when delaying may have been their best option. Hannibal was eager to fight a set battle; he needed to win and his whole strategy rested on gaining allies in the regions, and that could only be done by defeating the Romans.[23]

On a frigid, snowy day in mid-December, Hannibal readied his troops and set off to draw the Romans out of their camp. The detailed stories discuss how he fed his men well and oiled their skin to protect them from the cold. Winter fighting was not the norm and Hannibal planned to use this to his advantage. He meticulously staged the field, sending his youngest brother Mago with 2,000 cavalry to lie in wait in the marshlands. As his Numidian cavalry raced up to the Roman camp and drew them out on to the field, Hannibal marched up from the rear. The Romans rushed out to meet their enemy, buoyed no doubt by their much superior numbers and without giving much heed to the conditions. The Romans had almost double the number of infantry on the field but less cavalry, and as the battle rang out the two lines engaged in fierce fighting. The conditions were cold, foggy and marshy, dragging the Roman heavy infantry and slowing their progress. The Roman soldiers were unprepared for the elements, the Carthaginians more battle hardened and toughened by their trials. As the fighting between the infantry played out, Mago Barca and his cavalry sprang into action and swept around the back of the Roman troops to attack from the rear. So, even though the Roman infantry had broken through the Carthaginian lines in the centre of the fight, the Romans found themselves enmeshed in the enemy and were defeated comprehensively. Those Romans who could retreat did so, but many were killed by the banks of the river. Hannibal won a significant victory at Trebia, and if he hadn't it might have been all over for his adventure in Italy. Now he found himself the master of the Po Valley.

As the winter set in, all sides retreated. The Carthaginians received volunteers from across the region into their ranks. Hannibal had freed all the Roman auxiliary (non-citizen) troops he had captured without ransom and kept on the Roman citizen soldiers as captives.[24] The message he repeated over and over was that his fight was with Rome, not with her allies. Back in Rome a kind of panic set in. Hannibal's crossing of the Alps and quick victories took on epic proportions and the citizens in Rome turned to religion, with reports of omens in the sky and purification rituals. When Romans of the Republic lost battles and suffered disasters, they believed their gods had abandoned them and the only way forward was to win them back to their side with prayer, offering and sacrifice. Reports from that winter of 217 BCE say that they offered public prayers to all the gods and specifically mentioned are prayers and sacrifices at the temple of Hercules, a glimpse into the way that Hannibal's own myth management and use of the Melqart/Herakles deity as his patron played on the people and the priests at Rome.

In January, two new consuls were elected. They were Gnaeus Servilius and Gaius Flaminius, who spent the winter months raising new troops and 'mustering the allies' for support. They sent supplies and men to their bases in Ariminum (modern Rimini on the Adriatic) and to Etruria, indicating where they believed the fighting would take place the next season. Hannibal in his winter quarters was busy gaining an understanding of the lay of the land, planning his next moves and dodging assassins, according to reports. Livy tells us that the Celts tried to assassinate him, which we can rightly believe, and there must have been Roman agents embedded in the Celtic forces who had gone over to Hannibal just as the opposite was true among the Roman auxiliaries.[25] Hannibal was vulnerable at this moment, at the mercy of his allies. To end the whole invasion by cutting off the head that controlled it must have occurred to the Romans and they likely encouraged dissent among any of the Celts who would listen. Meanwhile, Hannibal tended to his soldiers' wellbeing and also to the animals, but it was the elephants who suffered that winter. By the time the Carthaginians moved out of winter camp towards the south, only one elephant had survived.

Hannibal moved down out of the Po Valley towards the south in the spring of 217 BCE. It is unlikely he moved until the Apennine mountain passes were clear, so it must have been May when he started south. The ground was wet and muddy, and the going was tough for his soldiers as they slogged through the flooded Arno River valley. The army advanced slowly with the Africans and Iberians and all the elite combat units leading the way while the baggage train was spread throughout. Hannibal had stationed the Carthaginian-allied Celts in the middle of the line, perhaps fearing they would change their mind and turn back, while his cavalry brought up the rear of the army. The rearguard command was entrusted to Mago Barca while Hannibal rode at the front on the last elephant. It was rough going and as they crossed through the soggy marshes of Etruria Hannibal began suffering from an eye infection which went untreated. As a result, Hannibal lost his sight in his right eye. The Roman satirist Juvenal, centuries later, wrote of 'the one-eyed general on his Mauritanian beast'.[26]

The new Roman consul Flaminius had taken up his position at Arretium (modern Arezzo in Tuscany) while Servilius was stationed further north at Ariminum. Flaminius was positioned where the boundary between Etruria and Umbria sat and guarded the road south to Rome. Hannibal camped near modern Florence and sent out his scouts to reconnoitre the situation. Flaminius had rushed up to Arretium as early as March so had been in position and spoiling to fight. In fact, he had been so eager to get to the field with his army that Livy and Polybius accuse him of not respecting the gods and not following through with the religious observances that a consul taking up office was supposed to participate in. These memories of disrespecting the gods may well be the reasoning for the events that followed in the early summer of 217 BCE, but we have seen before how important correct religious practice and superstitious beliefs were in the Roman Republic and for its military endeavours.

Hannibal and the Carthaginian army marched on and passed right in front of the Roman base at Arretium. They drew the consul and his army out, perhaps intending the Romans to believe they were marching towards Rome. The Carthaginian forces then veered to the east and proceeded to march along the flat ground that lay below the city of Cortona, keeping the lake, known as Trasimeno, on their right. The Carthaginian army burned the countryside as they went, enticing the Romans to engage, and Flaminius followed. He had about 25,000 soldiers with him, legions and auxiliaries, and was likely tracking the Carthaginians as they moved east while the other Roman consul Servilius moved down from the north. The Romans hoped to trap the Carthaginians between their two armies and to crush Hannibal, but it was not to be. Hannibal, marching into the narrow land between hill and lake, noticed how heavy the fog lay on the lake that time of year and realised he could trap Flaminius and his legions before they were able to trap him. The north side of the lake opens up to a small plain after a narrow pass and there Hannibal stationed his soldiers, in the hills and all around the whole space. He worked through the night to prepare his surprise ambush on the Roman army that was tracking him from behind.

Around the time of the summer solstice, perhaps even on the day itself, in the dense fog of a June morning the Roman army under Flaminius proceeded to follow Hannibal and the Carthaginians. It does not seem to have occurred to Flaminius that Hannibal could have hidden his army in this narrow defile on the north shore of Lake Trasimeno – and the Romans walked right into the trap. The fog was so thick that the Roman troops could not see that they were being attacked, but they could hear it. They were surrounded by enemy soldiers without being able to defend themselves. It was a complete rout, and the Carthaginian army destroyed the Romans, killing the consul and 15,000 of his men. Once the sun had broken through the fog on that summer day, the lake and the field were full of Roman dead. Hannibal was again gracious to the surviving non-Roman auxiliaries and freed them, keeping the Roman citizens as captives for ransom and allowing the rest to return home, or giving them the option to join the Carthaginian cause.

After Trasimeno, news of a further defeat reached Rome a few days later. The reports of Flaminius' death were followed quickly by an account of the cavalry defeat of the other consul, Servilius. Servilius had engaged with the Carthaginian cavalry under Hannibal's Numidian lieutenant and key commander Maharbal. The Roman cavalry lost completely, which left the two consular armies raised that year out of commission, one destroyed and the other without cavalry. The remaining soldiers were cut off from Rome by Hannibal's presence in central Italy. This was the moment, if it had been Hannibal's intention, that he might have moved south towards Rome. The path was now open to him, but he moved towards the east instead, into the region of the Piceni, on the east of the Apennines, perhaps ever wary of the Roman ability to raise another army, to come out again and again with new soldiers. There, in the modern region of Le Marche, among people who were long enemies of Rome, he set about tending to his animals and soldiers on the Adriatic coast. It is also possible that for the first time since he had left Iberia, he was able to directly communicate with Carthage.

The Romans, in crisis, had to choose a dictator to deputise for the consuls and decided to put a man named Fabius Maximus in charge. There was turmoil in Rome, as in the city people grieved and were panic stricken while the political classes fell prey to recrimination and bickering, with inter-familial rivalries under-lying much of the decision making. Fabius Maximus' master of the horses was a man named Minucius, a political opponent, reflecting the divided city at that moment. Fabius Maximus had a plan, and that was to avoid any engagement with Hannibal and the Carthaginian army. He would track the Carthaginians across the peninsula, use the Roman advantages of superior manpower to wear the army of Hannibal down, perhaps force him to make a mistake, and then pounce. He recognised that the longer they could keep Hannibal from fighting battles and winning, the less likely the Carthaginians were to succeed. There was a lot of hos-tility towards this strategy within the Roman military command, and Fabius Maximus was given a nickname, *cunctator* in Latin, which means the delayer, and this has remained his epithet for posterity.

From 217 BCE, through the autumn and into winter, Fabius, Maximus and the Romans tracked Hannibal as he moved south into the region of Apulia, into Campania, seeking to draw allies away from the Romans. The two sides did not engage in all-out war over this period but there were skirmishes and a long game of cat and mouse. The cities of these regions had to walk a fine line between two competing powers, trying to placate the angry Romans but also perhaps extend a curious look at Hannibal and the Carthaginians. Few were willing to commit to Hannibal's cause and he had to continually move his troops to avoid being caught between two Roman armies and their allied cities, while gathering supplies and making an effort to feed and support his army of almost 50,000. He needed to fight the Romans again, and he needed it to happen sooner than later.

Wintering in Apulia at the city of Geronium, Hannibal spent his time managing the large city that his travelling camp had become, sorting food supplies, fixing weapons and training new recruits. Most of all, he had to figure out how to set the stage for another battle with the Romans. At Rome, they elected new consuls over the winter of 217/216 BCE and gathered a huge army. The two men, Lucius Aemilius Paullus and Gaius Terentius Varro, took up office in March 216 BCE but did not join the armies in the field until June or July as they gathered and called up all the auxiliaries they could muster. The tactics of Fabius Maximus had provided the breathing space for the Romans to regroup, and in the summer of 216 BCE they felt ready to take on Hannibal. The Carthaginians had moved out of winter quarters and took a town called Cannae on the Apulian plain near the banks of the River Aufidus (now the Ofanto). This had been a grain store for the Romans and disrupting the supply lines was the trigger for a battle. Hannibal and the Carthaginian army waited at Cannae for the Romans to approach. The troop numbers available to both sides are difficult to know for certain: Livy and Polybius put the number of Hannibal's soldiers as 10,000 cavalry and 40,000 infantry and others, a neat 50,000 and almost double the number that had come down from the Alps. The Romans, in our records, had huge numbers with them; both Livy and Polybius record more than 80,000 soldiers. The intention was to end the war and they may well have outnumbered Hannibal and his forces 2:1.[27]

In late July 216 BCE the massive Roman army approached Cannae. The Romans camped close by, some 2km away from the town on the banks of the river. The two sides skirmished, they played out tactics, shifted positions. The two consuls in the field alternated command between them each day. One day Aemilius Paullus was in charge, and the next Varro. A slight discord in tactics and approach would have been an advantage to Hannibal and the Carthaginians, and to be fair, they needed any advantage they could muster at this moment. Movement of so many men and equipment was slow. The battle lines took two days to draw up, and this was done on the banks of the river across from where the Romans had set up camp. The men were anxious to engage, the air tense with anticipation. Finally, early one morning with a strong wind blowing from the south, the Roman commander Varro set up his lines for battle. His whole army faced the south, spread out in a long line, with cavalry on the flanks and the infantry in the middle. Hannibal moved his men out, adjusting formation to try to best counter the Roman numerical superiority.

All of Hannibal's soldiers were in place, his lieutenants ready to employ his plan. He had his brother Mago with him in the centre of the fight with his cavalry to the right and left. The Roman commanders on the field, including both consuls and the previous year's surviving consuls, commanded across the line. When the battle engaged, Hannibal's forces, because of their inferior numbers, hollowed out the centre of their line as the soldiers spread to the flanks instead. The Roman heavy infantry pushed forwards into the weakened centre – a move that Hannibal had planned for. He had intended the Romans to break through his infantry lines, as they had done at Trebia, so he kept his African infantry in reserve, behind the front line of Iberians and Celts. Slowly but surely the Romans pushed through the front and the line of the Carthaginians began the turn inwards around them. The African infantry attacked from the sides while the Numidian cavalry had won the

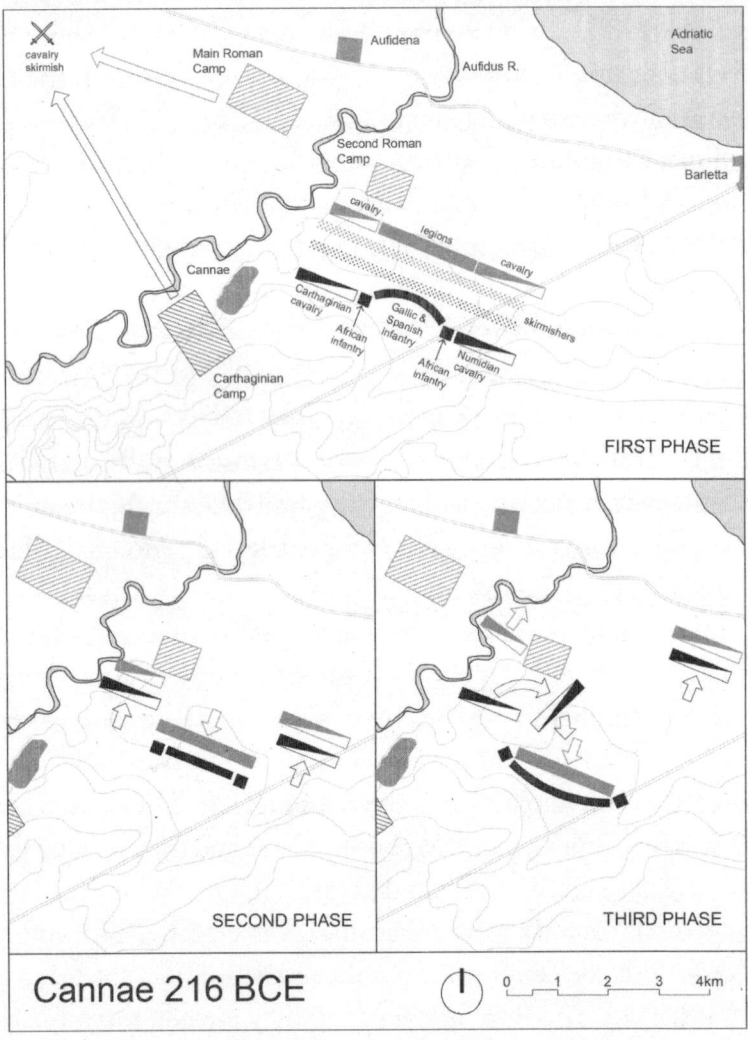

Fig. 23 Schematic of the phases of the battle of Cannae

fight on the flanks and was able to circle around and attack from the rear. The whole Roman force was eventually encircled by the Carthaginian army, then cut down and destroyed (Fig. 23).

It is impossible to get a sense of the numbers of dead; they are recorded as 45,000 on the Roman side. Livy's account has a listing of names that it seems he had access to from the Roman records. Among the Roman dead was acting consul Lucius Aemilius Paullus as well as 'both quaestors of the consuls . . . as well as twenty-nine military tribunes, some of whom were former consuls, praetors and aediles'. The list also named the ex-consul Servilius, the master of the horse Minucius and 'eighty senators or men who had held offices that qualified them for selection for the Senate'. The governing elite of Rome had been wiped out and it was a complete victory for Hannibal and his army. The Carthaginians had lost many in the fight as well, but at this moment Hannibal stood triumphant over Rome. He has, ever since that day in 216 BCE, been celebrated as one of the greatest military strategists of all time, feted across the millennia for his brilliance and creativity in the face of battle.[28]

CHAPTER 10

The Victor Is Not Victorious

The day after the battle of Cannae, the scene on that Apulian field was gruesome. Steam rose in the morning off the still warm bodies of the dead and injured, making the grim job of combing the field of battle and gathering the spoils shocking, even for those that had won. Ancient warfare was fought in very close combat by both the infantry and cavalry; they killed with swords and spears. Death came from injuries that may not have immediately killed, but incapacitated. At Cannae, the Carthaginians had been so outnumbered they had no choice but to try to disable as many of their enemy as quickly as possible. Livy's account depicts a gruesome scene, with severed thighs and knee tendons, where half-dead men struggle to rise from the chaos, only to be struck down again, while some plead for a swift end to their suffering. Hannibal undertook the solemn duty of burying his fallen soldiers and ensuring proper honours for the Roman consul's body as well. Then began the long task of collecting the loot and spoils of victory, of counting and parcelling it out among his men.[1]

His army had defeated the Romans so comprehensively that it may never have occurred to Hannibal that Rome would not sue for peace. His cavalry commander Maharbal urged Hannibal to march on Rome at that moment, to travel the 400km up towards the city and press home the victory. Hannibal declined and historians have pondered why he did so ever since. It is hard to know exactly what he was thinking. Perhaps he was still wary of the potential of Rome to raise more armies, and also knew that he too had lost many men on the field of Cannae. Or did Hannibal not even consider it? Had taking the city of Rome ever been his strategy? Perhaps he was convinced that the victory before him at Cannae was enough, that Rome had no choice but to come to terms. Conventionally the size of the defeat Rome suffered at Cannae would have led to a peace treaty in any other situation in the whole Mediterranean. Warfare seldom aimed at the destruction of a whole state or city but led to the imposition of the terms of the victor over the defeated.

Following convention, Hannibal sent ten Roman prisoners, accompanied by a Carthaginian named Carthalo, back to Rome to negotiate a deal. At the same time, he sent his brother Mago to Carthage with news of the victory. And after Cannae the story follows these two groups, leaving Hannibal and shifting to look at the Romans and their fight back. Up to this moment in the war, the sources followed the Barcid family of Carthage and its rise to power and prominence. After Cannae, the Roman sources tell of how, at the hour of their deepest crisis, great Roman men rose to challenge their most hostile enemy, and these men of the middle Republic were those upon whom all future Roman greatness rested. The story also shifts to follow Mago Barca back to Africa and the young Roman Publius Scipio from the field at Cannae to redemption. The whole plays out as a tale of two families, one Carthaginian and one Roman, and we often forget the intimate and familial nature of power in the period. This war was remembered as a battle between the Carthaginian Barcids and the Roman Scipios, these illustrious commanders who fought wars in an age of legends. At least, this was how the Romans wanted history to remember the story. The realities on the ground were much less noble and the truths of mass defeat much grittier.

There was panic in Rome in those days after Cannae. The Romans refused the peace deal offered by Hannibal and inside the city a state of hysteria took hold among the public. People turned on each other and looked to the gods. The impurity of two of the Vestal Virgins, the female keepers of the sacred hearth of the city of Rome, was held responsible for the defeat and one woman was buried alive while the other committed suicide. A dictator was chosen, more troops were raised and emergency consultations with the sacred texts of the Romans, the Sibylline books, were ordered. These religious texts instructed the Romans to make human sacrifices, so two Gauls and two Greeks, men and women, were ritually buried alive in a spot in the Forum Boarium in the city.[2] This was a place marked by stones where sacrifices had occurred before. The Romans sought divine help from further afield too. They sent a man named Fabius Pictor to the Panhellenic sanctuary at Delphi in Greece to consult the oracle of the god Apollo there. As the Roman poet Ennius wrote about the war, 'the victor is not victorious if the vanquished does not consider himself so.'[3] Hannibal had beaten a foe who did not consider itself defeated.

The Romans were not abandoned by all their allies in this moment of need. Many of the cities in Latin states and those from other areas held fast to their alliance. There were also many defections among the allies, as detailed in a list from Livy who noted that the people of southern Italy who had come over to Hannibal included the Bruttii from the region of modern Calabria, the Apulians, who had witnessed the defeat itself, and a number of the Samnites and Lucanians from the south-central region of the Italian peninsula who had so recently fought their own wars with Rome. Most significant of all was Capua, an important city in Campania and an old ally of the Romans, which also changed sides.[4] Other key cities were still undecided, and still more influenced by regional political issues than by Roman or Carthaginian force. The nature of the relationships between the different language groups and ethnicities in Italy meant that cohesion and cooperation were not simple tasks. The Romans held enough sway to keep Hannibal from accessing a major port on the west coast of Italy, and the piecemeal nature of the Carthaginian alliance meant Hannibal would spend much of the next few years defending his new allies from Roman attack rather than consolidating victory. Also, from the field of Cannae arose a new group of young Roman elites, all soldiers who had survived the battle and fled with the consul Varro to nearby Venusia (modern Venosa). There these men, numbering around 10,000 we are told, swore an oath to protect Rome and grew into a new kind of Roman commander. Among these was the younger Publius Scipio, whose father and uncle were in Iberia fighting the Carthaginians led by Hasdrubal Barca. The young Scipio and his companions had been schooled in fighting Hannibal over these few years. From this group rose the hope of Rome.

In this atmosphere of ritual and resistance Rome refused peace with Carthage. Meanwhile, Mago Barca stood in the senate in the city of Carthage and announced the victory and detailed all those who had been defeated. He then dramatically had all the golden rings of the Roman *equites* (knights) who had been killed, spoil from the field of Cannae, dumped in the entrance of the senate to emphasise the immensity of the victory. These golden rings piled high on the senate floor while news of the battle spread among the people of the city. Mago pressed the senate at Carthage for aid, reinforcements and more supplies for Hannibal and the army in Italy. Mago was granted his support, according to Livy, with 4,000 Numidian cavalry and 40 elephants sent along with an unspecified amount of funding, noted as 'talents of silver'. Mago and another unnamed Carthaginian commander were dispatched to Iberia with the funds to raise another 20,000 infantry and 4,000 more cavalry for the Italian fight.[5] The ongoing war in Iberia, where Hasdrubal Barca had been battling the Romans now co-commanded by the elder Scipios – the Roman proconsul Publius the elder and his brother Gnaeus – had been a struggle. Just as Mago Barca was to depart, news of a defeat in Iberia was received at Carthage. Mago and the troops meant for Hannibal were diverted to the Iberian Peninsula and would never reach Italy.

Over the years between the summer of 216 and 212 BCE the war hung in the balance and was fought across the whole western Mediterranean. The narrative is focused on the Roman commanders who fought back against Hannibal and the struggles in Italy but equally important were the battlefields in Iberia, Sicily and Africa, as the population of the western Mediterranean was pulled into the struggle. After Cannae and Hannibal's brilliant victory there, even the great kings of the east took an interest in what was happening in Italy. They largely watched from the sidelines, except the Macedonian Philip V who reached out to ally with Hannibal and Carthage in Italy. The Antigonid kings of Macedon, direct descendants of Alexander, ruled the region opposite the eastern shores of the Italian peninsula and had been in direct conflict with Rome over the regions of Illyria on the Adriatic coast. The treaty between Philip and Carthage was a way for both to try to contain the growing influence of Rome. We only know about the treaty because the ambassador sent by Philip and some of the Carthaginian senate were captured by a Roman patrol boat as they left the southern Italian city of Locri. It was perhaps the psychological impact of the alliance that most bolstered Hannibal's cause, although little ever came of the treaty.[6] The real issue that vexed Carthage and Hannibal was Rome's control of the coastal areas. Rome continued to illustrate its naval superiority, leaving Hannibal frustrated by lack of support directly from Carthage.

The reality for much of the population in these years was hardship and struggle. Many smaller polities caught between the two powers had to negotiate for their own survival and hope they chose the winning side for the vengeance from the other was sure to be harsh. Sicily, once again, became a theatre of war between Carthage and Rome, and the focus was on the city of Syracuse. Although a long ally of Rome, the Syracusans switched sides after Cannae once their old king Hiero II had died in circa 215 BCE. Syracuse as an ally boosted the Carthaginian cause; regaining ports in Sicily gave Carthage a counter to the Roman hold on the sea and Hannibal in Italy could be more directly supplied. Rome threw resources at Sicily, which led to, in 213 BCE, a large Roman army under the command of Marcus Marcellus putting Syracuse under direct siege. Marcellus was equipped with all the contemporary and advanced techniques of siege, and a fleet that carried floating engines and sophisticated catapults sailed into the port of Syracuse. The Roman siege weapons proved no match for the defences of Syracuse, however, which had some of the most advanced fortification walls and intricate systems of defence anywhere in the Mediterranean. The credit for Syracuse's defence rests with famed scientist and mathematician Archimedes, a Syracusan by birth. Archimedes was believed to have designed the defensive works and strategy at Syracuse, although it must have been a long time in construction to have been so effective, longer than the life of one man.[7]

Nonetheless, Roman memory and history have created a starring role for Archimedes in the defence of Syracuse. His story and that of the Roman commander Marcellus illustrate how the tales of the Second Punic War were distilled to epic across the ages and often reduced to the stories of individual men. Even if exaggerated, the record of Archimedes' counter-siege engines within Syracuse still seem miraculous. He was credited with the design of specific counter-siege weapons that functioned like catapults, or solid beams that dropped heavy rocks on ships, along with 'grappling irons and small catapults called scorpions'. The Syracusan defenders used these machines to great effect – they sunk enemy ships, ploughed through their lines of infantry and wreaked mayhem among opposition troops. For every strategy used by the Romans at Syracuse there was a counter attributed to the miraculous mind of Archimedes. So impressive was Archimedes' defence of the city that Polybius wrote, 'as long as he was present, they [the Romans] did not dare even to attempt an attack by any method which made it possible for Archimedes to oppose them.' Archimedes' ingenious contraptions proved incredibly effective in protecting the city from assault. As a result, the Romans opted to keep a safe distance from the walls and impose a blockade, aiming to compel Syracuse to surrender through starvation. They proceeded to cut off the city from both land and sea routes.[8]

By the spring of 212 BCE, Marcellus had made some headway at Syracuse, but the extent of the defensive walls and the intricate layers of entry to the city meant that he was only able to take part of it. The way ancient Syracuse was laid out, according to the Roman geographer Strabo, was as a *pentapolis* – a city made up of five towns.[9] As we saw in Chapter 4, the heart and centre of the city was the island of Ortygia, which sat between the two harbours. There were also neighbourhoods spread out along the mainland as well, and all were enclosed by the defensive land walls. The circuit walls of Syracuse enclosed both the island of Ortygia and the neighbourhoods on the mainland. The walls ran for 180 stadia (about 17km), according to Strabo, and to the north encompassed a vast plateau that was known as Epipolae.

Marcellus and the Roman troops had taken the plateau to the north, so held part of the city and could look down towards the centre, but that centre remained in Carthaginian hands. Carthage tried to break the blockade and lift the siege, but only sporadic supplies made it to the people trapped inside. A kind of stalemate ensued, with street fighting and little gains on either side over the long hot summer of 212 BCE. By the autumn, a plague had decimated both armies but seems to have affected the Carthaginians inside the city slightly more intensely, as is to be expected in close urban quarters. When the plague killed the Carthaginian general Himilco and the Syracusan/Carthaginian leader Hippocrates, only then did the city fall to the Romans and Marcellus.

The conquest of Syracuse by Marcellus marked a pivotal moment in the narrative of Rome's ascent to empire. The sight of the beautiful city laid out before him so moved the Roman general that he is said to have wept at the idea of destroying it. Nonetheless, Syracuse was looted and the wealth of this once great Greek entrepôt on the Mediterranean hauled back to the city of Rome. Marcellus had ordered that the soldiers seek out and spare Archimedes but even he did not survive the sack. Livy tells us that a Roman soldier in the process of all-out looting brought about the death of the 'greatest thinker of the age'. This soldier came across an old man intently drawing diagrams in the earth. When he did not respond to the questions posed to him by the soldier, he was killed. The genius was too distracted by his geometry, and so was lost to the brutality of war. This later moralising lesson of warfare, told centuries after the act, varies in other accounts, but the fact remains that Archimedes died in the sack of Syracuse.[10] While Archimedes could not be taken back to Rome as a prized captive, the wealth of Syracuse came to adorn the city of Rome. The trophies of war were used to decorate commemorative temples and, in some cases, were even fixed to the doors of houses.[11] Public and private spaces became mementoes of conquest and Rome's finances were boosted by the injection of huge amounts of silver and gold taken from the temple treasuries of Syracuse.

The years 212 to 209 BCE were the turning point for Hannibal in Italy and shifted the paradigm for Carthage in Iberia as well. Worn down by constantly having to protect his allies, and with the Romans raising more and more soldiers and coming back to fight stronger and stronger, he could not keep control of the territory he had won. First Capua and then Syracuse and Tarentum all came to support Hannibal, but one by one they fell to the Romans. Hannibal's army was geographically restricted in the south, hemmed in by the many Roman armies patrolling in Italy. Fabius Maximus' strategy of delay and divert had been employed by all Roman armies (or most anyway) with the overall goal of diminishing Hannibal's forces and his ability to operate. It was slow and expensive, with the numbers of soldiers Rome was able to raise in a single year amounting to almost 25 legions in the year 212 BCE, reflecting how its system of extracting military service from its allies and newly conquered territory was so effective in a long game. The influx of wealth from the sacked cities of Italy and Sicily rebooted the Roman economy, and the standard of Roman coinage, one that would last for the next four centuries, the silver denarius, was first issued in the year 211 BCE (Fig. 24). Wars were often won by sheer numbers in the pre-modern period and Rome's manpower, with over 200,000 soldiers in the field on an annual basis, would allow them to keep two-legion armies all over the south of Italy, and in Iberia and eventually Africa. There would continue to be victories for Hannibal and his armies in Italy but they are somewhat obscured by the sources. The Romans, in fact, would never again meet Hannibal in a big set battle in Italy, preferring

Fig. 24 New Roman silver denarius minted in circa 211 BCE with head of Roma (obv.), and Castor and Pollux (rev.)

to frustrate and contain him while they focused on winning back the cities they had lost.

The war had hung in the balance and these years were, in hindsight, the fulcrum. The Carthaginians stretched themselves to arm and support their war effort, cajoling their allies into ever more troops and cavalry to sustain them. Their focus had been on regaining a foothold in Sicily and holding on to Iberia in the face of Roman challenges. In fact, Carthage and its allies had been fighting the war in Iberia, and in Africa, largely unnoticed by the sources but from this period arise some of the most significant actors to dominate the last decades of Carthage's existence – the two Numidian kingdoms and their leaders who functioned as allies and support for the military effort of the Carthaginians in these years especially so. The Numidians ruled the regions west of Carthage, along the coast of what is modern Algeria and western Morocco, and inland to the Atlas Mountains. Syphax, king of the Masaesyli, had been courted and wooed by the Romans from early in the war and allied with them against Carthage. Diplomatic missions included Roman consular visits to the king's western capital, Siga (near modern Oran), along with the Carthaginian *sufetes*. The Romans considered

Syphax so crucial that they made significant gifts and recognition of his status. These included the curule chair (a particular seat reserved for consular power) and other consular attributes, which signalled him out as one of the most important of the Roman allies outside of Italy.[12] The soldiers of Masaesyli were, sometime in the year 214/213 BCE, ordered to desert the Carthaginians and became employed by the Romans fighting in Iberia. Syphax then staged a rebellion against Carthage in Africa. The wars on all fronts would be won by wooing the allies of enemy; resource and manpower was all.

Another key player, and one who seems to have been the catalyst for victory or defeat in the latter stages of the war, was Masinissa (see Fig. 25). Masinissa first appears in the sources fighting in support of the Carthaginians in Iberia in the years 212/211 BCE. He was a young prince of the Massyli who had been brought up and educated at Carthage. It is believed that he might even have been related to the Barcid clan through marriage, the elites of the Numidian royalty and Carthage having been closely related through marriage for centuries. Masinissa's aunt is thought to have been Hannibal's sister or niece and he was close in age to Mago Barca; both men were probably in their late twenties at this point.[13]

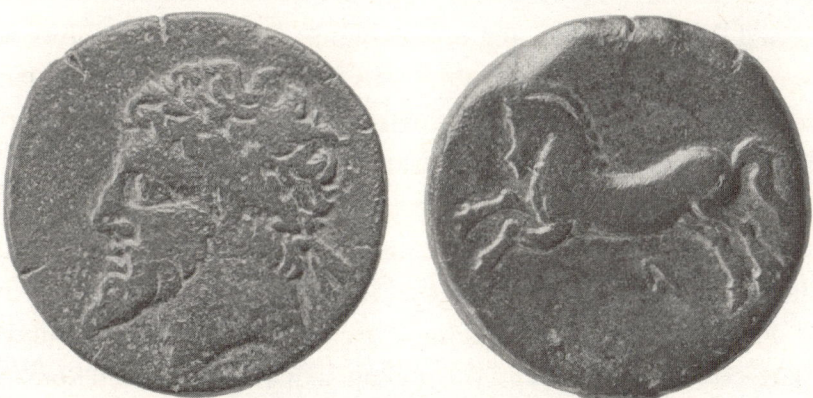

Fig. 25 Copper alloy coin of Masinissa, or possibly a son, second century BCE with diademed head left (obv.) and horse (rev.)

Masinissa had been sent by his father, King Gaia, to take charge of a unit of cavalry. He fought under the command of Mago Barca and quickly became instrumental in Carthaginian strategy. The two Barcid brothers, Hasdrubal and Mago, and two Roman brothers, Gnaeus and Publius Scipio (the elder), known by the epithet 'thunderbolts' of Rome, were involved in an intense war for control of the Iberian Peninsula.[14] Mago had returned to Iberia in the months after Cannae, and Publius Scipio had re-joined his brother and army in Iberia at some point after 217 BCE. The epic battles that ensued sapped a great deal of Carthage's resources and reduced the supply of troops and reinforcements that were available for Hannibal in Italy. By the spring of 211 BCE the Romans seemed so confident of victory that the two Scipio brothers left their winter quarters and set out to 'bring the war in Iberia to an end'.[15]

That spring there were three Carthaginian commanders in Iberia. The Carthaginians had come to terms with Syphax so perhaps freed up soldiers to support Hasdrubal and Mago. Each Barcid led an army, and another commander known as Hasdrubal, son of Gisgo, led a third. Hasdrubal Gisgo and Mago Barca joined armies to operate in sync while Hasdrubal Barca was stationed in the strategic region of the upper Baetis River.[16] The Roman commanders operated with two armies, separating to take on the two divergent Carthaginians forces. The joined-up and increased strength of the Carthaginian armies, along with new tactics and perhaps some overconfidence on the part of the Romans (news of the fall of Syracuse would have reached them), shifted the existing stalemate that summer.

First, Publius Scipio and his army were cut off and attacked by Masinissa's cavalry, and the proconsul was killed in the action. Then Mago Barca's army turned to support his brother Hasdrubal, and they managed to completely surround Gnaeus Scipio, who along with his army were largely lost fighting. In what seems like a flash, the Roman armies that had been so dogged in their pursuit of the Barcid brothers for almost eight years were wiped out in one season. The story preserved in Livy has serious flaws and gaps in both the chronology and details of the fighting. What we can say for certain is that, by 211 BCE, the elder Scipio brothers had died fighting the younger Barcid brothers in Iberia. Both died bravely in battle and Masinissa's presence seems to have been a key factor in the defeat. In this complex tale of soldiers and allies, it is easy to forget that the overall objective of the elder Scipio brothers had been to destabilise the Carthaginian alliances in Iberia and to occupy Hannibal's brothers, preventing any attempt to unify the armies of Carthage in Italy. In this they had succeeded.

The news of the victory of the Carthaginians over the Scipio brothers reached Rome late in 211 BCE and the Romans quickly dispatched a new army to contain the situation and held elections in Rome to appoint a new commander for Iberia. The chosen commander was the younger Publius Scipio, son of his namesake, who was now the head of a very powerful family in Rome. The 25-year-old Scipio was sent to avenge his father and his uncle. His father-in-law had been Lucius Aemilius Paullus, the consul who had died on the field at Cannae. This was very much a family affair. The sources describe Scipio as a new hero for a new Roman age, a new Hannibal. He was the same age as Hannibal had been when the Carthaginian came to lead the armies in Iberia. Scipio too is described as the ideal commander, young, strategic and inspiring to those who fought for him as well as always willing to work on new strategies of war. Scipio and his generation had learned their skills from Hannibal and would employ them against Carthage. From this moment onwards, Scipio takes on significant importance in the history of the rest of the war. Our main source Polybius had a very close relationship with the family and the descendants of Scipio. His history, written while he was a client of the family some 50 years later, is thought to reflect this insider's view; his history of the war with Hannibal is very much the official history of the family of the Scipios.

In 210 BCE Scipio left Rome. He went to Iberia with a fleet of 30 ships and first put ashore at the Roman-friendly port of Emporiae (established by the Greeks as Emporion; Empúries in modern Catalonia) (see page 170). There, Roman allies from Massalia and other cities gathered around him and formed a kind of coalition of allies. Scipio headed up this coalition as they looked to challenge the Carthaginians and their allies. The three Carthaginian armies in the Iberian Peninsula were reportedly spread out in different areas across the region. Scipio's reconnaissance that winter told him that none of the armies were anywhere near their capital city of New Carthage. The Carthaginians were so confident of the city's safety that they were off operating in the hinterlands in spring 209 BCE. Polybius noted that it did not seem to occur to them that the Romans would return in force.[17] Little of this makes any practical sense as reported. It seems more likely the Carthaginian armies were occupied elsewhere, perhaps with a rebellion or a recall to Africa. The Barcid brothers and their allies knew that the defeat of their proconsuls would not deter the Romans for long. Another Roman army was sure to return to avenge the deaths of the elder Scipios. Something is missing from our information.

In the spring of 209 BCE, to the surprise and shock of the Carthaginians, Scipio marched up to the walls of New Carthage and pitched camp to the north of the city with an army of 25,000 men. At the same time, his chief lieutenant, Gaius Laelius, sailed a fleet into the harbour, blockading the city from the sea. New Carthage was now under siege and was seriously undermanned. The city was well-fortified and protected on the land side by sophisticated walls and two large hills, yet there was only a small garrison of military inside the city itself. The population of New Carthage, artisans, merchant and sailors, must have felt a deep sense of security, for over the 20 years of warfare since its foundation, no armies had ever challenged its walls. Now they were facing more than 20,000 battle-hardened Roman soldiers and auxiliaries, and a determined fleet. The city fell quickly; those who could defended it bravely but they were outnumbered, and during a low-tide event the Roman marines had managed to cross the harbour and access the city via the port. It was taken in one day. Even Scipio must have been surprised by the speed at which he captured the Carthaginian capital of Iberia. Inside the city there was carnage and Livy reports that the Roman armies captured 10,000 male citizens and a huge volume of booty.[18]

Although there is no mention in the sources of the specifics or identities of those captured, the haul must have been significant and would have completely disrupted the Carthaginian alliance system in Iberia. The Romans captured the Carthaginian treasury, said to have amounted to 600 talents of silver. They also seized supplies, baggage and hostages when they took New Carthage. These were people who had been living at New Carthage and included the family members of the Iberian leaders who served with the Carthaginian troops. This was common practice on both sides, keeping members of allies' families close at hand as guests/hostages in exchange for loyalty. So, when the sources mention the 'baggage' they mean the wives, the children and the belongings of the soldiers fighting with the Carthaginians. It is entirely possible that Hasdrubal and Mago Barca (and even Hannibal) had wives and families in New Carthage. This was a disaster of unmitigated proportion for the Carthaginian war effort and

Scipio was now firmly in charge of the war for Iberia. Hannibal in Italy must have despaired at the news: Syracuse, Capua, New Carthage all lost, and soon Tarentum would be too.

Carthage must have ordered the Barcid brothers to fight back and try to reclaim their capital and reputations, but allies were deserting them, and the capture of New Carthage had left the brothers in disarray. The information on their movements over the next months is scarce and incomplete but the view narrows in on Hasdrubal Barca in the spring of the following year, 208 BCE, and his efforts to face Scipio in battle. The two armies met at a place near the town of Baecula, which held a strategic position. The location is now believed to be just south of the River Baetis in a region known as the High Guadalquivir. This lay just to the east of the Carthaginian strongholds of Castulo and Illurgia in the modern province of Jaén (see page 170). We know the location from archaeological excavations that have helped to pinpoint the landscape in which this epic battle took place. It is so rare to know the exact location of an ancient battle but on the field near the town of Turruñuelos were found distinctive javelin tips used by the Numidian cavalry of the time, lead projectiles of Balearic slingers, armour and Carthaginian coins dated to the period of the battle. This has convincingly led excavators to identify the site as Baecula.[19]

Scipio approached the field of battle from the south, for Hasdrubal Barca had chosen the site carefully and the sources emphasise that Hasdrubal's superior position made any engagement difficult for Scipio. The Roman commander needed to be careful not to get trapped between armies, as his father and uncle had done. But Scipio was confident in his soldiers' abilities and drew up in formation. He had fewer troops than Hasdrubal and had to use his formation creatively by putting his light troops, his skirmishers (lightly armed troops used in the front lines), into battle first and then having the heavy infantry challenge the flanks. The description of the battle, of Scipio's superior troops vs Hasdrubal's greater numbers, is almost the exact reverse of many of Hannibal's victories over the Romans. It is always worth considering how much of this is the literary construction of an ideal strategic victory rather than the true facts of the day. The mayhem of ancient battle and the lack of perspective from eyewitnesses mean that the reconstruction of events after they occurred must be somewhat idealised based on results. In this case, the story has Hasdrubal sensing his army was in trouble and pulling up and retreating north across the River Baetis.[20]

He then kept going. With two-thirds of his soldiers, his treasury and elephants, Hasdrubal Barca left the field of Baecula and marched his army up and over the Pyrenees and across Gaul, headed for the Alps. He was going to Italy to finally join up with his elder brother Hannibal. Nothing emphasises how little we know about what was happening on the ground more than this story. The departure of Hasdrubal Barca to Italy was no mad dash across Europe but must have been carefully planned out. In fact, we should consider whether the battle at Baecula was an attempt by Scipio to stop Hasdrubal leaving Iberia. None of the sources tell us anything about the preparation or strategy. That this was a carefully thought-through plan is only emphasised by the fact that a new army was sent from Carthage to replace Hasdrubal under the general Hanno.

Hannibal's areas of operation in Italy were largely restricted by the time Hasdrubal set out to join his brother. He still had allies in the region of the Bruttii and with the cities of southern Magna Graecia, and these needed protection from the Romans. So, while the area he could reside in was limited, he still managed to elude Roman power and continued to inflict the occasional stunning defeat on the many different armies he faced. He was far from conquered but also had no opportunity to advance. The coming of Hasdrubal must have restored in Hannibal a glimmer of hope, perhaps believing that the joined-up Carthaginian armies could inflict another massive setback on the Romans. But it would have to be one big enough to shift the momentum in Italy. Hannibal must have often thought of the Epirot king Pyrrhus and his words about Rome from a few decades earlier: it was like the many-headed hydra from mythology, whose heads grew back if you chopped them off and who was thus impossible to kill. For every victory Hannibal and the Carthaginians inflicted on the Romans, they came back with more; for every consul killed the Romans picked themselves up and sent out another.

Hasdrubal Barca crossed the Alps early in the spring of 207 BCE. His journey was quicker and easier than his brother's had been ten years earlier.[21] It is possible the southern pass along the Durance Valley was open and available, which would bring the Carthaginians directly into the Po Valley. There he gathered recruits and volunteers for his army as he moved quickly south. What did Hasdrubal Barca know about his brother's situation? How much contact was there between the two? We don't have answers but, again, there must have been a plan. The Roman manpower in this year in Italy was astounding. There were 23 legions in action across all theatres of the war that year, with 15 of these being in Italy. The Carthaginians were outnumbered at least threefold, and the Roman consuls leading those armies were far less arrogant and much more strategic after ten years of war. They divided their armies and tracked the two brothers, one in the north and one in the south. Hasdrubal expected his brother to move north and rendezvous with him but as Hannibal attempted to do so he met with the consular army under Claudius Nero near Grumentum. Soon he had to set off south again into Magna Graecia to protect his allies. Hasdrubal sent scouts south to find

Hannibal, whom he thought was near the city of Metapontum on the south coast of Italy. The scouts had orders to arrange a meeting in Umbria between the two armies but were intercepted by the Romans. Hannibal was now camped in Apulia near Canusium and held there by the consul Claudius Nero and his army. He never heard news from his brother.

Hasdrubal moved his army south and was camped near the modern Adriatic coastal town of Senigallia hoping that any day now he would hear from Hannibal. He soon realised that the Roman army that moved to meet him was bigger than he had first thought, and the two Roman consuls had somehow joined forces. With Hannibal nowhere in sight, Hasdrubal faced two experienced commanders with superior numbers and no support. He felt he had little choice but to evade the Roman armies and pass through the mountains into Umbria, so left his camp in the night. His army, probably around 30,000 strong, was made up of Carthaginian, Numidian, Iberian and Celtic troops, cavalry, recruited foot soldiers and elephants. They were near the River Metaurus when the Romans caught up with Hasdrubal and forced a fight. It was an epic battle with big losses on both sides, but the Carthaginians were outmanoeuvred and outnumbered. The elephants caused mayhem on both sides when they were caught between the armies, and Hasdrubal himself was killed in the fighting. The Romans counted this as a massive victory, and they remembered it as payback for Cannae, so destructive was it to the Carthaginian forces.[22]

Hannibal had no idea that this battle had taken place and for someone who had always prided himself on staying a step ahead of his enemy, he was surprisingly ill-informed. The first he heard of the battle of the Metaurus was when the victorious Roman consul, Claudius Nero, returned to the part of his army he had left in Apulia and had Hasdrubal's head catapulted into the

Carthaginian camp. Claudius Nero then released two captured African prisoners so they could share the details of what had happened. It is difficult to comprehend how the Carthaginian army felt when the head of the famed younger Barcid brother was used as a projectile into their camp or how Hannibal must have reacted. It was 207 BCE and the war in Italy was essentially over, yet Hannibal remained there for another four years. This was perhaps a particular strategy of the Carthaginians, for even if he was not winning victories, the very presence of Hannibal meant that Rome could not fully focus its military on Carthage and Iberia; it had to keep armies in Italy. Nevertheless, the action in the war fully shifted away to other theatres, and for now we leave Hannibal on the south coast of Italy, near the city of Crotona and the temple of Juno Lacinia, where he inscribed his column with the events of the war and the historian Polybius was able to read about it.

The final stages of the Second Punic War unfolded in Iberia and Africa. Scipio continued to win territory and allies in Iberia and a year after Metaurus, in 206 BCE, at a place called Ilipa (possibly near modern Seville), he defeated the combined Carthaginian forces under the command of Mago Barca and Hasdrubal Gisgo. The significance of this victory was profound; the whole of the peninsula was soon in Roman hands. Cádiz was the last holdout. Mago retreated there with the remnants of his army while Hasdrubal Gisgo returned to Africa. Mago was ordered to go to Italy and, in the story, he left Cádiz, then tried to return – but his entry was blocked. Even the old alliance of western Phoenicians no longer wanted to host a Barcid, as the Romans were now firmly in control. Mago then sailed with his armies to the region of Liguria in northern Italy, where he landed and took the town of Genoa.

Scipio founded the first Roman colony in the Iberian Peninsula on the Guadalquivir River, near modern Seville. It was called

Italica and Scipio settled his veterans there and gave the city colonial status, making the inhabitants Roman citizens. Resistance to Roman power would rumble on in Iberia for another two centuries, but the dominance of the Carthaginians was ended. It was after Ilipa that the Massyli prince Masinissa approached the Roman Scipio. The two men negotiated an alliance that would see the Massyli fighting for the Romans. Rome was now closely allied with one of the most significant powers in Africa, and the relationship Masinissa built with Scipio would shift the balance in Africa and ultimately seal the fate of Carthage. As Livy remembered it, Masinissa had flattered Scipio when the men met and remarked that Carthage could not last long if the Roman Scipio was their enemy.[23] The Numidian prince then returned to Africa, where he had to deal with pressing family issues that had arisen in his absence. This story will follow him as the final years of the war played out in the home regions of the Numidians, taking us back to Carthage.

CHAPTER 11

The Full Circle

As the history of the Second Punic War turns to Africa, the individuals there start to emerge from our Roman historians with more clarity and focus. One such figure is the beautiful Sophonisba, a young woman who grew up in Carthage and led the life of an elite daughter belonging to one of the ruling families of the city. She would have been educated at home by tutors and was fluent in Greek, sophisticated in the ways of the Mediterranean and considered an asset to the city. In that role she was married to the king of the Masaesyli, Syphax, a man many decades older than her. He ruled a large kingdom that spanned two capitals, from Cirta (modern Constantine) in the east to Siga (near modern Oran) in the west. We have already seen that both Rome and Carthage courted Syphax, who was a significant player in the African theatre of the war. He took on the role of a moderator between the two enemies and tried to balance his relationship with both Rome and Carthage to preserve his own land and rule. The changing landscape of alliances would have placed Syphax in a difficult position. He had started the war as an ally of Carthage but switched to the Romans after being wooed by the elder Publius Scipio. A friend of both the Scipio family and Carthaginian leaders, in the year 206 BCE he was approached by Hasdrubal Gisgo, who had just been defeated at Ilipa. As Scipio returned triumphant to Rome and won the right to prepare a

245

full-scale invasion of Africa with proconsular power, the Carthaginians knew they needed Syphax on their side more than ever. To woo him over and keep him loyal to Carthage, the king was offered a close alliance with the leader of Carthage, and given Sophonisba as his bride.

As we know from the Barcid examples, intermarriage between elite Carthaginians and Numidian royalty was a long-standing tradition and there was nothing unusual about this arrangement. But the way the Roman historians focused on this marriage is unusual, putting great significance on the Carthaginian woman who became the centrepiece of this episode of the war. The story of Sophonisba must have passed down via contemporary romances or dramas associated with the history of the wars as a romanticised tale for the popular imagination. So, when the Roman writer Appian tells us that Sophonisba had once been engaged to the Massyli prince Masinissa, who had gone to school in Carthage and grew up there, we perhaps glimpse another episode in a larger lost drama.[1] The romanticised and tragic tale of Sophonisba's life presents us with another of the few female historical characters in the whole history of Carthage. The narrative is Roman, and she was used as a foil to reflect weaknesses in the enemy and also to dramatise the events of the war. Yet Sophonisba is still an intriguing character who opens a view on to the role that elite women in Carthaginian society played. It was the women and children of Carthage, and of Rome, who would have felt the brunt of the long war and massive loss of life, of their husbands, brothers and sons. These are the primarily ignored hardships in the ancient tales of great wars; Sophonisba was one of many pawns in this larger game.

Sophonisba is the Latinised version of the Punic name Saphonbal (SPNB'L). Her name, like Hannibal and Hamilcar, was theophoric and meant something like 'Saphon is protected by Ba'al'. The Roman sources gave her a great deal of agency in the story. She was held personally responsible for coaxing the Masaesylian king Syphax back to Carthage. After her marriage, the old king even sent formal envoys to Scipio and delivered the message that he would now be 'obliged to fight for the land of Africa' and protect it against a Roman invasion. Sophonisba is credited by the Roman historian Livy with turning the Numidian king back to his heritage. Much of this tale plays into the construction of a Carthaginian femme fatale, a woman whose beauty and seductive ways woo an old foolish king away from the Roman cause. In Livy, Syphax is controlled by desire for his younger wife, a timeless tale of a man's judgement overwhelmed by lust. The Roman historian intended it to reveal to the audience the deep flaw in the man. Syphax, in the Roman mind, was essentially too steeped in his 'barbarian' otherness to control his passions.[2]

While Syphax reunited with the Carthaginian cause, the young Masinissa had returned from Iberia and was fighting to capture the Massyli kingdom of his father Gaia. Inheritance patterns in the Numidian royal families transferred sideways across the male line. This meant that when Gaia had died while Masinissa was in Iberia, the kingdom had gone directly to the oldest living brother, not the son. Masinissa's uncle had then been overthrown by a distant relative, who now held the throne. Masinissa aimed to take the kingdom for himself. After treating with Scipio in Iberia, he landed in the western regions of North Africa, crossing over from near Cádiz. This was the kingdom of the Mauri (roughly modern Morocco) and there he raised a small army. His force of supporters grew and Masinissa defeated the usurpers to his Massyli throne. He was now a king with a kingdom of his own, and Rome had an established ally in North Africa. With Syphax allied to Carthage and Masinissa to Rome, even before the actual Roman invasion of Africa, a proxy war started. The Carthaginians urged Syphax to attack his Massyli neighbour and to contain the threat he posed. The two sides met first in a skirmish and then a larger and fiercely fought battle took place between the towns of Cirta (Syphax' eastern capital) and Hippo (Hippo Regius, modern Annaba). Syphax was the undisputed winner, but Masinissa escaped with 60 horsemen and plunged madly into the Bagradas River to evade Vermina, Syphax's son, who was in pursuit. Masinissa was now a king without a kingdom and took refuge in the region referred to as the Lesser Syrtis, roughly 300km to the south and east. There he waited for the Romans to arrive.[3]

Syphax's victory alleviated some pressure, yet Carthage still prepared for the worst-case scenario. The Romans were coming, and the memory of Agathocles and Regulus was not far from their minds. Laelius, Scipio's chief lieutenant, had spent much of the year 204 BCE raiding the African coast with a fleet of 60 ships, reminding the Carthaginians and the rural population in their agricultural heartland of what was coming. The countryside was pillaged, and the Romans sent out scouting parties to reconnoitre the landscape. It was the turn of the Carthaginian population inside the city walls to panic at the idea of a heroic Roman commander, who had so recently taken Iberia from them and defeated Hannibal's Barcid brothers. Carthage reached out to all its allies to try to divert the Romans. Reinforcements were sent to Mago Barca in Liguria, where he did what he could to disrupt the Romans, achieving some success. Hannibal, still lingering in the south of Italy among the Bruttii, was so close to Scipio in Sicily that there was little chance to supply him. Neither of the surviving Barcid brothers could, at this point, do enough to distract the Romans from their main focus – the invasion of Africa.

As early as was possible in the year 204 BCE Scipio launched his offensive, sailing from the Sicilian city of Lilybaeum. The Roman consul landed in Africa at a place called Cap Farina, north of Utica, with his full invasion force. Scipio may have intended to land at Kelibia on Cap Bon, the place that both Agathocles and Regulus had started their invasions, but the wind sent the fleet off course to the west (see page 170). As soon as Scipio made shore, he set up camp and was immediately joined by Masinissa, who had been waiting for his friend and ally. Masinissa had travelled north to meet Scipio, accompanied by only a few horsemen, his kingdom in tatters. He eagerly joined with Scipio in his pursuit of victory over Carthage, for that would mean victory over Syphax as well. Masinissa's only chance of regaining his throne lay with the Romans.

Scipio's arrival brought dread to the citizens of Carthage. Columns of rural men, women and children all driving their animals clogged the roads as people moved towards the walled city for protection. Livy notes that the Carthaginians had not seen a Roman army for over half a century. The city gates were bolted, men were posted as sentries and an imminent attack was expected. The Carthaginians sent out commanders to skirmish with the Romans, to test their intentions, but these cavalry encounters ended badly for Carthage. By late summer, Scipio felt ready to move and lay siege, not to Carthage but first to Utica, Carthage's northern neighbour and ally. Hasdrubal Gisgo and Syphax combined their forces and moved to relieve the siege. They had superior numbers, the combined Carthaginian and Numidian armies forcing Scipio to give up and move off from Utica. By the end of the campaigning season of that year, Scipio had built a heavily fortified winter camp that encompassed his whole land army and his fleet. The Romans were secured on a small peninsula in the delta of the Bagradas River and spent an insecure winter there.[4]

Over that first winter in Africa, Scipio was determined to try to lure Syphax back to the Romans. Syphax, on the other hand, was interested in negotiating some kind of peace deal between the two sides. Syphax might even have been negotiating on behalf of Carthage's leaders when he proposed a deal that would see Hannibal recalled from Italy and Scipio leave Africa. Did Scipio really consider this an option? It seems unlikely, and I suspect that Scipio was biding his time, giving himself longer to collect allies and gather intelligence. The Roman commander did not feel capable of facing the combined forces of Syphax and Carthage; he was vastly outnumbered and without local allies of any substance. Livy revels in describing how much Sophonisba, the old king's young wife, was able to keep him loyal to Carthage and includes plenty of innuendo about Syphax's inability to control his lust. The Roman cultural stereotype of the Numidian king illustrates their generalised othering of peoples they considered enemies. This tends to undermine our appreciation of the strength of Syphax's kingdom and his military importance.[5]

Most of the winter of 203 BCE was taken up with the negotiation between Scipio and Syphax, with the envoys moving back and forth between the two camps. This meant that Scipio was kept well informed of the Carthaginian and Numidian armies' activities and the state of their winter camps. He strung his enemies along, while Syphax and Hasdrubal Gisgo seemed to believe that a truce was possible. Scipio's real plan was a bold attempt to neutralise the numerical superiority of his enemies before they had even engaged in battle. He moved part of his army out of their winter quarters towards Utica, pretending to begin anew the siege, and then sent Laelius and Masinissa with the rest of his forces to attack and capture the Carthaginian/ Numidian camps. The winter camps were made of temporary structures constructed by the soldiers with locally available materials. There were huts and buildings of wood, reed and thatch. Noting how flammable these were, and perhaps how dry the late winter had been, Laelius and Masinissa had their cavalry race up to the camps and hurl flaming projectiles into them. The Romans took their enemies completely by surprise with this ambush and wreaked havoc in the camps as fires quickly ignited and structures burned. The two commanders, Syphax and Hasdrubal, escaped with some of their soldiers, but a huge number were reportedly caught off guard and trapped. The camps would also have been full of the soldiers' families and hangers-on, people who supplied and lived off a travelling army. All of these were burned in their makeshift huts or struck down by the Roman soldiers, stationed at the exits of the camps to kill any who tried to flee. The estimate in Livy is that as many as 40,000 soldiers were killed and the camps captured.[6] Such numbers, as we know, were intended to reflect the sheer scale of the losses, which included thousands of soldiers, elephants, weapons and supplies.

Just days after the attack on the camp, the two sides met in battle at a place called the Great Plains in the Bagradas River's valley (see page 148). The Carthaginians and Syphax had pulled together their remaining, demoralised soldiers and gathered as many extras as they could press into service. It was a motley crew, and the Carthaginians were cut down and roundly defeated by Scipio's army and Masinissa's cavalry. Once again, Hasdrubal Gisgo and Syphax both survived the fight and fled the field of battle. Scipio moved to take Tunes, the city just 12km south of Carthage, while Masinissa and Laelius chased Syphax west towards his fortified city of Cirta. On 23 June, a date noted centuries later by the Augustan poet Ovid's *Fasti*, Masinissa captured Syphax.[7] During a clash of cavalry, the elder monarch was thrown from his horse and seized by his youthful adversary. Prior to surrendering Syphax to the Romans, Masinissa publicly displayed him in shackles before the fortified walls of his seemingly invincible citadel, Cirta. Witnessing their ruler subdued and captive, the populace yielded to the victorious Masinissa, who claimed the city for himself.

Masinissa captured Cirta and Syphax's whole kingdom, including his beautiful wife Sophonisba. She flung herself at the feet of the conqueror when he stormed into the palace. Sophonisba begged Masinissa to kill her, to free her from the coming humiliation of being bound and paraded through Rome at the feet of Scipio in a triumphal parade. Masinissa was swayed by her beauty, bravery and nobility in defeat, and decided that he would marry her himself to protect her from the Romans. As the wife of a conquered king, it was within Masinissa's rights to marry her, but in the Roman mind she was a war prize. Scipio was furious with Masinissa for taking the prize from his possession, removing this beautiful Carthaginian queen from his control – for nothing adorned a Roman triumph as nicely as a beautiful enemy woman. Nor was Scipio a romantic; he insisted that Masinissa hand Sophonisba over to him, that her value was enormous to Scipio, and that Masinissa had stepped outside his authority in marrying her. The drama ended with Masinissa secretly delivering a cup of poison to his new wife. The beautiful Sophonisba bravely took up the cup and in Livy's version of the tale uttered a last sentence: 'I accept this wedding gift . . . it is not unwelcome, if my husband has found it impossible to give his wife a greater one.' Sophonisba then drunk down the draught and collapsed. So ends the story of the woman who challenged Rome through her beauty and persuasion. The tale of Sophonisba was popular with later Romans, and early medieval and Renaissance historians, poets and artists represented her repeatedly (see Fig. 26 in plate section). Her bravery meant Scipio was denied his full trophy by the wiles of a woman and Syphax was sent alone in chains to Rome to be paraded in triumph for the people.[8]

In this moment, Carthage had essentially lost the Second Punic War, but the fighting did not end here. With few allies left, the Carthaginians had run out of options. Gathering supplies, the population prepared for a protracted siege while the city magistrates debated in the senate about the next move. Hannibal and his army were still in Italy and in no position to help – he was essentially as trapped as they were. The Carthaginians sent a delegation of 30 of their most eminent senators to the Roman commander at Tunes. The men fell prostrate before Scipio and begged for leniency. They blamed the whole war on the Barcid family, on Hannibal himself, and asked for a pardon. Scipio was persuaded by the delegation and began to draw up peace terms. Roman generals in the field, like the Carthaginian ones, were granted leeway to settle terms and make peace deals when warranted. Although most of these would have to be ratified through the senate in Rome, a commander far from home exercised wide autonomy. The terms dictated by Scipio were exacting indeed. They included specific details about the armies left in Italy and Gaul being recalled, meaning those of Mago Barca in Liguria (known as Cisalpine Gaul) and Hannibal in Bruttium. The Carthaginians could never attempt to return to Iberia, plus they had to abandon the islands between Italy and Africa (i.e. Malta and Pantelleria). Carthage would have to surrender its navy, all but 20 warships, and supply Rome with massive amounts of wheat and barley, along with a substantial war payment.[9]

Carthage had three days to consider the terms and a delegation of the city's elders travelled to the Roman senate. The two sides met in Rome at the Temple of Bellona. Bellona was the archaic Roman goddess of war whose temple was used to debate matters of war, a place for victorious generals to appear when they returned from campaign and to receive foreign dignitaries. What happened there is very difficult to clarify because our Roman sources disagree. Livy and Polybius chose to present different versions, suggesting this history was contested in their lifetimes, and conflicting tales existed. Livy constructed the whole story as a giant ruse on behalf of Carthage to trick the Romans into letting their guard down so they could get their armies back to Africa and fight on. Polybius, generally considered our more reliable source, insisted that the treaty was ratified, and that the peace was being seriously negotiated by both sides. Another Roman historian throws his views into the mix as well: Cassius Dio refuted all of this, saying the Romans would never have received Carthaginian senators in Rome while Mago Barca and Hannibal were still in Liguria and southern Italy, and any ratification would have waited until the enemy armies had departed.[10]

The result of these negotiations was that Mago Barca and Hannibal were ordered to prepare to return to Africa. Hannibal had been encircled by Roman armies but still held his own. He would now have to abandon many allies who had remained loyal to the end. He attempted to do what he could and refortified some towns, but he also faced resistance from his Italian recruits who did not want to return to Africa with him and leave their families and lives in Italy. Livy records harsh treatment of those who dissented. Hannibal had ultimately failed to protect those who had been loyal to him for so long and all knew that Roman retributions in the region would be extremely harsh. When Hannibal finally sailed, he took with him some of the existing army – the estimates are that 10,000 to 12,000 made the crossing to Africa – but very few of his cavalry. Presumably they could not transport the horses, many of which were slaughtered to prevent them falling into Roman hands. He landed with his army near the region of Hadrumetum (modern Sousse) where his family is said to have had an estate. There they set up camp and waited. Mago Barca had been fighting the Romans in Liguria and causing all kind of trouble in the north but had been seriously injured in an engagement just before being loaded on to a ship to sail back to Carthage. He died on the journey. Hannibal was 45 years old, the only Barcid brother left and the only one to return to Africa after 35 years.

At Carthage a kind of inertia had set in. The city was under a blockade and the Romans were both north and south of the city, with Scipio and the fleet near Utica and the army at Tunes. A stalemate or truce was in place but there were tensions on all sides. Long spans of time would have passed to allow for the travel and communication needed between Rome and Carthage, and in the winter particularly, when it was treacherous to sail. All sides held their breath until the spring of 202 BCE, when a fleet of Roman ships – warships and cargo – were blown widely off course in a storm in the bay off Carthage. Some Carthaginian citizens decided to launch their ships and tow the Roman supply vessels to the city's port. The people were starving, and the city had been blockaded for months. These were ships meant to supply Scipio's Roman forces and the population of Carthage knew they were full of grain and barley.

Scipio was furious. Confrontations took place between the two sides inside the city of Carthage, violence broke out and Roman envoys were attacked. Although Polybius claimed that the envoys left the city unharmed, there were skirmishes between triremes in the bay and some were wrecked. These events then triggered a full-blown, furious attack by Scipio on the towns and cities of the Carthaginian heartland. The truce was forgotten and the peace deal evaporated while towns and farms were looted, with people captured and sold into slavery. It appears Scipio was provoking the Carthaginians into a full battle or trying to force an all-out surrender. The Roman historians believe that the presence of Hannibal and his army at Hadrumetum had given the Carthaginians some renewed hope. Perhaps Scipio relished the idea of taking on the famous Carthaginian general himself. He had already defeated two of the Barcid brothers and was now in a stronger position than any Roman who had ever faced Hannibal before. It was Scipio's chance for a final and complete glory over Carthage and the great Hannibal.

For his part, Hannibal seems a reluctant warrior in this phase of the story. He received messengers from Carthage imploring his help in countering Scipio. He gathered his forces and whatever allies he could muster and moved them inland from Hadrume-tum. His army was disjointed, made up of his own loyal troops and those remnants of Mago's forces who had joined him from Liguria. There were Carthaginian and Libyan recruits, but he was very short of Numidian allies and their essential cavalry, despite having some 80 elephants. Hannibal could hardly have been com-fortable in a landscape in which he had barely spent any time after childhood. Scipio roamed across the countryside, sending messages to Masinissa to gather his cavalry and join with him. Masinissa had been busy consolidating his victory over Syphax and building his kingdom. He appeared with a strong force of cavalry and once with Scipio they moved together towards Hannibal. Scipio sent messengers to his rival commander that he was ready to meet.

The two men met at a place called Zama. According to Polybius, the whole of the western Mediterranean was gripped in anticipation: 'not only all the inhabitants of Italy and Africa, but those of Iberia, Sicily and Sardinia likewise were held in suspense and distracted, awaiting the result.' The armies were in place when Scipio and Hannibal rode out towards each other to meet in person. They had each started with a few compan-ions but broke away and spoke to each other privately, although each man brought an interpreter with them. Such was the power play on the field of battle that the two men, both fluent in Greek, would only speak in their native tongues, Punic and Latin. Livy added that they were silent for a while, sizing each other up, 'the two greatest commanders of their age', before Hannibal spoke first. He greeted Scipio as the younger man and first rued the wars between their cities. Hannibal asked that Scipio negotiate a fair peace so that both Carthage and Rome could thrive. He compared their careers, even saying (if we can believe any of these words were his) that 'today you are just what I was at Trasimeno and at Cannae.' Scipio spoke in his turn but refused any peace and blamed Carthage for the wars. He demanded complete surrender or a fight. The two commanders then returned to their armies and prepared for a battle to be fought on the next day.[11]

It was the autumn of 202 BCE, perhaps October, when the Battle of Zama took place. At daybreak on the morning after the commanders had met, the two sides moved out of their camps and set up position on the field. The armies may have contained similar total numbers, but the Carthaginians were lacking enough cavalry and Scipio had Masinissa with the combined strength of the Massyli and Masaesyli. The Roman army was easily the better fighting force at this moment. Battle hardened after long years together in Iberia and now Africa, it was the seasoned and experienced force. Hannibal's more makeshift army noted above also included some Numidian cavalry from a distant relative of Syphax who had joined the fight. The generals gave their speeches to their troops but unusually Hannibal did not address his army as a whole. Instead, he left his lieutenants to deliver a message to each of the separate parts on the field. I think Polybius must have included this detail as a symbol of how disjointed Hannibal's forces were, because the Carthaginian general had never not addressed his whole army before a battle, and the absence of a speech was perhaps meant to imply that Hannibal knew he couldn't win and was almost resigned to losing.[12]

It was a brutal and hard-fought battle, and the sources still marvel at how well Hannibal was able to do, even when he had the notably inferior army. Close hand-to-hand combat raged around the field. Polybius provides us with details of how the Carthaginian troops behind the first line of Hannibal's soldiers would not come to the aid of the front line. So, when the front eventually collapsed against the Roman pressure and turned back, they were destroyed. The discord in Hannibal's army was clear when these front-line forces, mostly made up of foreign soldiers, then turned on the Carthaginian forces behind them in fury. As Hannibal's army began to fight among themselves and against the Romans at the same time, they were cut down. It was carnage. Hannibal commanded his core troops to hold the line and not allow the retreating fighters to join them. The retreating soldiers were then forced out to the flanks and the ground became soaked in blood and covered in 'slippery corpses . . . fallen in heaps'. The Romans advanced over the dead and moved to take on Hannibal's crack troops. This was a fierce and equal fight, and the Romans were only relieved when Masinissa and Laelius returned to the field after pursuing the opposing cavalry. Scipio's cavalry fell on Hannibal's troops from behind, surrounded them and cut them down. It was a messy and brutal defeat with at least 20,000 of Hannibal's army reported killed and many were captured.[13]

As the survivors of the defeated army galloped off the field of battle with Hannibal, Carthage prepared to surrender. The senate summoned Hannibal to the city and the population must have turned out to watch him, the last-surviving Barcid, make his way to meet with the leading men of the city. Standing in the senate Hannibal conceded defeat and advised the Carthaginians to sue for peace. Scipio dictated terms and these were ratified by 201 BCE. The peace was harsh to Carthage, which had to pay financial reparations to Rome consisting of an immediate payment and then a further yearly instalment. The Carthaginians would deliver a war indemnity to Rome every year for 50 years, amounting to 13,500 Euboean talents, the equivalent of 350,000 kilograms of silver. Carthage was forbidden from waging war outside of Africa, and even in Africa it had to first ask the Romans for the right. Furthermore, Carthage could not take any military action against its neighbours without the permission of Rome. The war elephants were surrendered, and all its warships were taken into the bay and burned while the population watched from the walls. One hundred hostages were given over to Rome, young men chosen by Scipio himself. These youths, from age 14 to 30, were taken to Rome to be guarantors of the treaty. The city of Carthage preserved most of its territory, although without the actual right or ability to defend it. Masinissa was formally made king of the Massyli and the Masaesyli kingdoms, and he was recognised as a client king of Rome. As its firm ally, he was now the most powerful man in North Africa.[14]

Scipio earned the epithet Africanus after this victory and was the first of many Roman commanders (and later, emperors) to be given the name of the region or people they had conquered. A magnificent triumph took place through the city of Rome, described in detail by the historian Appian. As trumpeters processed through the city, they were followed by wagons full of spoils. There were constructions of towers representing the cities captured in the campaign and painted pictures showing the exploits of the war, re-enacting the major battles and the heroic moments. After the scenes of victory came the looted gold and silver coin and bullion and all the other valuables that had been captured. There were crowns to be given to the successful commander by all the allies and cities of the realm, then white oxen and elephants and captives – the elite Carthaginian and Numidians who adorned the procession. Then the lictors of the Roman senate, carrying the symbols of the magistrate's power, then musicians and pipers wearing golden crowns singing and dancing and insulting the enemy with gestures and jokes. Then incense bearers and finally the victorious commander himself, Scipio Africanus, wearing a crown of gold and precious stones and dressed in a purple toga embroidered with golden stars. Scipio bore a sceptre of ivory and a laurel branch – the Roman symbols of victory. He wound his way through Rome to the cheering of crowds and, accompanied by his family and commanders and lieutenants, the triumphal procession made its way up to the Capitol in Rome where Scipio held a feast for the victory and dedicated the spoils to the temple of Jupiter.[15]

At Carthage, the second war with Rome was over, but despite the harsh and damaging peace terms, it did not take long for the city to recover. It may have had to pay a huge indemnity to Rome and had no war fleet, but Carthage thrived as the Mediterranean became more deeply connected than ever. Carthage had been forced to shift its commercial focus east in the aftermath of war with more contact and trade moving back and forth between the kingdoms of the Seleucids and Ptolemies. The sources are sketchy regarding the events that followed right after the war, but within a decade the economic bounce-back was visible. There is speculation about why this prosperity happened so quickly. Increased trade was likely one factor, but Carthage's inability to spend its funds on waging war must also have alleviated a huge expense from the public purse in a city that was used to hiring paid soldiers from abroad.

The archaeology of the city reveals new buildings and creative design in these post-war years. The still-visible, innovatively designed ports were built in this period and we have a vivid description of them from Appian (see Fig. 27 in plate section). There were two joined-up harbours sharing a common entrance to the sea that was 20m wide. This entrance could be closed off with iron chains. The first port, a rectangular space, was for merchant vessels and ships' tackle. Inside the second port, which was circular, was an island with 'embankments' that were full of shipyards with a capacity for 220 vessels. Resting above were magazines for the tackle and furniture. There were two ionic columns in front of each dock that worked as a portico to link both the harbour and the island with an architectural decoration. On the top of the island was the admiral's house and from there the chief naval officer oversaw everything; signals were sent out by horn and orders delivered by messengers. The island sat right near the entrance to the harbour. It was built up to a height that allowed the admiral to observe what was going on out at sea, but anyone approaching by water did not have a clear view of the inside of the port. Even merchant ships coming into the rectangular port had no view of the docks, 'for a double wall enclosed them, and there were gates by which merchant ships could pass from the first port to the city without traversing the dockyards'.[16]

The ports at Carthage and their operation reflect advanced engineering, sophistication and strategic planning. These famous structures offered state-of-the-art infrastructure for Mediterranean shipping. There was also new elite housing built at Carthage on the hills neighbouring the Byrsa. These homes were large and luxuriously constructed with porticoes and courtyards and beautiful views out to the bay. Other recent research on the economic resilience of Carthage has focused on the residual evidence for lead-silver mining in the heartland along the Bagradas (Medjerda) River basin. This new hypothesis explains that Carthage could rely on locally sourced metal and mineral resources in times of external pressure and stress, once again emphasising the resilience and wealth of the location of Carthage itself that the Phoenician colonists had chosen all those centuries ago.[17] After the war, the city was so prosperous that it was able to offer to pay off the entire war indemnity owed to Rome 40 years early, in the year 191 BCE. The Roman senate was extremely irked by the offer and refused.

What the visible prosperity in the archaeological record at Carthage cannot reveal to us is the state of the citizens. The post-second war environment in the city was politically fraught and the traumas of the citizens and the families of Carthage were deeply felt. These years are best captured by the story of Hannibal in the aftermath of war. After so many years as an international military figure of heroic dimension, his domestic reception was more bruising than he was used to abroad. In Carthage, Hannibal was a deeply divisive figure both within the governing elite and among the wider populace. Both Romans and Carthaginians were happy to lay all the blame for the disasters of the recent war squarely on Hannibal's shoulders. Cassius Dio wrote that 'Hannibal was accused by his own people of having refused to capture Rome when he had a chance to and of having appropriated the plunder from Italy', although Dio also noted that he was not convicted of any charges. Dio reported that Hannibal was elected to the highest office in Carthage and became one of the two *sufetes* in the year 196 BCE. Hannibal is said to have led a period of governmental reform and imposed anti-corruption laws on the city, although how much of this is made up by the Roman historians is difficult to know.

The election of Hannibal Barca to *sufet* was too much for many of his enemies in the city. Within the senate at Carthage were families that had opposed the Barcids during all those years Hannibal fought in Italy. These were now in the majority, and they were willing to work with the Romans to try to remove the last Barcid from power. Livy described how Hannibal accused some of his fellow senators of embezzlement of public funds and bribery, and claimed that there were financial irregularities, including the payment of the war indemnity to Rome in coin with a debased silver quantity. Hannibal's enemies in the senate then turned to the Romans and accused Hannibal of plotting against them and planning to renew hostilities by entering into discussions with the Seleucid king, Antiochus III.[18]

Hannibal's conqueror, Scipio Africanus, spoke up and defended his old enemy in Rome but it was no use. An envoy from Rome was sent to Carthage demanding that Hannibal be charged with 'plotting war' with Antiochus against Rome. At Carthage, Hannibal was declared an enemy of the state and charged with breaking the treaty with Rome. His house was attacked and destroyed by a rival faction, and he was exiled from the city.[19] Hannibal fled Carthage, leaving Africa and sailing to Tyre, where he was greeted as a celebrity conqueror, and making his way to the court of King Antiochus to act as an advisor. Hannibal would live for the next decade as a never-ending opponent of Roman imperialism until his death by suicide in 182 BCE. The sketchy yet fascinating details reveal that the fiscal and financial prosperity visible in the archaeological record at Carthage does not equal political prosperity. Carthage was a deeply traumatised and divided city in these same years that visible signs of wealth appear.

A fuller picture of what was happening on the ground comes through a comic play written after the Second Punic War by the Latin playwright Plautus, called the *Poenulus* ('the little Punic'). It is an intriguing and sympathetic view into the Carthaginian people in this period. The protagonist of the play, a man named Hanno, embodies so much of the struggles and realities of life for Carthaginians in the aftermath of great defeat. In the play, Hanno travels the seas looking everywhere for his daughters, who have been captured and sold into slavery. Hanno searches far and wide, voyaging to ports and visiting all the brothels. Here is both innuendo by the playwright and the full understanding of the fate of thousands of young girls, boys and women who had been caught up in the conflict and carried off as prizes of war. Hanno's character, despite being a figure of fun in a Roman comedy about a Carthaginian, is nonetheless an interesting study of the people and their customs and even how they looked. He was a devout father, yet at the same time made fun of for speaking the Punic language, which is projected as a kind of incomprehensible babble to the Latin audience. In Hanno we can glimpse how the Carthaginians were visually perceived by others – of note are his pierced ears and long tunics. Elsewhere, Plautus tells us that the Carthaginians were 'porridge eaters', probably consuming wheat or barley porridge as a staple food.[20] Hanno the Carthaginian appears both as a sympathetic character, a victim of war like so many others would have been, and a figure of ridicule.

The play, the *Poenulus*, also shows us how close the links between Carthage and Rome were and how well the two people knew each other. The ties were much closer than is usually understood or discussed, and while this is never explicitly stated in other historical sources there are intriguing mentions about familial ties between elite families in the two cities. One example took place during the battle for the city of Tarentum in 209 BCE when the Carthaginian commander Carthalo, one of Hannibal's close lieutenants, was killed. Livy describes how Carthalo had laid down his arms during the battle and been on his way to see the Roman consul, Fabius Maximus. Livy states that Carthalo wanted to remind Fabius Maximus of the ties of hospitality that existed between their fathers. He never got the chance because Roman soldiers struck him down before the two men could meet. This close link between a Carthaginian commander and a Roman senatorial family goes almost without comment – it was clearly nothing unusual.[21] This means it must have been well understood at the time how closely connected the elites of both cities were, and this would become even more developed in the period after the end of the war.

New archaeology and old literature present a different Carthage in the post-war years. For the first time, there is a glimpse of the broader population who lived there, underneath the grand historical narrative of warlords and ambitious colonialists who usually dominate our picture of the ancient Mediterranean. There was chaos and deep resentment between factions in the political arena. There were the personal traumas of the defeated Carthaginians – their deep losses make the history of the city a very human one for the first time. Meanwhile, the visible economic growth and prosperity of the city would provoke a belligerent Rome to cause its final downfall.

CHAPTER 12

And the Commander Wept

'Carthage must be destroyed.' These are the most infamous words ever spoken about Carthage. In Rome, the senator Cato repeated this phrase every time he stood up to speak in the senate. This mantra followed a visit to Carthage by Cato and other Roman magistrates in 153 BCE. A senatorial delegation had gone to the city near the end of the 50-year period that required Carthage to make annual war reparation payments to Rome (due to end in 151 BCE). Cato was a grizzled old senator, a hawk and an extreme Roman patriot. Skirmishes and tensions between the Numidian kingdom of Masinissa and the Carthaginians had flared up and, as the treaty demanded, the Romans had been called in to negotiate. Cato and his fellow senators were amazed by the thriving metropolis, the busy ports, the rich landscape and the people coming and going from across the Mediterranean. Carthage had continued to thrive and the increased wealth and growth of the Numidian kingdom of Masinissa only added to its prosperity as the conduit for trade in and out of Africa. Cato was alarmed to see the possibility of a strong Carthage once more. The Roman state of mind in the mid-second century BCE was one of conquest and domination; it was rarely interested in peace. Cato urged his fellow Roman senators to destroy their old enemy while they could and, in an infamous scene, the old senator even dropped some fat juicy figs on the floor of the senate and claimed he had brought them from Carthage – to emphasise that it was only a few days' sail away. This was a gesture designed to scare the Romans with old ghosts of Hannibal in Italy and the death of so many of the Roman elite on the fields of Cannae. It was also clear that not everyone in the Roman senate agreed with Cato. As many times as he filibustered in the senate about how Carthage must be destroyed, his nemesis and descendent of the conqueror of Hannibal, known as Publius Cornelius Scipio Nasica, returned with 'Carthage must be saved.' The political power of Rome was fractured and the rivalries between elite factions intense. But also essential were deep connections between the two peoples, with many Carthaginian elite families related through friendship and patronage to families in Rome, especially the Scipios.[1]

The source for these final years of Carthage is Appian. A native of Alexandria, he wrote a Roman history in the Greek language in the second century CE. Appian's version of the tale relies heavily on Polybius' telling and, most importantly, Appian included parts of the original Polybian history that we no longer have preserved. Polybius was in the entourage of the Roman commander Scipio Aemilianus, who was the adopted grandson of Scipio Africanus. Appian's story essentially preserved much of Polybius' eyewitness account of the war between the Carthaginians and Numidians that led to the Roman siege and destruction of Carthage. The ancient tale is as close as we can get to seeing the action unfold through the eyes of the Roman participants. It is a vivid and detailed picture of ancient violence, politics and destruction.

The action leading up to the final destruction of Carthage, conventionally called the Third Punic War, also starts with the Numidian kingdom of Masinissa. The old king was in his late eighties by the 150s BCE and he and his kingdom had thrived in its newly enhanced position as the most powerful state in North

Africa and ally of Rome. Just after the end of the Second Punic War, around 195 BCE, Masinissa had seized a large part of the Carthaginian territory for his own realm, claiming that it had once belonged to his Massyli kingdom. Carthage could do little but had protested to the Romans who, as the treaty demanded, sent moderators to decide on the case. Appian tells us that the outcome was fixed, and the Roman negotiators had been told to decide in favour of Masinissa. The Numidian kingdom became the dominant military power in North Africa in the inter-war years and territorial disputes like this between the two sides rumbled on over the next decades. The story repeated itself many times, with Masinissa's Numidians encroaching on Carthaginian territory, the Carthaginians appealing to Rome and the Romans deciding in favour of the Numidians. The Romans in this period were off fighting in many different regions, east against the Seleucid and Macedonian kingdoms and west in the Mediterranean in Iberia. Masinissa's sons and their Numidian cavalry continued to participate and fight as auxiliaries with the Roman forces. The sources place them in Iberia, where dissent and rebellion lingered on among the Celtiberians of the central and northern peninsula. It is worth considering how much of this dissent was fuelled by pro-Carthaginian tribes and remnants of the Phoenician diaspora in Iberia, but there is no mention of the connection in the sources.[2]

At Carthage in these inter-war years different political factions sprang up. They themselves were shaped by and depended on their relationships around the Mediterranean. By the 150s BCE there was, in the words of Appian, a pro-Roman party, a democratic party and a party that favoured the Numidians. The pro-Roman party was led by Hanno, the democratic party by two men known as Hamilcar the Samnite and Carthalo, and the pro-Numidian party by a man named Hannibal the Starling. As the city grappled with new influences and had to balance the demands of the peace with the reality of its aggressive neighbours, there were calls to raise forces and to fight back. Decades of capitulation, of having to swallow every aggressive move by their neighbours and turn the other cheek, had played on the Carthaginian psyche and identity. The Romans had conceded to Masinissa's seizure of Carthaginian lands across four decades. Masinissa had grown his kingdom and had many children, the last of whom was born when he was 86. According to the historian Polybius, who knew him personally, he was a cultivated man who endowed the sanctuary of Apollo on the island of Delos and had his sons educated in Greece. Masinissa represented a new North African identity, a kind of Graeco-Numidian-Punic culture born of these wars and the increasing contact between cultures in the Mediterranean.

Things came to a head in 152 BCE when 40 of the pro-Masinissa faction in Carthage were expelled from the city. The expelled citizens went to Masinissa and urged him to declare war, and the old king sent two of his sons, Micipsa and Gulussa, to Carthage to negotiate the return of their allies. Violence erupted when Hamilcar the Samnite attacked and injured some of the Numidian delegation, and war followed not long after. The commander of the Carthaginian forces, another man named Hasdrubal, raised an army to march to war. In 151 BCE the treaty signed at the conclusion of the Second Punic War ended with the final payments of war indemnity. Carthage was once again able to function outside of the yoke of Rome and had been arming itself in anticipation. The army raised by Carthage consisted of 25,000 infantry and some hundreds of cavalry, but they were soon joined by 6,000 Numidians who had deserted Masinissa's sons and fought with the Carthaginians. Somewhere near a town called Oroscopa (perhaps in western Tunisia today) the field of battle was set.[3] An eyewitness account comes from the Roman commander Scipio Aemilianus, who recalled the scene and must have told it to Polybius. Scipio had travelled to Africa from Iberia, where he had been fighting as a Roman legate under the consul Lucullus. He came to find Masinissa to procure elephants, the animals having proven so successful for Carthage in their battle against the Iberians 70 years earlier that the Romans were going to employ them as well.

The grizzled octogenarian Masinissa was preparing for battle when he heard of Scipio's arrival and sent some cavalry to meet and install him in a safe place to watch the day unfold. The residual image of the old king suiting up to take the field and lead his armies is impressive. The story is full of admiration for Masinissa as a man who still led out his troops personally and was a vigorous fighter, despite his age. Appian described how the Numidians rode bareback into battle, and in the admiring Roman eye were long lived and robust generally. Scipio was positioned on high somewhere off the field of battle and watched as the fighting began. He described it 'as one views a spectacle in a theatre' while Masinissa and Hasdrubal drew their armies up to face each other. The fighting lasted all that day but towards the evening the opponents ceased and regrouped. Scipio approached the camps. He went to Masinissa and when the Carthaginians heard that the Roman was in the area they came and appealed to him to broker a peace. Terms could not be agreed so no peace was made, and the next day the battle continued. Masinissa was eventually able to encircle the Carthaginian camp and blockade the army inside. So, a kind of stalemate set in and Scipio departed with his elephants. Official envoys from Rome were on their way to try to settle the dispute. The Roman envoys were instructed to not let Masinissa lose, or to ensure Carthage lost, but otherwise to stay out of the fighting.

Inside the Carthaginian camp the situation was dire. The soldiers were 'weakened by hunger and they were incapable of attacking their enemies'. They were desperate and resorted to eating their pack animals and horses, and even boiled their leather straps for sustenance. They were trapped in a small camp, unable to move and exposed to the scorching heat. The lack of food and, exercise, and exposure to the harsh African summer, caused them to fall ill with various diseases. With no wood left for cooking, they were forced to burn their shields for fuel. They were unable to carry out the dead bodies or even burn them due to Masinissa's strict ring that held them in their camp. This led to the spread of a terrible disease. Finally, beaten, the Carthaginians negotiated with the Numidians, agreeing to take back into the city those who had been exiled and to pay an indemnity. They had to withdraw from the camp with nothing and leave their weapons and armour with the victors. Just wearing tunics, they filed out past the Numidian forces. When one of Masinissa's sons charged on the Carthaginians, they had no strength to resist and it was a slaughter. Only a few, including their commander Hasdrubal, made it back to Carthage alive, according to Appian. The Carthaginians' first foray to war in 50 years had been a disaster.[4]

The Carthaginian senate condemned their commanders Hasdrubal and Carthalo to death for the calamity while the Romans began to raise a new army. A war was already in motion, but the build-up continued for many months. The Carthaginians sent envoys to Rome but there were no remediations offered; the Romans were going to war, and the expedition was enthusiastically embraced by the Roman people. Appian tells us that thousands signed up for an opportunity to go to war against the old enemy and an army of 80,000 was raised with a new fleet. Utica, long-time ally and rival of Carthage on the coast to the north of the city, sent delegates to Rome and surrendered their city. From the reaction of Utica, it is clear that there was little question in most people's minds what the outcome of this war was going to be. Without allies, without soldiers, Carthage stood alone and was desperate. Then Hasdrubal, one of the condemned commanders, rebelled against his death sentence and gathered another army outside the city. With the dual threat of civil war and invasion, Carthage again sent envoys to beseech the Romans to call off the invasion. The senate of Rome told the Carthaginian envoys to send hostages – 300 of the children of their elite families – as security and the 'freedom and autonomy' of Carthage might be preserved. Carthage did as it was told, gathering the children and sending them to the Roman commanders in Sicily. The citizens were bereft. Appian described the scene at the port where the children had gathered to board the ships to Sicily – how mothers clung to their children with 'frantic cries and tore at the anchors and ropes of the ships' and threw themselves at the sailors to try to stop them leaving port. How some of the women even swam far out into the sea after the ships as they sailed away.[5]

The Romans at Sicily took the Carthaginian children and sent them to Rome. They told the Carthaginians to meet them in Utica and crossed over the sea with their army. The Roman consul Lucius Marcius Censorinus received the Carthaginian envoys at Utica and after listening to their pleas he demanded that they give up all their armaments. They were ordered to 'bring all their weapons and engines of war, both public and private', to the consul at Utica. They agreed and two Roman magistrates, Scipio Nasica and Gaius Cornelius Hispanus, accompanied the Carthaginians to the city. Wagons were loaded up with all the weapons. Appian describes 'complete armour for 200,000 men, besides innumerable javelins and darts, and 2,000 catapults for throwing pointed missiles and stones', which made for a spectacular sight. After all this, the Carthaginians stood in front of the

Roman consul Censorinus in anticipation of reprieve. That was when he delivered the crushing blow. The citizens of Carthage would have to now leave their city, to take themselves and their families and move inland at least 15km from the sea, and never again occupy the land upon which Carthage had been founded. The Romans were going to burn it to the ground.

The Carthaginian envoys were astounded. They could not believe their ears. They had complied with every demand, acquiesced to each request and it was still not enough. They were being asked to abandon their homes, their history and legends, and their rights to live by the sea – to abandon their very identity. The Roman consul patronisingly explained that it was not because of any ill will towards the Carthaginians that they demanded these sacrifices, but for the sake of the Carthaginians themselves; that the city on the sea's edge was too tempting for them and they just couldn't help but cause trouble by their very location. This is a common rhetorical theme in Roman philosophy – that cities on the sea were somehow dangerous, filled with multilingual people mixing cultures and thriving as emporia of sin and deceit. In the Roman rhetoric, all the Carthaginians had to do was become good farmers like the Romans and all would be well.

The envoys returned to Carthage. Citizens watched from the walls as the dejected men approached, moving slowly. It was bad news indeed and when the population of Carthage heard the new demands they erupted in 'fury and weeping'. They turned on the ambassadors and anyone they could find. They had given up their children, their weapons and now they had nothing. The senators at Carthage declared war on Rome, brought their rebellious commander back into the fold and prepared to defend their city. They named another commander for operations inside the city, also called Hasdrubal, who was a grandson of Masinissa, the son of one of his daughters who had married a Carthaginian.

Again, this emphasises how closely connected and mixed the different ethnicities in North Africa were. It was the city itself that made the citizens, and these citizens readied for a war they knew they could not win. The whole place became a workshop and forge. Appian describes how all the sacred places, the temples and any unoccupied space saw 'men and women working together day and night without rest'. They made swords and shields and missiles for catapults, javelins and any other weapons they could, working without pause.[6]

It was 149 BCE when the attack began. The Roman commanders had delayed the assault, waiting at Utica for the Carthaginians to cede to all their demands, reasoning that they had no other choice. Eventually the consuls realised they were going to have to fight – that the Carthaginians were not going to leave their city. The Roman forces moved from Utica by land and sea to prepare to lay siege to Carthage. The city, as we know, was heavily defended and fortified: its location on a small peninsula encircled on the land side by triple walls, 15m high, and expanding 17km to encompass the Megara region of the city, the agricultural land attached to it. As we have already discussed, these walls were like living defensive structures as well, divided into upper and lower parts, with the bottom spaces used as stables that could house up to 300 elephants and 4,000 horses and had places for fodder and grain. There were also barracks for soldiers and the walls were surrounded by a deep ditch as well. A seawall stood facing the water. When an initial attempt to overrun the land and seawalls by the two Roman consuls resulted in their being repulsed by the newly rearmed citizens of Carthage, the Romans retreated and regrouped. Their plan had been to scale the seawalls with ladders and to focus on the one point of weakness in the land walls, where the land wall met the harbour, but they had not expected such fierce resistance from within.

The attacks on the city continued throughout the year, with the Romans bringing huge siege engines into play and battering at the walls. By night, the Carthaginians would fix any damage they could and even snuck out to try to burn the Roman engines, damaging them enough to make them inoperable. Some of the Carthaginians were only armed with clubs and stones yet the resistance continued. Outside the city, there were two Carthaginian armies operating against the Romans, one led by Hasdrubal and the other by Phameas. These two armies fought successfully, trapping the consul Censorinus and chipping away at Roman morale. The Carthaginians under Phameas fiercely attacked the Romans, ambushing them and fighting a kind of guerrilla war. His encounters with the younger Scipio Aemilianus form a large part of the narrative of the war in this year. Scipio was the one Roman who shone in these encounters, showing wisdom and bravery against the enemy. There is, in Appian's account, criticism of the Roman consuls but never of Scipio, who was then only a commander operating underneath the two consuls who had led the attack. This is, of course, a narrative that Scipio told himself and was originally written down by his ward, the Greek Polybius, so it is perhaps no surprise that he is the star of the story.

Scipio turned the tide of war by bringing one of the sons of Masinissa into the conflict against Carthage and by convincing Phameas and 2,200 of his cavalry officers to switch sides. When the old king Masinissa had died in the late autumn or early winter of 149/148 BCE and three of his sons inherited his kingdom, Scipio had been called in as executor and emerged from the process with the youngest son, Gulussa, as his ally. At Carthage the stalemate continued, the summer heat had caused pestilence in the Roman camp and through the autumn the struggle continued. The length of the siege and the strength of Carthaginian opposition and resolve had obviously surprised the Romans. The city remained unbreeched by the year's end.

Early in 148 BCE Scipio returned to Rome with the Carthaginian Phameas, who was rewarded for his treason. The Senate praised Scipio's actions and presented Phameas with gifts. The list of gifts is fascinating and gives us a view into what was considered of great value at the time. He received a purple robe with gold clasps to emphasise his authority, a horse with gold trappings, a complete suit of armour displaying his marshal prowess, and 10,000 silver drachms. They also gave him 100 minas of silver plate and a completely furnished tent. The Roman senators told him that he could expect more if he would just cooperate with them to the end of the war. This Phameas promised to do, and returned to Africa, sailing directly for the Roman winter camp. One of the new consuls, Calpurnius Piso, and his legate Lucius Mancinus sailed to Carthage in the spring of 148 BCE, taking charge of operations there. The Romans maintained the Carthaginian blockade but seem to have largely focused on resistance in the countryside.

The strength and bravery of the resistance Carthage had shown in the face of overwhelming odds had encouraged others across the countryside to hold out against the Romans. Roman supply ships were attacked and towns in the hinterland offered help and resistance, pushing back against the Romans. The Carthaginians rallied and sent out envoys to the cities of Africa and decried the Roman aggression. They even sent envoys to the Antigonid king Perseus in Macedonia, who was fighting a war with the Romans and promising aid and support. Two of the sons of Masinissa were hesitant to join in the Roman expedition and while they spoke of their loyalty to the Roman envoys, they did not engage in the conflict but held back and waited to see the outcome.[7]

What was it like to live in Carthage in these years of siege? The idea of Carthage had been so dominant in the narrative of Rome in the 50 years between the wars that we understand the deep psychological trauma the Romans had suffered from the Hannibalic war dominated many of their decisions. Inside the city of Carthage, the citizens and their families must have been equally haunted by their relentless persecution by the Romans. The Carthaginian memories do not survive, but tensions and conflict within the city do appear throughout the story. Imagine the grief and sorrow when their commander Phameas chose to save himself and his family; the elation when the defence of the city seemed to hold. These feelings are not remembered but must have led to deep stress and turmoil. The commander Hasdrubal who had fought successfully outside the city wall all the previous year now aspired to power inside the city. This position was held by the other Hasdrubal, the grandson of Masinissa. This also made him the nephew of Gulussa, who had been actively fighting on the side of the Romans. One Hasdrubal accused the other of planning to betray the city to his Numidian uncle and in the popular assembly at Carthage there was an uproar. Violence broke out and the man who had so successfully defended the city from the Roman siege was beaten to death.

The atmosphere in Rome was fraught as well. The consuls operating in Africa faced fierce criticism for not taking the city quickly and easily, for seeming to lose ground to the Carthaginians. Factionalism and elite rivalries underpin these criticisms, but there seemed to be serious anger about the fact that it was taking so long to win this war against an enemy who had been disarmed. The popular assembly at Rome demanded that Scipio Aemilianus be made consul for the following year, 147 BCE. Scipio was only standing for the election to the position of aedile in the city. He was too young to be consul as the Roman *cursus honorum* (course of honours), a strict ladder of senatorial appointments, existed so that a young elite had to rise through each stage before reaching the top of the Roman state. The Roman tribune proposed changing the law that declared a consul must have reached the minimum age of 42 so that Scipio could take the position.[8] This proposal allowed Scipio Aemilianus to hold the consulship, and he had Gaius Livius Drusus as his colleague. Again, the popular assembly stepped in to demand that Scipio get the command in Africa as well. This use of the popular assembly at Rome to push through populist political choices was unprecedented and would become more and more significant in the years after the war. It would lead to civil violence in Rome and was one of the reasons the republican system became so broken in the first century BCE.

Another new army was recruited for Scipio and he set sail to Africa to re-join the war effort there and rescue his fellow Romans from their precarious position at the walls of Carthage. In his assessment, the Roman army was in a dire state. The soldiers had become idle, greedy and prone to looting. There was a 'swarm of merchants' who had infiltrated the ranks and trailed around the army solely for the spoils. These merchants even joined unauthorised raids for plunder. Despite the legal consequence of desertion for straying beyond the sound of the trumpet during wartime, forays into the countryside for rape and pillage were rampant. Scipio is said to have recognised that the commander bore responsibility for the failures of his troops and that the sole pursuit of plunder led to internal strife and a decline in morale. There were disputes over loot, including goods and women, that frequently escalated into violence, resulting in injuries and even fatalities among comrades. Considering these challenges, Scipio concluded that victory over the enemy could only be achieved by first restoring discipline and order within his own ranks. Appian's description of the discipline within the army provides an explicit criticism of the previous consul, Piso, but also great insight into the life and environment around a military camp in these years.[9]

The Carthaginians now had to deal with Scipio leading a more disciplined attack on their city. The region of the Megara, the urban garden space of Carthage that had allowed the city to survive the siege and blockade, was the focus of an attack. The Romans scaled the walls and burst open a gate. The Carthaginians rallied and Scipio and his men withdrew – but the damage done to the psyche of the defenders was enormous and emphasised how vulnerable they were. The city commander, Hasdrubal, behaved like a tyrant, not the head of a republic. After the breach of the Megara walls, Hasdrubal took Roman prisoners up to the parapets and tortured and mutilated them in front of the enemy, tossing their bodies down off the walls. The assembly at Carthage was horrified by his actions, so he put those who had protested to death. This gruesome story of torture and mutilation serves to portray Hasdrubal as the unstable and vicious foil for the noble and disciplined Scipio, but also reinforces the extreme pressure the Carthaginians were under, constantly, for all these years.

Scipio focused on the ports and the Roman forces managed to block the entrance, piling up huge stones to make it impassable to the ships inside as well as to any that snuck past the blockade to resupply Carthage from outside. The Carthaginians responded by digging a new entrance to their harbours. The original entrance had been to the south so they began excavating the new entrance in a section of the harbour wall that was positioned facing outward into the middle of the sea towards the east. This made constructing a high bank for protection unfeasible due to the water's depth and the force of the wind. We are told that everyone, even women and children, participated in the digging effort that took place from the inside, covertly. At the same time, the Carthaginians recycled and reclaimed materials to construct new ships, building triremes and quinqueremes and, as Appian notes, 'demonstrated remarkable courage and determination'. They supposedly were able to keep the work secret, to the extent that not even captives could tell Scipio what was happening. Reports from inside the city only noted 'a persistent commotion in the harbour, day and night'. Finally, when all their preparations were complete, the Carthaginians dramatically unveiled the new harbour entrance one day at dawn, sailing out with a fleet comprising 50 triremes and other smaller vessels. There were ships from other cities in the bay around Carthage at that point. Ports like the city of Side came to the aid of their Roman allies in the siege. Side, just southeast of Antalya in modern Turkey, was a key ally of the Romans with a long seafaring tradition. Mostly unmentioned but certainly at play were soldiers and ships from allies and enemies across the Mediterranean fighting on both sides for the soul of Carthage.[10]

The Carthaginians desperately defended their city, using all their 'considerable technical and martial abilities' to foil every attempt the Romans made at entry. They even crossed the bay by night, through the water, to burn a Roman siege engine. As always, each time the relentless Romans came back, with new siege engines and more ships to tighten their blockade. Inch by inch the Romans came closer to taking the city and as the winter of 147 BCE set in they had gained enough of a foothold near the port to build a wall up against the defensive wall of Carthage. Before making his final move, Scipio needed to settle the disrupted countryside and spent much of the early winter months taking back the city of Nepheris (somewhere south of Carthage), which had been held since the previous year by pro-Carthaginian troops under the command of a man named Diogenes. When Scipio won with the aid of the Numidian Gulussa and took back the city, he also defeated a large force of pro-Carthaginians fighters. The stage was set for the final assault.

One spring day in 146 BCE the Romans took the circular harbour of Carthage with a huge effort. They had scaled the walls and launched an attack with relentless numbers. Over the course of that day, the fighting spread into the city itself. First the Romans crossed into the agora (marketplace) adjacent to the harbour. The next morning, with 4,000 fresh troops, Scipio entered the precinct to the temple to the god Resef (Apollo), which dominated the marketplace. A golden statue, housed within a shrine that was crafted from beaten gold, stood resplendent in the temple. The statue weighed 1,000 talents and the soldiers pillaged it, hacking away with their swords, defying their officers' orders until they had divided the spoils among themselves. 'Only then did they resume their fight in the streets of the city.'

Scipio had his soldiers move swiftly to attack the Byrsa hill, the city's strongest position and the location of its original foundation. Many of the population left in the city had sought refuge there while others had stayed in their homes to defend them. There were three streets that ran up from the forum to the citadel, lined with tightly packed six-storey houses. The citizens of Carthage hurled down projectiles on the soldiers as they tried to advance up the hill. The Romans then entered the houses and took them one by one. Street to street, house by house, the fighting progressed. Roman soldiers took one house, then threw planks across the roofs to take the next, hurling the people they found in their homes down on to the streets, killing them all. Once Scipio reached the Byrsa he ordered the houses all burned and the streets cleared of the debris of bodies so that the Roman troops could take the remaining part of the city. So many dead cluttered the way that 'sweepers' were needed to remove them.

The eyewitness account of the destruction preserved in Appian is brutal and vivid as it reveals the death throes of the city and the real victims of war. As the fire in the streets spread and carried on from house to house, as the buildings fell and the sound of their crashing grew louder, the many corpses fell with the stones into the streets. Some citizens were still alive, old men, women and young children who had hidden in the 'inmost nooks of the houses, some of them wounded, some more or less burned, and uttering piteous cries'. Other people fell into the fires from the heights with the collapsing stones and timbers of their houses, and were 'torn apart in all shapes of horror, they were crushed and mangled'.[11]

On Byrsa hill, remnants of Carthage's defenders held out for six days and nights while the city burned around them. The Romans brought in fresh soldiers each day to alleviate their own fighters. Appian's text states this had to be done so that the Roman soldiers would not be worn down by the 'toil, slaughter, want of sleep, and the horrid sights'. The Carthaginian commander Hasdrubal and his wife and children were among those who had sought refuge in the precinct of the temple of Eshmun on the hill.[12] This place was the richest and most sacred of the temples in Carthage, and after seven days of slaughter, envoys from the last holdouts in the temple grounds appeared to Scipio carrying olive branches as symbols of peace and surrender. Scipio granted these envoys their wish of accepting surrender and spared their lives, except for any deserters from the Roman army among them. The refugees from the temple filed out. Appian numbers them at 50,000, which hardly seems credible, even if the temple precinct was large enough to hold that many. It was certainly a large number, though, and in the thousands. Not long after this event the commander of Carthage, Hasdrubal, presented himself in surrender to Scipio, while his wife and children and the Roman deserters and other holdouts remained in the temple. The last survivors climbed on to the roof of the temple and from there the famous scene from the last days of Carthage played out. Hasdrubal's wife berated her husband as a traitor and threw herself and her children into the funeral pyre that their city had become.

Scipio watched the drama unfold and shed his own tears. Appian wrote that the Roman commander was deeply moved while gazing upon this metropolis, which had prospered for seven centuries since its foundation, and 'had ruled over numerous territories, isles, and oceans'. It had been a city with an abundance of weaponry and naval forces, elephants and wealth, talented citizens and creativity, a city rivalling the most powerful empires and one that had surpassed them in courage and resilience. Scipio's remembrances 'turned to the people who had endured relentless warfare for three years without ships or arms and amid famine'. Now, as he watched its demise 'in utter ruin' he wept and openly mourned the fate of this great adversary of Rome.[13] This literary trope of the destroyer weeping for the destroyed was common in Graeco-Roman traditions when describing acts of great brutality, but we can also imagine that the personal ties and long history moved the commander to some degree.

Carthage, after standing proudly on the north coast of Africa for 668 years, had lost and lost completely. The city and its stories became the property of Rome. The year Carthage was burned to the ground the prosperous port city of Corinth in Greece was totally destroyed by Roman troops as well. Both these cities, with their strong and independent identities and long histories, were disposed of and taken over for their commercial potential. They would become key localities of Roman colonies in their future empire and would be integral to Roman success and control of the Mediterranean. The difference with Carthage was that the culture it represented disappeared too. And if the wider perspective tells us how important the strategic location of the city of Carthage was to Rome, it was its wealth and independence and the very thriving culture of the Carthaginians that the Romans subsumed. Carthage was destroyed as much for Roman control of the Mediterranean than for any real fear Rome had of a prosperous old enemy. With this final act of destruction Rome took not only the city of Carthage for itself but also the whole long history and memory of the Carthaginian people as well.

CHAPTER 13

Let There Be No Love or Treaties

At the end we must return again to the beginning and to myth and legend. To when the Augustan poet Virgil wrote achingly of the young Trojan hero Aeneas and his flight across the Mediterranean. To when Aeneas landed on the shores of Africa and met Dido, the wandering queen who had led her people as refugees from Tyre to the new lands of Carthage, to found the new city. Aeneas' tales of Greeks and Trojans at war and the destruction of Troy catapulted the story of Rome and Carthage into the same epic heights. When Aeneas and Dido fell in love, star-crossed lovers became symbols of two great cities on the Mediterranean. But when Aeneas moved on because he had a job to do – to be a founding father of the Roman people – the rupture was permanent. When Dido was left abandoned on the shores of the Mediterranean, she was distraught, betrayed and alone. When Dido committed suicide, hurling a curse on her departed lover and all his descendants, calling for a conqueror to make the Romans pay for his infamy, she became the ultimate woman scorned.

This I pray, these last words I pour out with my blood.
Then, O Tyrians, pursue my hatred against his whole line

and the race to come, and offer it as a tribute to my ashes.
Let there be no love or treaties between our peoples.
Rise, some unknown avenger, from my dust, who will pursue
the Trojan colonists with fire and sword, now, or in time
to come, whenever the strength is granted him.

Virgil, Aeneid 4.621–7[1]

The *Aeneid*, written for Rome's first emperor Augustus late in the first century BCE, used Carthage as the foil for this new imperial age. The poem was a celebration of all things that were dominant about Rome, folding Rome's recent past into its deeper memories of that great war and great victory over Carthage. In the subtext of the *Aeneid*, Dido is the woman who is Carthage, but is also any other woman who has ever tempted a Roman man to ruin. Dido is dangerous; she is Cleopatra, she is all the powers the Romans have conquered. Dido in the *Aeneid* is the enemy feminised and forced to take her own life in the face of Rome's inevitable rise to domination. The first and last women of Carthage both sacrifice themselves, and Rome wins, taking Carthage and its history and memory captive.[2]

This is the most famous and enduring example of how, repeatedly, the story of Carthage was told in Rome in the years after the Punic Wars. As the total obliteration of the Carthaginian people faded into memory, their story became part of the fabric of Rome itself. The epic battles and the woeful destruction of a people and a culture all played out in performances – mock naval conflicts in the amphitheatres and theatres of the whole empire, and in the schoolrooms of Rome – where the characters of Carthage's history were used to fill the souls of young Roman men with moral lessons and a history of long ago.

'Dido's Lament' from Henry Purcell's seventeenth-century opera *Dido and Aeneas* repeats the refrain 'remember me', sung as she watches the man who has spurned her sail off to other lands. And remember her we still do. We understand how the story of these events passed into the popular imagination of the whole Mediterranean through Rome's rise to empire.[3] When a Roman general celebrated a triumph, he paraded through the streets of Rome in a war chariot followed by a long train of loot made up of the enslaved people – men, women and children – who would be sold off as profit. Alongside the captured citizens were the statues, gold and silver, furniture and anything portable from his conquest. These triumphs were also accompanied by scenes from the war that unfolded in front of the eyes of the public. The Romans who fought the wars with Carthage, the successful commanders whose names became legendary – the Scipios, the Fabii, the Marcelli – would have celebrated their own family's successes in funeral speeches, in public monuments and victory temples. The memorial landscape of the Roman victory over Carthage would have crowded the city in the years after the wars. The spoils of Carthage would have been everywhere in the city of Rome in the decades that followed. In this way, the events of all wars were passed into the public view, visually with real captives and imagined action, architecturally through commemoration. What it must have been like to be a descendent of surviving Carthaginians in these years after the war we just do not know but can well imagine the hidden and internalised emotions as the public celebrated and revelled in the story of destruction and death.

The Roman memories only ever told one side of the story and from the moment Scipio Aemilianus triumphed over Carthage the records of his deeds were written down by the Greek Polybius, and by the Roman historians, poets, senators and the wider population. People remembered, vilified and even sympathised with the Carthaginians; it was never a simple tale, but the long residue of these memories has obscured the story. The complexity of this once-great, sophisticated and multicultural African city with a history of innovative technologies, brave warriors and deep religious beliefs was gone. Carthaginian voices did not carry across the centuries, so by the first centuries BCE/CE, when the Roman Empire was formed after long centuries of conquest, the Roman story of Carthage had a starring role in the process. The history of a defeated Carthage was passed on in this way through to the early medieval period in European and Islamic historical accounts, and then translated into vernacular languages across Europe in the early modern period. This pathway turned the story of Carthage and Rome into dramatic tales in English, French, Italian and German, in plays such as Christopher Marlowe's *The Tragedy of Dido, Queen of Carthage* and operas like Berlioz' *Les Troyens* and Purcell's *Dido and Aeneas*, along with more recent outputs like the masterful 1914 silent film *Cabiria* or Thomas Harris's *The Silence of the Lambs* in 1988. Carthage even made an appearance as the wealthy city of Qarth in season two of the original *Game of Thrones* TV series in 2011. The drama of Carthage lives on with us today.

But what of Carthage and the culture of the Carthaginians that survived into the Roman period in the new province of Roman Africa? This new Carthage grew up and prospered in the first centuries CE after the ruins of the destroyed city had smouldered on the shores of Africa for decades. In the direct aftermath of the destruction of Carthage, the exact status of the city was somewhat unclear. The Roman Cicero claims that Scipio consecrated the soil, which would have made it sacrilege to reoccupy the land. Appian only records that the senate ordered Scipio to curse anyone who would settle on the land but did not actually consecrate it.[4] In Appian's exact words, 'the senators decreed that if anything was still left of Carthage, Scipio should raze it to the ground, and that nobody should be allowed to live there.' The place was never forgotten nor was it abandoned for very long, but the curse placed on the city meant that Roman occupation there was, for quite a while, a complicated process.

The Romans did not immediately resettle Carthage but they did occupy Carthaginian territory and created the new Roman province of Africa from it. The organisation of the province of Africa was concurrent with the settlement of the Numidian kings who had supported the Romans in their final assault on the city. A portion of the former territory of the Carthaginians was given to the three sons of Masinissa. These gifts were payment for their support during the war and consisted of the region of the middle Bagradas River. A boundary between the Roman and Numidian territories was marked out by a ditch, which was called the *fossa regia*. This ditch ran roughly from Thabraca (modern Tabarka) on the northern coast to Thaenae on the southeastern coast (roughly equivalent to modern Sfax). The Punic cities that had sided with Rome against Carthage in the final war – places like Utica and Hadrumetum – were recognised with a special status that translates roughly into 'free and immune citizens' (*civitates liberae et immunes*). They were independent cities with free possession of their territories and not subject to heavy Roman taxation. The remaining land in the new province became 'public land' (*ager publicus*) of the Roman people. The senate made some of this land available to Roman/Italian investors to buy or lease. The rest of the land was assigned as 'stipendiary land' (*ager stipendarius*), which meant the native population could keep it but the land was subject to heavy taxation. This was the administrative set-up of the province and the sources tell us that by the end of the second century BCE there were formal associations of Roman citizens existing both within and outside of the new province of Africa.

The territory of the Carthaginians was extremely attractive to the Romans. It was agriculturally wealthy and close to Italy. There were, even before the city fell, a fair number of Roman businessmen around in the period of the Third Punic War. The word 'carpetbaggers' is the modern term for what was going on. The potential of the agricultural wealth, the grain trade, was the major lure for the Romans and other Italians wanting to exploit this new resource.[5] Ultimately, the site of Carthage was too rich, too strategic, too beautiful and too liveable for it to be abandoned for long. Just 24 years after the destruction of Carthage the first Roman colony there was planned. The first attempt at the foundation of a colony was organised by C. Sempronius Gracchus in 122 BCE. The colony was planned on a very large scale, with 6,000 colonists receiving allotments of land of about 53 hectares each. The planning of overseas colonies was a key platform in C. Gracchus' reforming legislations aimed at alleviating land issues in Italy. The new colony was described as being 'on the soil of the destroyed Carthage', despite the curse of Scipio, and the city was renamed Junonia. Juno was one of the Romanised versions of the Punic goddess Tanit, who had been so important to the city. But shortly after Gracchus had returned from his new colony in Africa he was defeated in the Roman senate and assassinated by his political enemies. The colony did not outlast his death but some of the colonists had already set out and taken up their land and so were granted possession of it under a specially issued land law.[6]

The long period of civil violence and unrest that shook Rome after the demise of the Gracchi means that no further formal attempt was made to colonise the site of Carthage for almost 80 years. The Jugurthine War between the Numidian king Jugurtha, an illegitimate grandson of Masinissa, and the Romans (112–106 BCE) did not formally change the situation in Africa and even with the eventual defeat of Jugurtha by the Romans the Numidian kingdom retained a nominal independence and the border between the Roman province and the kingdom remained the same.

During this period the number of Italians and Romans who migrated to the province of Africa continued at a steady pace. Eventually the province was drawn more fully into the civil wars of the Roman Republic's final decades. In these decades the ruined city of Carthage sat smouldering on the shores of the Mediterranean, watching like an audience while the great generals of the Roman Republic destroyed themselves in civil wars. Destroyed Carthage even plays into the narrative of these wars, with the Roman general Marius imagined as seated among the ruins of the city as he hides from his enemy Sulla.[7] This particular scene was one that captured the imagination of later European artists so that the nineteenth-century painting *Marius among the Ruins of Carthage* projects the brooding power of a Roman general dominating the remains of the destroyed enemy (see Fig. 28 in plate section). Next was the turn of the Roman Pompeius Magnus (better known as Pompey the Great) to visit Carthage in 81 BCE.[8] The general stopped to see the famous place of Roman victory while his soldiers were occupied rooting around on the site looking for coins and treasure.

It would not be until the civil war between Pompey and Caesar that any real change took place in terms of how Rome organised its African province. After Caesar's victory over the Pompeian faction at Pharsalus and then Pompey's death in Egypt in 48 BCE, the remaining pro-Pompey forces rallied in Africa under the leadership of Cato the Younger and Metellus Scipio. The king of Numidia, Juba I, also joined their cause. In 46 BCE Julius Caesar was victorious and there was nothing left for Cato the Younger and Juba I to fight for. Both took their own lives in the aftermath of the battle.[9] With Juba's death Caesar annexed the Numidian kingdom and created the province of Africa Nova (New Africa). The boundary between the two provinces remained as it was and there were then two provinces in Africa, Vetus and Nova (old and new). The historian Sallust was appointed as the first governor of the new province. Caesar, in a short time, revived the populist policies of Gracchus towards overseas colonies and established several citizen colonies in Africa and in Hispania. Settling the urban masses of Rome in newly conquered territory was a way to alleviate population pressures in the city and establish centres of Roman citizens in new territories. Caesar's death saw the rise of his nephew Octavian (who became Augustus) and for the most part Caesar's policies of colony building continued under the new regime. As Appian tells it, Caesar was inspired by a dream when he was camped near the site of Carthage during the civil wars. When he awoke, he wrote a memo about it, to refound the city.[10]

Appian tells us that Caesar assigned land at Corinth and Carthage to the poor, that Augustus built the city of Carthage according to Julius Caesar's memo, and that Carthage was repopulated 102 years after its destruction, making it 44 BCE. Cassius Dio says that Augustus was responsible for a new group of colonists in 29 BCE. The colonists of Carthage were Roman citizens and Caesar called his new city *Colonia Concordia Iulia Karthago*, but it remained known as Karthago. At some point in the post-Julius Caesar/pre-Augustus civil wars, the two provinces were amalgamated into one and called Africa Proconsularis, which continued to be a province until the reorganisation of Africa by the emperor Diocletian in circa 285 CE. In 35 BCE, the new Roman city of Carthage became the seat of the provincial governor and became the administrative centre of the new province. From the start, Augustus intended his city to be a grand one. We have, in the *Aeneid*, the description of what is supposedly Dido's Carthage being built, but most accept it is a description of Augustus' new provincial capital. Pliny's *Natural History* describes how 'the colony of Carthage [was built] on the remains of Great Carthage', and the archaeological remains attest to this.[11]

Can the foundation of a Roman colony on the original site of Carthage be considered 'survival'? What did the Roman town planners hope to achieve with their new city, and did they take into consideration the one that had existed before? As the first emperor of Rome built the new city of Carthage, Virgil immortalised the founding queen Dido as a remorseless, scheming woman trying to keep Aeneas from his destiny, and at the same time Livy wrote the history of the wars between Carthage and Rome into orthodoxy. As a new Roman Carthage appeared, the new Rome created a narrative from which the story of Carthage and its battles with Rome were immortalised in the eye of the conqueror. The Byrsa hill at Carthage became the centre of the Roman city, the forum. There the Romans established their core power in a huge construction project. They widened and flattened out the top of the hill, driving huge brick pylons into the ground as the platform for the new forum (see Fig. 29). On the top of the Roman city was a basilica for law courts and a temple, the centre of civic life.

There is more evidence that Carthage and its institutions 'survived' in the broader regions of Africa. There is a bilingual Punic/Latin inscription where magistrates who used the Carthaginian term *sufetes* are attested to in Lepcis Magna in the first century CE, and in Volubilis, now in Morocco, the word *sufet* appears on inscriptions as well. So, across North Africa the words of Carthaginian administrative power continued to be used for

Fig. 29 Carthage, Byrsa hill view with Roman brick pylons in background and Punic houses in foreground

more than a century after its destruction – and words matter. In fact, it is believed that Africa was never so Punic as it was after Carthage was destroyed, for any surviving Carthaginians would have sought refuge across the landscape and created a kind of Punic diaspora. There is clear evidence of religious survival as well. There is a stone-carved stele now in the British Museum (see Fig. 30) that preserves all kinds of imagery directly related to Carthaginian religious beliefs, including the distinctive sign of Tanit and the caduceus connected to the deity Eshmun.

There is a Punic inscription as well, and it tells us that the name of the person who set up the stele was Gaius Julius Arish, son of Adon-Ba'al. We can tell from the name Gaius Julius that this Arish was a Roman citizen, as new citizens of the Roman Empire took on the names of the consuls in the year they were granted citizenship – so here the name comes from the family of

Fig. 30 Stele of Gaius Julius Arish

perhaps Gaius Julius Caesar or his adopted son Augustus. This carved stone gives us evidence for a Carthaginian father and a Roman citizen son on a Punic-styled commemoration. It captures the ways people adapted in and around Carthage during these years. The religion of the Carthaginians merges into Roman cults so that we have the Temple of Juno Caelestis built on the site of the Tophet in Carthage in the Roman period, and the worship of Saturn across the landscape.[12] These deities, Juno Caelestis and Saturn, absorbed the religious attributes of Tanit and Ba'al. The culture of the Carthaginians continued to exist beneath the façade of Roman citizenship.

It is not until the second century CE that Carthage appears fully formed again in literature. It was called 'the muse of Africa' by a second-century writer named Apuleius and was of great symbolic importance to the Romans. The city's post-destruction evolution into a Roman provincial capital and centre for western Christianity, an economic hub with a rich heritage, dominated its history in the post-Punic years. Underneath it all, although most of the people of the original Carthage had been killed or enslaved by the Romans, there were survivors dispersed across Africa and the Iberian Peninsula. We can trace vestiges of the old Carthage and of cultural survival in the former Phoenician cities of North Africa and Iberia through the residue of their language and religions.

Apuleius again serves to illustrate how underneath the veneer of *Romanitas*, of being Roman, lay the vernacular language of the Carthaginians, Punic, which was considered quaint, backward and provincial in the face of the languages of power and culture that dominated the Mediterranean world in these centuries, Latin and Greek. He notes in a document that contains much autobiographical information that his stepson (who had brought a suit against him) 'never speaks except in Punic and from his mother a few words in Greek. He is neither willing nor able to speak Latin.' Here we have the sophisticated multilingual author making fun of his accuser through his reference to the Punic language. So, from Apuleius we learn that the language was still there but had lost its authority and power with the end of Carthage. Punic became a local language, one subsumed by the Roman conquest and its Latin language.[13]

More interesting is the way that Apuleius self-identified as Numidian. He emphasised that he came from a town situated between Numidia and Gaetulia. He expresses his identity in an educated and ironic way of a distant past and its glorious stories when he states that

> I don't know what I should be ashamed of, any more than Cyrus the Great who was also of mixed birth – half Mede and half Persian . . . I did not say this out of any embarrassment of my home town, even if we were still the city of Syphax. When he was defeated, we were graciously allowed by the Roman people to join king Masinissa. (Apuleius, *Apologia* 24.7)

Just a few decades after Apuleius wrote, an African man of Punic heritage became the emperor of Rome. The family of Emperor Septimius Severus (r. 195–203 CE) hailed from the former Punic town of Lepcis Magna. This city, along with Sabratha and Oea (modern Tripoli), were the cities we discussed as the 'emporia', places of Phoenician origin and Carthaginian alliance. The Roman sources express, with some admiration and sarcasm, that the Severan family is so sophisticated that the emperor's uncle did not even have a Punic accent.[14] Even the great Christian bishop and foundational thinker of western Christianity, St Augustine, reminded us that the people in the fields working around his hometown still spoke the Punic language as late as the early fifth century CE. In the late second century CE the African emperor and his relationship to an epic past were explored more fully when Caracalla, also emperor and son of Severus, rebuilt the tomb of Hannibal at a place called Libyssa in Asia Minor. The monument to a glorious Carthaginian past became a place people remarked upon, even paid homage too, well into the medieval period.[15] Severus even officially installed the cult of the goddess Caelestis (*Dea Caelestis*) in Rome – that deity connected to the Romanised version of the worship of the Carthaginian goddess Tanit. In the same period, the city of Tyre began to mint coinage that depicted the tale of Dido building Carthage, illustrating the circle of myth and legendary past that allowed the stories of ancient Carthage to be reinstated in the common language and tradition of the Roman Empire, three centuries after its destruction.

Perhaps the most profound impact on the story of Carthage was its role in the creation of the notion of empire and imperialism in the European imagination, and the knock-on effect on European colonial aspirations. Carthage and the wars it fought with Rome were credited with creating the Roman Empire.[16] The history and tales of the wars preserved in Latin and Greek passed through to early modern traditions so by the sixteenth century there were translations of many ancient texts like Livy into the vernacular languages of Europe. Suddenly, in English, French, Italian and German the story of the epic battle of conquest and imperial domination was widely accessible, and Carthage played a starring role as the defeated enemy. The conceptions of power, conquest and empire in Europe and then North America were modelled on that of republican and imperial Rome, and fundamental to that story were its wars with Carthage. As a result, the identity of the Carthaginians was shaped and remembered through these conflicts. Napoleon famously saw himself as Hannibal crossing the Alps but the British Empire preferred to evoke the Roman victories. More recently the Irish playwright Frank McGuinness used the paradigm to explore British colonial occupation in the aftermath of the 1972 Bloody Sunday events in Northern Ireland in his 1989 play, *Carthaginians*. The tale of Carthage has become mutable depending on who is employing these battles of the past to tell their own stories.

The history of Carthage still resonates and fascinates. The city and its people came up against an implacable enemy who could no longer tolerate their existence – and they were destroyed. Despite the best efforts of the Romans to control their story in the aftermath, we have seen how the physical remains of Carthage are emerging to tell a different narrative of the lost Carthaginians. We can now meet the heroic warriors, beautiful queens and intrepid explorers, the colonisers, villains and victims, along with the priestesses, artists, farmers, merchants, parents, children and grandparents. The story of Carthage is an epic tale that we have followed over the long course of its mythical rise, flourishing power and influence, and ultimate demise. Along this journey we have met many Carthages as it grew from a struggling colonial outpost to a grand city-state and naval power with multicultural and multilingual citizens living in a cosmopolitan city on the sea. This was a place of long history and aspiration populated by proud citizens who cherished their beautiful city, their myths, stories and traditions, and who fought desperately to save it all. Today, the vividly described and horrific destruction still captivates us, but the real Carthaginians can only be understood by joining all the different narratives and the archaeology together. In this way, we can, as Dido demanded in her lament, properly remember them.

Notes

INTRODUCTION: THE BURNING PYRE

1. Appian, *Punic Wars* 8.131; text from Appian's *Roman History*, trans. Horace White. This text is used throughout with some modifications and cited by chapter number in the *Punic Wars* (as *Pun.*) unless the book is otherwise noted.
2. For more on the story of 'Punic' see Prag 2006; also more broadly the various articles in Quinn and Vela 2014 including van Dommelen 2014.
3. See Biggs 2020 on the poetics of the First Punic War and its foundational role in Latin literature.
4. There are many histories of Carthage written in many languages: in English see Miles 2010; also still excellent is Lancel 1995a; all the books of Dexter Hoyos listed in the bibliography offer extensive coverage of key topics; Melliti 2016 and Fantar 2000 provide excellent overviews in French. The essays in Docter et al. 2015 provide an excellent overview of the vast range of material available to study Carthage.

I. CHILDREN OF PHOENIX

1. Translation adapted from Williams 1910.
2. See Giusti 2018 here on Virgil's Dido and also Biggs 2020 on Naevius' and Ennius' roles in the creation of the myth.
3. Justin, *Epitome of Pompeius Trogus* 18.4–6 preserves this account (cited below as Justin, *Ep.* + passage).
4. Appian, *Pun.* 1.1.
5. Other, fourth-century, versions of the story exist too (see FGrH 566 F47) that name two Tyrians, Azoros and Karchedon, as the founders who also appear in *Pun.* 1.1; see Dridi, 2019.

6. See Lopez-Ruiz 2021, pp. 36–7.

7. See Álvarez Martí-Aguilar 2017 on the networking connections between Tyre, Carthage and Gadir/Cádiz.

8. Quintus Curtius Rufus, *History of Alexander* 4.2.2.

9. Possibly Kition on Cyprus carried the same name; Lopez-Ruiz 2021, p. 156. For a counter version of Tyre's history and more balanced contextualisation of the sources see Schmitt 2024.

10. See Cardoso et al. 2016 for the details of the feast and faunal remains. The ancient sources for Utica's foundation are Pliny *Natural History* 16 216; Velleius Paterculus 1.2.4; Silius Italicus 3.241; see Weech et al. 2016 for Utica's history and context.

11. See López Castro et al. 2020 for recent research on Utica and its archaic networks.

12. Justin, *Ep.* 18.5.

13. See Lipiński 2004; Aounallah and Trannoy 2018.

14. Livy, *Ab urbe condita* 1.57.

15. See Giusti 2018 on the Virgil story and the drama of the tale and its meaning.

16. Docter et al. 2005.

17. Polybius, *Histories* 1.73.3–6 (cited below as Polybius + passage).

18. See Katz 2008 on the Uluburun and Tyrian networks.

19. References here from *Iliad* 9.168, 432; and *Iliad* 14.321.

20. See Ezekiel 27:12.

21. Diodorus Siculus, *Library of History* 5.19–20 (cited below as Diodorus Siculus + passage).

22. Herodotus, *The Histories* 5.58 (cited below as Herodotus + passage). For an alternative view see Waal 2022.

23. Homer, *Iliad* 11.632–7. The Euboic Greek alphabetic script is used on the cup. See Gaunt, 2017 on Nestor's cup and its long reception.

2. THE SIGN OF TANIT

1. Description from Gauckler 1915, p. 398, with this translation adapted from Lancel 1995a, p. 77, who notes with a chuckle that Flaubert himself could not have written the description better.

2. For an early sign of Tanit at Megiddo, see Arie 2017.

3. Maybe related to the deity mentioned in Exodus 14:2–4.

4. Inscription found in Marseille assumed to have come from Carthage listed as KAI 69 (CIS 1.165).

5. Translation here from Lupu 2005, Appedix A, KAI 69 (CIS 1.165).

6. 2 Kings 23:10; Jeremiah 7:31.

7. Most of these masks were not found in situ so their full meaning is difficult to assess; they do appear in situ from Tophet sites at Motya on Sicily and Sulci on Sardinia.

8. Melchiorri 2023, 268 for a similar figure from Motya.

9. See Quinn and Vella 2014. There is a large bibliography to – for recent excavations see Ben Jerbania et al. 2020, and also McCarty 2019, Xella 2013, Quinn 2011, Bonnet 2011.

10. For the metallurgical analysis see Kaufman et al. 2016 on the results from excavations at Bir Massouda.

11. Justin, *Ep.* 18–19.

12. This date and reading from Hoyos 2010, p. 26.

13. See Verhelst 2021 for a recent look at the *sufetes*.

14. Or, as Devillers 2000 argues, based on Justin, they were the Hannonids rather than Magonids.

15. Aristotle, *Politics* 2.1273a–b.

16. The many works by Dexter Hoyos on Carthage, especially his *Carthage: A Biography* and *The Carthaginians*, detail what is known about the governmental functions.

17. Here the assumption is made based on later Roman colonial foundations and there is little evidence to prove this point.

18. See Krings 2008 on the agricultural significance of Carthage in the Roman sources; Bechtold and Docter 2010 recorded 80 to 85 per cent local and regional fabrics in the early stratified contexts (seventh to fifth century BCE) at Carthage.

3. BEYOND THE PILLARS OF HERAKLES

1. The original date is debated; my preference is fifth century BCE but for an analysis of the different dates preferred by different scholars see Mederos Martín 2015. Estimates range from the late sixth to the early third century BCE.

2. The two manuscripts are the *Palatinus Graecus* 398 now in Heidelberg, and *Vatopedinus* 655 in the British Museum and Bibliothèque nationale, Paris. Translations are available online at the Internet Archive (used here along with that cited in note 9 below). Pliny, *Natural History* 2.169a; Arrian, *Indica* 43.11–12; possibly Herodotus 4.196ff also refers to these events.

3. See Cunliffe 2023 for an up-to-date assessment of the text in the context of Africa in the ancient world.

4. Herodotus 4.42.6 trans. A.D. Godley.

5. See Rollinger 2023 for an excellent contextualisation of the Achaemenid Persian world around which this story hovers.

6. Herodotus 4.42.4.

7. The map is visible at the Digital Maps of the Ancient World website: https://digitalmapsoftheancientworld.com/ancient-maps/ptolemys-map/.

8. Rollinger 2023.

9. An online version of the text can be read here, https://livius.org/articles/person/hanno-1-the-navigator/hanno-1-the-navigator-2/. The number of ships is surely exaggerated. For Libyphoenician, see the Introduction.

10. Liverani 2000 and Lancel 1992 both clearly set out the details; see also Harrison 2022. Herodotus 4.196 (here translation is adapted from de Selincourt).

11. As there is no agreement in modern scholarship on the interpretation of all the variant parts of the document, this is a version taking a literal approach to the range of travel and intent. Some scholars argue the whole thing is a literary exercise, while Mederos Martin 2015 argues for an expedition to the Canary Islands. The word 'gorilla', used here to refer to the large primates of the name, comes into the Greek vocabulary much later – we do not know what the Carthaginians used in the original.

12. Pliny, *Natural History* 6.198–205.

13. See Melliti 2016, pp. 65–76, on Carthage as an African city.

14. Diodorus Siculus 5.16.

15. Herodotus translation here adapted from Godley.

16. For Cadmus and the links to Phoenicians see Waal 2022.

17. Thucydides, *History of the Peloponnesian War* 1.13.6 and all further references to Thucydides from the same text

18. Or perhaps the alliance was more broadly with west Phoenician city-states rather than just Carthage.

19. See Camporeale 2016 on the Etruscans in the Mediterranean and context for the *tessera hospitalis*; and a variant translation from Naso 2006, p. 190, who reads 'I belong to Piunel the Carthaginian' as the text.

20. Polybius 3.22–7.

21. For the research on Rome and Italy in the early period see Bradley 2020. On the treaties see Serrati 2006 for a full discussion.

22. Polybius 3.23.

23. Sallust, *Bellum Jugurthum* 79.

24. Strabo, *Geography* 3.5.5; Pliny, *Natural History* 5.28.2.

25. The recent reading on the altars of the Philaeni brothers by Quinn 2019a is adopted here.

4. THE THREE-SIDED ISLAND

1. There are variations to the story, and the number of seeds or the months spent shifts, but the essence remains the same.

2. The fascinating story in Diodorus Siculus (4.23.1–3) of Herakles fighting the Sicilian king Eryx for dominion here and the syncretised god, Melqart/Herakles, only enriches the tale of local and wider stories mingling together.

3. Thucydides 6.46.

4. The map shows today's location; there has been land reclamation and sea-level shifts since its ancient occupation.

5. Thucydides 6.2.

6. See Bechtold 2022 and Bechtold and Docter 2010 on the ceramic evidence from Carthage in Sicily.

7. See Visonà 2018 on early Carthaginian coinage.

8. See Prag 2010, especially on the use of the story in Syracusan politics.

9. Herodotus see note 10 p. 306 7.165–7.

10. As told in Diodorus Siculus 11.4ff.

11. See Diodorus Siculus 11.24. The more confusing tale in Herodotus seems to conflate Hamilcar with celebrations of the annual rite of

Melqart, or Carthaginian tales that told of his suicide in the face of the military disaster.

12. Diodorus Siculus 11.1; Herodotus 7.165–7.
13. See more in Rood 2018.
14. The results were published by Reitsema et al. 2022 and Viva 2020.
15. Diodorus Siculus 11.72.3.
16. Pilkington 2019 on Carthaginian imperialism from the Carthaginian source material offers a useful shift of perspective here.
17. Thucydides 6.88.6, 6.34.2.
18. See Pilkington 2019, pp.150–53.
19. Discussed in detail in Pilkington 2019, pp.150–54.
20. Didorus Siculus 14.48.2–14.50.4.
21. Pilkington 2019, p. 155 argues this point.
22. For the sybils in a Greek context, see Ustinova 2009, pp. 156–76.

5. THE AGE OF WARLORDS

1. The best primary source is Diodorus of Sicily 19.5–31.17, based mainly on the now fragmentary history of Timaeus of Tauromenium (Taormina), who hated Agathocles and whose biases are surely embedded in this version; also key is Justin, *Epitome of Pompeius Trogus* – both are used extensively here.
2. For a new history of Agathocles and his time see de Lisle 2021 (pp. 201–28 for Agathocles and Carthage); Justin, *Ep.* 179 for the quote on Agathocles.
3. Plutarch, *Life of Timoleon* 1.
4. Menander, *Aspis* 1.34–7.
5. Diodorus Siculus 18.10.1.
6. Ibid.
7. See Prag 2010 on the Sicilian despots who used Carthage as a foil for their ambitious expansion.
8. Justin, *Ep.* 21.6.1–7.
9. Diodorus Siculus 18.4.4; Justin, *Ep.* 21.6.1–7, these sources were likely trying to make the events in the western Mediterranean and Roman conquests as important as Alexander's.
10. Justin, *Ep.* 21.6.7.

11. Justin, *Ep.* 22.6.

12. Diodorus Siculus 20.8.3–4.

13. This recorded by Justin, *Ep.* 22–3.

14. Diodorus Siculus 20.14.4–7.

15. Diodorus Siculus 20.5–69; Justin, *Ep.* 22–3.

16. Plutarch, *Pyrrhus* 9–10; Diodorus Siculus 21.4, 22.8.2. See Carney 2011 for more on the early Hellenistic queenships.

17. See Lomas 2016 for a good summary of Tarentum in the *Oxford Classical Dictionary*.

18. Justin, *Ep.* 18.1.

19. Strabo, *Geography* 16.2.10. For an in-depth analysis of the Seleucid rule, its ideology and the role of the elephants, see Kosmin 2014.

20. Justin, *Ep.* 18.1.

6. THE BOXING MATCH

1. See van Regenmortel 2024 on soldier's wages and the economic impact; Theocritus, *Idyll* 14, 58–9; and for the high pay offered by Carthage, see Diodorus Siculus 16.81.4.

2. Polybius 1.5.1.

3. Polybius 1.16.

4. Polybius 1.3.7.

5. See de Ligt 2012 and Erdkamp 2011 for assessments of manpower in this period.

6. See Rankov 2011 for a breakdown of these.

7. Thucydides 6.4.4.

8. Polybius 1.17.4–5.

9. Diodorus Siculus 23.9.1; we might be suspicious of this story since Diodorus Siculus 13.19.4 presents a remarkably similar narrative to this one for the Carthaginian sack of the same city in 405.

10. Polybius 1.20.1–2.

11. Polybius 1.20.1–9.

12. Its sister ship was reburied for preservation's sake. See Frost 1981 for the excavation report; also there are excellent resources and visuals available from the Honor Frost Foundation website https://honorfrostfoundation.org/the-punic-ship-of-marsala/.

13. On the Carthaginian Navy see Rawlings 2010.
14. Steinby 2007 on the Romans and their naval experience.
15. Polybius 1.20.15.
16. Polybius 1.20.9.
17. Polybius 1.25ff for the details. See Hoyos 2015, pp. 45–7 on numbers.
18. Diodorus 19.106.3.
19. Valerius Maximus 6.6.2 and Cassius Dio 11, frag. 43.21a.
20. Polybius 1.29.5–6.
21. Polybius 1.29.9.
22. Polybius 1.30.4–15.
23. Polybius 1.31.7–8.
24. Polybius 1.33.5.
25. Polybius 1.36.5.
26. Polybius 1.38.6.
27. Diodorus 24.12; for elaborations on the death see Horace, *Odes* 3.5; Appian *Roman History*, *Pun.* 4 and *Sicelica.* 2.1. See Lazenby 1996a, p. 122 on Regulus.
28. Polybius 1.46.4–13. Is he related to Hamilcar Rhodanus mentioned in Chapter 5? It seems likely but we do not know.
29. Polybius 1.57.1.

7. TRUCELESS WAR

1. See Maraoui Telmini 2011 for references and that most evidence does not come from Carthage itself but more from other sites in North Africa that were not destroyed in the final carnage that burned the city to the ground.
2. The long tunics and pierced ears appear in Plautus, *Poenulus*, circumcision in an offhand comment by the Greek Aristophanes about the Phoenicians; for porridge see Cato, *De Agricultura* 85 and Plautus, *Mostellaria* 828.
3. See Hill 2020 on the Barce connection.
4. Polybius 1.55.7–10, 1.58.2–3.
5. Appian, *Roman History*, Sic. 5.1.
6. Polybius 1.58.9.

7. Polybius 1.61.5–6.
8. Appian, *Roman History*, Sic. 2.1.
9. Polybius 1.66.1.
10. Polybius 1.66.6–67.7.
11. Pliny, *Natural History* 5.24.
12. Hoyos 2007, 39 for the calculation of the coin's value.
13. Polybius 1.68.12; Appian, *Iberica* 4.
14. Polybius 1.67.10–11.
15. Polybius 1.70.6–71.2.
16. Polybius 1.74.9.
17. Polybius 1.74.2–4.
18. Polybius. 1.75–6.
19. Polybius 1.78.9–15.
20. Diodorus Siculus 20.3.3.
21. Polybius 1.79.4.
22. Polybius 1.83.1–5.
23. Eutropius 2.27 and Valerius Maximus 5.1.1 supply the details; Polybius does not.
24. The Roman Livy, whose history now comes into the story, claims five years, *Ab urbe condita* 21.2.1; see also Diodorus Siculus 25.5.6.
25. Livy 21.1 – all quotations from Livy following are from his *Ab urbe condita* (adapted from Yardley's translation as *Hannibal's War*) unless otherwise noted and cited as Livy, plus the book and chapter numbers.
26. Polybius 1.65.6.

8. IMPLACABLE ENEMY OF ROME

1. Strabo, *Geography* 3.5.5.
2. Hercules Gaditanus, as the deity was known in the Roman world; ancient sources continue to mention the temple at Cádiz up until the fifth century CE.
3. Strabo, *Geography* 3.5.5.
4. See Fear 1991 for full details on sources.
5. Justin, *Ep.* 44.5.1–4.

6. The Latin word in Justin, *Ep.* 44.5.1–4 is *consanguineis* – so kin, blood relatives or family implied. See Álvarez Martí-Aguilar 2017 for a full and recent assessment of the passage and its significance.

7. Discussion and full sources in Álvarez Martí-Aguilar 2017, p. 126.

8. For the story see Livy 21.1; Polybius 3.11.5–7. For more details see MacDonald 2015.

9. Valerius Maximus 9.3.2.

10. Cornelius Nepos, *Hamilcar* 4.1 (all references to Nepos found in *On the Great Generals of Foreign Nations*); Diodorus Siculus 25.12.

11. Diodorus Siculus 25.10.1–3.

12. Diodorus Siculus 25.10.3.

13. Álvarez Martí-Aguilar 2017.

14. Cassius Dio frag. 48.

15. Diodorus Siculus 25.10.3.

16. Livy 21.1.1; Diodorus Siculus 25.10.4; Polybius 2.1.8; Cornelius Nepos, *Hamilcar* 4.2.

17. Seibert 1993a.

18. I have written previously about Sigmund Freud's fascinating views on the relationship between Hamilcar and Hannibal, see MacDonald 2015, pp. 43–4

19. Cornelius Nepos, *Hamilcar* 3.3; Livy 21.2.4.

20. Livy 21.4.2–5.

21. Livy 21.4.2–10.

22. On Hasdrubal's marriage see Diodorus Siculus 25.12; Polybius 3.8.1–5.

23. Polybius 2.13.3–7.

24. Zonaras 8.21; Cornelius Nepos, *Hannibal* 13.3.

25. Polybius 3.13.4–8 for the first part of Hannibal's rule.

26. Polybius 3.14.2–10.

27. Livy 21.6.3–6.

28. Polybius 3.15.8. Both Eckstein 1984 and Erdkamp 2009 offer full discussions; see also Hoyos 1998.

29. Polybius 3.30.1.

30. Polybius 3.17.9 and Livy 21.15.3ff cover the events in some detail.

31. Silius Italicus, *Punica* 1.271–2; Livy 21.8.10–12, 21.11.3–5.

9. ON HIS MAURITANIAN BEAST

1. Polybius 2.20.5.
2. Arrian, *Anabasis* 5.26
3. Livy 21.17.1–9.
4. Polybius 3.20.1–7.
5. Cassius Dio 13.54.5.
6. Plutarch, *Pyrrhus* 19.
7. Livy 22.33.1.
8. Polybius 3.33.5–16.
9. Polybius 11.19.4.
10. Polybius 3.39; Livy 21.4.5–8.
11. Polybius 3.35.6.
12. This is the speed of a heavy infantryman based on calculations and research by Anthony Curtis for his PhD (forthcoming, 2026) shared with me over many discussions. Lazenby 1998 is still one of the best treatments, and provides the itinerary followed here.
13. Polybius 3.42.1–4.
14. A recent discussion with full analysis is in Charles 2020.
15. A good analysis of the feasibility of the ancient accounts is in O'Bryhim 1991, pp. 121–4.
16. Extensive bibliography in Mahaney et al. 2017; see also Kuhle and Kuhle 2012 for a contrary view with references.
17. The story includes the felling of trees, which is highly improbable as they would have been above the treeline. Livy 21.37.2–4.
18. According to the measurements of Polybius 3.39. Lazenby 1998 is an excellent and detailed account of the timing and distance.
19. Polybius 3.56.4; Livy 21.38.5.
20. Napoleon's thoughts on Hannibal can be found in Plon and Dumaine (eds.), vol. 29, p. 88f, and vol. 32, p. 307.
21. Polybius 3.47.6–9.
22. Livy 21.41.7.
23. Polybius 3.66.10–67.3.
24. Polybius 3.77.3–7.
25. Polybius 3.75.5; Livy 22.1.1–4.
26. Juvenal, *Satires* 10.158.

27. For the numbers, see Livy 22.36.1–2 and Polybius 3.109.4.
28. Livy 22.49.15–18.

10. THE VICTOR IS NOT VICTORIOUS

1. Livy 22.51.5–52.4.
2. This from Livy (22.57.6), with Roman records of this particular custom of human sacrifice, of Gauls and Greeks, recorded on two other occasions in the Republic (in 228 and 114/113 BCE). The practice was eventually banned by a senatorial decree in 97 BCE (Pliny, *Natural History* 30.12).
3. Ennius, *Annales* frag. 31.493.
4. Livy 23.11.7–12.
5. Livy 23.13.7–8.
6. Livy. 23.33–4 and Polybius 7.9 cover the events of the treaty in detail. The First Macedonian War would be fought in 206/205 BCE by the Romans while the war with Carthage was ongoing.
7. Diodorus Siculus 14.18.4–8.
8. Plutarch, *Marcellus* 15.1–17.4; Polybius 8.7.9; Livy 24.34.16.
9. Strabo, *Geography* 7.2.4.
10. Livy 25.31.9 on Archimedes' death; there are versions in Valerius Maximus 9 and Cicero, *De Finibus* 5.50. Plutarch, *Marcellus* 19.4–6 offers a similar but slightly different account, where Archimedes refused to go to Marcellus until he had finished his equation.
11. See Livy 38.43.9–10 for the loot of Syracuse.
12. Livy 27.4.8.
13. Appian, *Pun.* 67–73.
14. See Valerius Maximus 9.3 ext. 2; Silius Italicus, *Punica* 7.106; Cicero, *Pro Balbo* 34.
15. Livy 25.32.1–2.
16. Livy 25.32.9.
17. Polybius 10.36.3.
18. Livy 26.47.1–2.
19. See the full account in Bellón et al. 2016, pp. 73–104
20. Polybius 10.38.7–10.
21. For the crossing see Livy 27.39.7; Polybius 11.1.1.

22. Livy 27.49.5.
23. Livy 28.35.11.

11. THE FULL CIRCLE

1. Appian, *Pun.* 27.
2. Livy 29.23.1–5.
3. Livy 29.30–33.
4. Livy 29.27–9.
5. For example, see Livy 30.3.4–5.
6. Livy 30.3–6.
7. Ovid, *Fasti* 6.769.
8. See Livy 30.13.1–15.8 for this dramatic scene.
9. Livy 30.16.10–13.
10. Livy 30.23.8; Polybius 15.1.3–4; Cassius Dio 17.74.
11. Polybius 15.3.4; Livy 30.30.11.
12. Polybius 15.10–11.
13. Polybius 15.13–14.
14. Polybius 15.18.1–2; Livy 30.37.2.
15. Appian, *Pun.* 9.66.
16. Appian, *Pun.* 14.96.
17. See Delile et al. 2019 for the publication of the evidence on metalliferous ore mining.
18. Livy 32.2.1–2.
19. For the events leading to Hannibal's exile see Livy 33.47–9; Cornelius Nepos, *Hannibal* 7; Justin, *Ep.* 31.1–2.
20. Plautus, *Mostellaria* 828.
21. Livy 27.16.5.

12. AND THE COMMANDER WEPT

1. Plutarch, *Cato the Elder* 27.1; much of the rest of this chapter is entirely reliant on the events described by Appian and preserved in his *Roman History*. I have cited the passages at the end of each paragraph and used direct quotations in places. A version can be read online: www.livius.org/sources/content/appian/appian-the-punic-wars/.

2. Appian, *Pun.* 10.69–71.

3. Appian, *Pun.* 11.78 records the place but the location is unknown otherwise.

4. Appian, *Pun.* 15.101–4.

5. Appian, *Pun.* 16.105–11.

6. Appian, *Pun.* 19.127–32.

7. Appian, *Pun.* 22.133–6.

8. The *Lex Villia Annalis* i(Livy 40.44.1)n 180 BCE was a law regulating the minimum age for political office along the stages of the *cursus honorum*. See Beck 2005, pp. 51–60.

9. Appian, *Pun.* 17.115.

10. Appian, *Pun.* 18.123.

11. Appian, *Pun.* 19.129.

12. Called the temple of Aesculapius in Appian, *Pun.* 19.130 – the Greek deity considered equivalent to the figure of Eshmun in the Punic pantheon.

13. As paraphrased from Appian, *Pun.* 19.132, who said it as well as it could be written.

13. LET THERE BE NO LOVE OR TREATIES

1. Translated by A.S. Kline © 2002.

2. Giusti 2018 discusses these points in detail and analyses the feminised Carthage for the Roman reader.

3. Here see Quinn 2017.

4. The famous story that the land of Carthage was sown salt is an early modern addition to the destruction. See Ridley 1986, who chases down the story; Cicero, *De Lege Agrarian* 1.5 and 2.51; Appian, *Pun.* 8.135 and *Bellum Civile* 1.24.

5. Polybius 36.7.

6. See Appian, *Pun.* 20.136; Livy, *Epitome* 60; Plutarch, *C. Gracchus* 11. The *Lex Agraria* in 111 BCE, FIRA i. 102–21.

7. For Marius among the ruins see Velleius Paterculus 2.19.4 and Plutarch, *Marius* 40.

8. See Plutarch, *Pompey* 11–13; Appian, *Bellum Civile* 1.80.

9. Cicero, *De Lege Agrarian* 1.5 and 2.51, mentions Rullus' attempt at a colony in 63 BCE.
10. Appian, *Pun.* 20.136.
11. For Cassius Dio see 52.43.1 and 43.50.5; Pliny, *Natural History* 5.24.
12. See Hurst 1999.
13. Apuleius, *Apologia* 98.8; See Harrison, S. 2012.
14. Statius, *Silvae* 4.5.
15. See Moscovich 1990 for the Severan interest in Hannibal and, for Byzantine comment on the tomb, see Johannes Tzetses, *Chiliades* 1.789.
16. For a recent look at this, see Lange 2024.

Bibliography

Altekamp, S., *Karthago: Archäologische Stadtbiographie* (Berlin, Boston: De Gruyter, 2024). https://doi.org/10.1515/9783111333311

Altekamp, S. and Khechen, M., 'Third Carthage: struggles and contestations over archaeological space.' *Archaeologies: Journal of the World Archaeological Congress* 9; 3 (2013): 470–505

Álvarez Martí-Aguilar, M., 'The network of Melqart: Tyre, Gadir, Carthage and the founding god.' In T.N. del Hoyo and F.L. Sánchez (eds.) *War, Warlords, and Interstate Relations in the Ancient Mediterranean* (Leiden: Brill, 2017), pp. 113–50

Aounallah, S. and Trannoy, M.C., 'De Byrsa a Carthage: naissance d'un topynome Carthage.' In A. Aounallah and A. Mastino (eds.) *Carthage: Maîtresse de la Méditerranée, capitale de l'Afrique (IXe siècle avant J.-C.–XIIIe siècle)* (Tunis: Agence de mise en valeur du patrimoine et de promotion culturelle Institut national du patrimoine, 2018), pp. 57–64

Arie, E., 'The earliest known "sign of Tanit" revealed in 11th century BCE building at Megiddo.' *Journal of the Institute of Archaeology of Tel Aviv University* 44; 1 (2017): 61–71

Aubet, M., *The Phoenicians and the West: Politics, Colonies and Trade* (Cambridge: Cambridge University Press, 1993)

Bechtold, B., 'Some remarks on amphorae circulation at Palermo (sixth–second centuries BCE).' In R.F. Docter, E. Gubel, V. Martínez Hahnmüller and A. Perugini (eds.) *Amphorae in the Phoenician-Punic World: The State of the Art*, Ancient Near Eastern Studies Supplement 62 (2022), pp. 211–36

Bechtold, B. and Docter, R., 'Transport amphorae from Punic Carthage: an overview.' In L. Nigro (ed.) *Motya and the Phoenician Ceramic Repertoire between the Levant and the West, 9th to 6th century BC,*

VIII Giornata di Studi Moziesi 'Antonia Ciasca' (Rome, 2010),
pp. 85–116

Beck, H., *Karriere und Hierarchie: Die römische Aristokratie und die Anfänge des cursus honorum in der mittleren Republik*. Klio Beiträge zur Alten Geschichte 10 (Berlin: Akademie Verlag, 2005)

Bellón, J.P. et al., 'An archaeological analysis of a battlefield of the Second Punic War: the camps of the battle of Baecula.' *Journal of Roman Archaeology* 29 (2016): 73–104. https://doi.org/10.1017/S1047759400072056

Bénichou-Safar, H., *Les tombes puniques de Carthage. Topographie, structures, inscriptions et rites funéraires* (Paris: CNRS, 1982)

Bénichou-Safar, H., *Le Tophet de Salammbô à Carthage: essai de reconstitution* (Rome: Collection de L'École Français de Rome, 2004), p. 342

Ben Jerbania, I. et al., 'Nouvelles fouilles dans le sanctuaire de Ba'l Hamon à Carthage.' In S.C. Pérez and E.R. González (eds.) *Un viaje entre el Oriente y el Occidente del Mediterráneo*, IX Congresso Internacional de Estudios Fenicios y Púnicos, Mérida, MYTRA, Monografías y Trabajos de Arqueología, Instituto de Arqueología 5 (2020): 1141–56

Biggs, T., *Poetics of the First Punic War* (Ann Arbor: University of Michigan Press, 2020)

Bingham, S., and MacDonald, E., *Carthage: Archaeological History* (London, New York: Bloomsbury Press, 2024)

Bockmann, R., 'African Rome: the city of Carthage from its Roman (re-) foundation to the end of the Byzantine period.' In R.B. Hitchner (ed.) *A Companion to North Africa in Antiquity* (Hoboken, NJ: John Wiley & Sons Inc., 2022), pp. 117–41

Bockmann, R., et al., 'The SW quarter of Carthage and its main monument: new results on the topographical context, construction and development of the circus, based on fieldwork 2015–17.' In J.H. Humphrey (ed.) *For the Love of Carthage* (Portsmouth, RI: Journal of Roman Archaeology Supplementary Series 109, 2020), pp. 50–74

Bondì, S., Botto, M., Garbati, G. and Oggiano, I., *Fenici e cartaginesi: una civiltà mediterranea* (Rome: Istituto Poligrafico e Zecca dello Stato, 2009)

Bonnet, C., 'On gods and earth: the Tophet and the construction of a new identity in Punic Carthage.' In E.S. Gruen (ed.) *Cultural Identity in the Ancient Mediterranean* (Los Angeles: Getty Research Institute, 2011), pp. 373–87

Bradley, G., *Early Rome to 290 BC: The Beginnings of the City and the Rise of the Republic* (Edinburgh: Edinburgh University Press, 2020)

Brett, M. and Fentress, E., *The Berbers* (Oxford: Blackwell, 1996)

Burgeon, C., *La troisième guerre punique et la destruction de Carthage* (Paris: L'Harmattan, 2015)

Camporeale, G., 'The Etruscans and the Mediterranean.' In S. Bell and A.A. Carpino (eds.) *A Companion to the Etruscans* (Chichester: John Wiley & Sons, 2016), pp. 67–86

Cardoso, J.L., et al., 'What the people of Utica (Tunisia) ate at a banquet in the 9th century BCE: zooarchaeology of a North African early Phoenician settlement.' *Journal of Archaeological Sciences* 8 (2016): 314–22

Carney, E., 'Being royal and female in the early Hellenistic period.' In A. Erskine and L. Llewellyn-Jones (eds.) *Creating a Hellenistic World* (The Classical Press of Wales, 2011), pp. 195–220

Cazeau, M., 'Massinissa et Syphax. Un diptyque barbare chez Tite-Live.' Formes du portrait (Paris: Classiques Garnier, 2017), pp. 189–210

Charles, M.B., 'The African elephants of antiquity revisited: habitat and representational evidence.' *Historia* 69; 4 (2020): 392–407

Chelbi, F., 'Recherches sur la topographie Carthaginoise: neapolis et mégara: l'extension urbaine de carthage du IVe s. jusqu'à 146 av. j.-c' in *AFRICA Revue des études et recherches préhistoriques, antiques, islamiques et ethnographiques* vol. 24, (INP, Tunis, 2017): 13–28

Crawford, M., *Roman Republican Coinage*, vols 1 and 2 (Cambridge: Cambridge University Press, 1974)

Crawford, M., *Coinage and Money under the Roman Republic* (London: Methuen, 1985)

Crawford, M., *The Roman Republic*, 2nd edn (London: Fontana, 1992)

Crawford, M. (ed.), *Imagines Italicae: A Corpus of Italic Inscriptions*, 3 vols (London: The Institute of Classical Studies, University of London, 2011)

Cristofori, A., 'The maritime city in Graeco-Roman perception. Carthage and Alexandria: two emblematic examples.' In L. François and

A. Isaacs (eds.) *The Sea in European History* (Pisa: Edizioni PLUS, 2001), pp. 1–24

Cullingford, E., 'British Romans and Irish Carthaginians: anti-colonial metaphor in Heaney, Friel and McGuinness.' *Publications of the Modern Language Association* 111; 2 (1996): 222–39

Cunliffe, B., *Facing the Sea of Sand: The Sahara and the Peoples of Northern Africa* (Oxford: Oxford University Press, 2023)

Dalaine, L., 'Par quel col Hannibal est-il passé? Une literature sans fin ... ' In J.-P. Jospin and L. Dalaine (eds.) *Hannibal et les Alpes: une traversée, un mythe* (Gollion: Infolio Editions, 2011), pp. 126–37

Daly, G., *Cannae: The Experience of Battle in the Second Punic War* (London: Routledge, 2002)

Delile, H., et al., 'Economic resilience of Carthage during the Punic Wars: insights from sediments of the Medjerda delta around Utica (Tunisia).' *Environmental Sciences* 116; 20 (2019): 9764–9

De Ligt L., *Peasants, Citizens and Soldiers: Studies in the Demographic History of Roman Italy 225 BC–AD 100* (Cambridge: Cambridge University Press, 2012)

De Lisle, C., *Agathokles of Syracuse: Sicilian Tyrant and Hellenistic King* (Oxford: Oxford University Press, 2021)

Devillers, O., '"Magonides" ou "Hannonides"? A propos de Justin, Historiae Philippicae, XIX, 1, 1.' *ACFP* IV, 1, Actes du quatrième Congrès des Études Phéniciennes et Puniques, Cadix, 2–6 Octobre 1995 (Cádiz: Servicio de Publicaciones, Universidad de Cádiz, 2000), pp. 147–51

Doak, B. and López-Ruiz, C. (eds.), *The Oxford Handbook of the Phoenician and Punic Mediterranean* (Oxford: Oxford University Press, 2019)

Docter, R., 'Carthage and its hinterland.' In S. Helas and D. Marzoli (eds.) *Phönizisches und Punisches Städtewsen (Iberia Archaeologica 13)* (Mainz: P. von Zabern, 2009), pp. 179–89

Docter, R., Boussoffara, R. and ter Keurs, P. (eds.), *Carthage: Fact and Myth* (Leiden: Sidestone Press, 2015)

Docter, R., et al., 'Carthage Bir Massouda: preliminary report on the first bilateral excavations of Ghent University and the Institut National du Patrimoine (2002–2003).' *BABESCH* 78 (2004): 43–70

Docter, R., et al., 'Radiocarbon dates of animal bones in the earliest levels of Carthage.' In G. Bartolini and F. Delpino (eds.) *Oriente e*

Occidente: metodi e discipline a confronto: Riflessioni sulla cronologia dell'età del ferro in Italia (Pisa, Rome: Istituti Editoriali e Poligrafici Internazionali, 2005), pp. 557–75

Docter, R., et al, 'Punic Carthage: two decades of archaeological investigations.' In J.L. López Castro (ed.) *Las ciudades fenicio-púnicas en el Mediterráneo Occidental* (Almería: Centro de Estudios Fenicios y Púnicos, 2007), pp. 85–104

Dridi, H., 'Early Carthage: from its foundation to the battle of Himera (ca. 814–480 BCE).' In B.R. Doak and C. López-Ruiz (eds.) *The Oxford Handbook of the Phoenician and Punic Mediterranean* (Oxford Handbooks, 2019; online edn, Oxford Academic, August 2019), pp. 140–54

Eckstein, A., 'Rome, Saguntum and the Ebro Treaty.' *Emerita* 52; 1 (1984): 51–68

Erdkamp, P., 'Polybius, the Ebro Treaty and the Gallic invasion of 225 BCE.' *Classical Philology* 104; 4 (2009): 495–510

Erdkamp, P., 'Manpower and food supply in the First and Second Punic Wars.' In D. Hoyos (ed.) *A Companion to the Punic Wars* (London, New York: Blackwell Publishing Ltd, 2011), pp. 58–76

Erskine, A., 'Hannibal and the freedom of the Italians.' *Hermes* 121; 1 (1993): 58–62

Fantar, H., *Carthage: approche d'une civilisation* (Paris: CNRS, 2000)

Fear, A., 'The dancing girls of Cadiz.' *Greece and Rome* 38; 1 (1991): 75–9

Fentress, E., 'Romanizing the Berbers.' *Past and Present* 190; 1 (2006): 3–33

Fentress, E. and Docter, R., 'North Africa: rural settlement and agricultural production.' In P. van Dommelen and C. Gómez-Bellard (eds.) *Rural Landscapes of the Punic World* (London, Sheffield, Oakville: Equinox, 2008), pp. 101–28

Ferjaoui, A. (ed.), *Carthage et les autochtones de son empire du temps de Zama.* Colloque international organisé à Siliana et Tunis due 10 au 13 mars 2004 par l'Institut National du Patrimoine et l'Association de Sauvegarde du site de Zama, hommage à Mhamed Hassine Fantar (Tunis: Institut national du patrimoine, 2010)

Ferjaoui, A. and Redissi, T. (eds.), *La vie, la mort et la religion dans l'univers phénicien et punique.* Actes du VIIème colloque international des études phéniciennes et puniques (Tunis: Institut national du patrimoine, 2019)

Franko, G., 'The use of *Poenus* and *Carthaginiensis* in early Latin literature.' *Classical Philology* 89; 2 (1994): 153–8

Franko, G., 'The characterization of Hanno in Plautus' Poenulus.' *American Journal of Philology* 117; 3 (1996): 425–52

Fronda, M., *Between Hannibal and Rome: Southern Italy during the Second Punic War* (Cambridge: Cambridge University Press, 2010)

Fronda, M., 'Hannibal: Tactics, Strategy, and Geostrategy', in D. Hoyos (ed.), *A Companion to the Punic Wars* (Oxford: Blackwell, 2011): 242–259

Frost, H., 'The Punic wreck in Sicily, second season of excavation.' *International Journal of Nautical Archaeology* 3; 1 (1974): 35–40

Frost, H., et al., 'Lilybaeum (Marsala) – the Punic ship: final excavation report.' *Notizie degli scavi di antichità* 8 (Supplement vol. 30, 1976) (Rome: Accademia Nazionale dei Lincei, 1981)

Fumadó Ortega, I., 'Colonial representations and Carthaginian archaeology.' *Oxford Journal of Archaeology* 32; 1 (2013): 53–72

Fumadó Ortega, I., 'Punic Carthage.' In R. Hitchner (ed.) *A Companion to North Africa in Antiquity* (Hoboken, NJ: John Wiley & Sons Inc., 2022), pp. 81–100

Gaunt, J., 'Nestor's Cup and Its Reception'. In *Voice and Voices in Antiquity* (Leiden, The Netherlands: Brill, 2017): 92–120

Gauckler, P., *Nécropoles puniques de Carthage* (Paris: Picard, 1915)

Giusti, E., *Carthage in Virgil's 'Aeneid': Staging the Enemy under Augustus* (Cambridge: Cambridge University Press, 2018)

Goldsworthy, A., *The Fall of Carthage* (London: Cassell, 2003)

Goldsworthy, A., *Cannae* (London: Phoenix, 2007 [2001])

Gruen, E., 'The consular elections for 216 BC and the veracity of Livy.' *California Studies in Classical Antiquity* 11 (1978): 61–74

Gruen, E., *The Hellenistic World and the Coming of Rome* (Berkeley: University of California Press, 1986 [1984])

Gruen, E., *Studies in Greek Culture and Roman Policy* (Berkeley: University of California Press, 1990)

Gruen, E., *Culture and Identity in Republican Rome* (Ithaca: Cornell University Press, 1992)

Gruen, E. (ed.), *Cultural Identity in the Ancient Mediterranean* (Los Angeles: Getty Research Institute, 2011)

Gruen, E., '*Punica fides.*' In *Rethinking the Other in Antiquity* (Princeton, Oxford: Princeton University Press, 2011), pp. 115–40

Harrison, S., '*Milesiae Punicae*: how Punic was Apuleius?' In T. Whitmarsh and S. Thomson (eds.), *The Romance Between Greece and the East* (Cambridge: Cambridge University Press, 2012), pp. 211–24

Harrison, T., 'History as contagion? Herodotus on silent trade (4.196).' *Syllogos* 1 (2022): 1–30

Hill, A., 'Hamilcar of Barce? Discerning Barcid proto-history and Polybius' *Mixellēnes.*' article not included elsewhere e.g. *Journal of Roman Archaeology Journal of Hellenic Studies* 140 (2020): 69–105

Hobson, M., 'Carthage after the Punic Wars and the Neo-Punic legacy.' In B.R. Doak and C. López-Ruiz (eds.) *The Oxford Handbook of the Phoenician and Punic Mediterranean* (Oxford Handbooks, 2019; online edn, Oxford Academic, 12 August 2019)

Hoyos, D., *Unplanned Wars: The Origins of the First and Second Punic Wars* (Berlin: Walter de Gruyter, 1998)

Hoyos, D., *Hannibal's Dynasty: Power and Politics in the Western Mediterranean, 247–183 BC* (Oxford: Routledge, 2003)

Hoyos, D., *Truceless War: Carthage's Fight for Survival, 241–237 BC* (Leiden: Brill, 2007)

Hoyos, D., *The Carthaginians* (Oxford, New York: Routledge, 2010)

Hoyos, D., *Mastering the West: Rome and Carthage at War* (Oxford: Oxford University Press, 2015)

Hoyos, D., *Carthage: A Biography* (London: Routledge, 2021)

Hunt, P., 'The locus of Carthage, compounding geographical logic.' *African Archaeological Review* 26 (2009): 137–54

Hurst, H., 'The sanctuary of Tanit at Carthage in the Roman period: a re-interpretation.' *Journal of Roman Archaeology*, Supplementary Series Number 30 (1999): 1–95

Katz, H., 'The ship from Uluburun and the ship from Tyre: an international trade network in the ancient Near East.' *Zeitschrift des Deutschen Palästina-Vereins (1953–)* 124; 2 (2008): 128–42

Kaufman, B., 'The political economy of Carthage: the Carthaginian constitution as reconstructed through archaeology, historical texts, and epigraphy.' In P.S. Avetisyan and Y.H. Grekyan (eds.) *Bridging Times and Spaces: Papers in Ancient Near Eastern, Mediterranean, and Armenian*

Studies. Festschrift in Honour of Gregory E. Areshian on the Occasion of His Sixty-Fifth Birthday (Oxford: Archaeopress, 2017), pp. 201-13

Kaufman, B., et al., 'Ferrous metallurgy from the Bir Massouda metallurgical precinct at Phoenician and Punic Carthage and the beginning of the North African Iron Age.' *Journal of Archaeological Science* 71 (2016): 33-50

Kosmin, P.J., *The Land of the Elephant Kings: Space, Territory, and Ideology in the Seleucid Empire* (Cambridge, MA: Harvard University Press, 2014)

Krahmalkov, C., *Phoenician–Punic Dictionary, Studia Phoenicia XV* (Leuven: Orientalia Lovaniensia Analecta 90, 2000)

Krings, V., *La civilisation phénicienne et punique: Manuel de recherché* (Leiden: Brill, 1995)

Krings, V., *Carthage et les Grecs, 580–480 av. J.-C.* (Leiden: Brill, 1998)

Krings, V., 'La critique de Sosylos chez Polybe III 20.' In G. Schepens and J. Bollansée (eds.) *The Shadow of Polybius: Intertextuality as a Research Tool in Greek Historiography*, Studia Hellenistica 42 (Leuven, 2005), pp. 223-36

Krings, V., 'Rereading Punic agriculture: representation, analogy and ideology in the classical sources.' In P. van Dommelen and G. Gómez Bellard (eds.) *Rural Landscapes of the Punic World*: *Studies in Mediterranean Archaeology*, vol. II (London: Equinox, 2008), pp. 22–43

Kuhle, M. and Kuhle, S., 'Hannibal gone astray? A critical comment on W.C. Mahaney et al. "The Traversette (Italia) rockfall: geomorphological indicator of the Hannibalic invasion route." *Archaeometry* 52; 1 [2010]: 156–72).' *Archaeometry* 54; 3 (2012): 591–601

Kunze, C., 'Carthage and Numidia, 201–149 BC.' In D. Hoyos (ed.) *A Companion to the Punic Wars* (Malden, MA: Wiley-Blackwell, 2011), pp. 393–411

Kuttner, A., 'Representing Hellenistic Numidia, in Africa and at Rome.' In J. Crawley Quinn and J. Prag (eds.) *The Hellenistic West: Rethinking the Ancient Mediterranean* (Cambridge: Cambridge University Press, 2013), pp. 216–72

Lancel, S., 'La renaissance de la Carthage punique. Réflexions sur quelques enseignements de la campagne international patronnée par l'UNESCO.' *Comptes rendu des séances de l'Académie des Inscriptions et Belles-Lettres* 129; 4 (1985): 727–51

Lancel, S., *Carthage* (Paris: Fayard, 1992)

Lancel, S., *Carthage: A History*, tr. Antonia Nevill (Oxford: Blackwell Publishers, 1995a)

Lancel, S., *Hannibal* (Paris: Fayard, 1995)

Lancel, S., *Saint Augustin* (Paris: Fayard, 1999)

Lange, C.H., *From Hannibal to Sulla: The Birth of Civil War in Republican Rome*, Studies in Ancient Civil War, vol. 1 (Berlin, Boston: De Gruyter, 2024)

Lazenby, J., *The First Punic War* (London: UCL Press, 1996a)

Lazenby, J., 'Was Maharbal right?' In T. Cornell, B. Rankov and P. Sabin (eds.) *The Second Punic War: A Reappraisal* (London: Institute of Classical Studies, University of London, 1996b), pp. 39–48

Lazenby, J., *Hannibal's War: A Military History of the Second Punic War*, paperback edn (1978) (Norman: University of Oklahoma, 1998)

Lazenby, J., 'Rome and Carthage.' In H. Flower (ed.) *The Cambridge Companion to the Roman Republic* (Cambridge: Cambridge University Press, 2004), pp. 225–41

Le Bohec, Y., 'The "Third Punic War": the siege of Carthage (148–146 BC).' In D. Hoyos (ed.) *A Companion to the Punic Wars* (Malden, MA: Wiley-Blackwell, 2011), pp. 430–45

Leigh, M., *Comedy and the Rise of Rome* (Oxford: Oxford University Press, 2004)

Leveau, P. and Mercalli, L., 'Hannibal et les Alpes: l'identification du col franchi et son context environmental.' In J.-P. Jospin and L. Dalaine (eds.) *Hannibal et les Alpes: une traversée, un mythe* (Gollion: Infolio Editions, 2011), pp. 94–106

Levene, D., *Livy on the Hannibalic War* (Oxford: Oxford University Press, 2010)

Lewis, D.M., 'Punic Carthage' In *Greek Slave Systems in their Eastern Mediterranean Context, c. 800–146 BC* (online edn, Oxford Academic, 20 September 2018). https://doi.org/10.1093/oso/9780198769941.003.0014, accessed 4 April 2024

Lipiński, E., *Dieux et déeses de l'univers phénicien et punique* (Leuven, 1995)

Lipiński, E., *Itineraria Phoenicia*, Studia Phoenicia 18, Orientalia Lovaniensia Analecta 127 (Leuven, 2004)

Lo Cascio, E., 'Recruitment and the size of the Roman population from the third to the first century BCE.' In W. Scheidel (ed.) *Debating Roman Demography* (Leiden: Brill, 2001), pp. 111–37

Lomas, K., 'Rome, Latins, and Italians in the Second Punic War.' In D. Hoyos (ed.) *A Companion to the Punic Wars* (Malden, MA: Wiley-Blackwell, 2011): 339–56

Lomas, K., 'Tarentum.' *Oxford Classical Dictionary* (2016)

López Castro, J.L., et al., 'Nouvelles recherches sur la période archaïque d'Utique.' In J.L. Castro (ed.) *Entre Utica y Gadir: navegación y colonización fenicia en el Mediterráneo Occidental a comienzos del I Milenio AC* (Granada, 2020): 55–80

López-Ruiz, C., 'Tarshish and Tartessos revisited: textual problems and historical implications.' In M. Dietler and C. López-Ruiz (eds.) *Colonial Encounters in Ancient Iberia: Phoenician, Greek and Indigenous Relations* (Chicago: University of Chicago Press, 2009), pp. 255–80

López-Ruiz, C., *Phoenicians and the Making of the Mediterranean* (Cambridge, MA: Harvard University Press, 2021)

López-Ruiz, C. and Doak, B. (eds.), *The Oxford Handbook of the Phoenician and Punic Mediterranean* (Oxford: Oxford University Press, 2022)

Lupu, E., *Greek Sacred Law: A Collection of New Documents (NGSL)* (Leiden, Boston: Brill, 2005)

Ma, J., *Antiochus III and the Cities of Western Asia Minor* (Oxford: Oxford University Press, 1999)

MacDonald, E., *Hannibal: A Hellenistic Life* (New Haven: Yale University Press, 2015)

MacDonald, E. and Bingham, S., 'Piracy, plunder and the legacy of archaeological research in North Africa.' In R. Evans and M. De Marre (eds.) *Piracy, Pillage and Plunder in Antiquity: Appropriation and the Ancient World* (London: Routledge, 2020), pp. 170–84

Maes, A., 'L'Habillement masculin à Carthage à l'époque des guerres punique.' In H. Devijver and E. Lipiński (eds.) *Studia Phoenicia X: The Punic Wars* (Leuven, 1989), pp. 15–24

Mahaney, W., *Hannibal's Odyssey: Environmental Background to the Alpine Invasion of Italia* (Piscataway, NJ: Gorgias Press, 2009)

Mahaney, W., 'Comments on M. Kuhle and S. Kuhle (2012): "Hannibal gone astray? A critical comment on W.C. Mahaney et al. 'The Traversette (Italia) rockfall: geomorphological indicator of the Hannibalic invasion route' (*Archaeometry*, 52; 1 [2010]: 156–72)."' *Archaeometry* 55; 6 (2013): 1196–204

Mahaney, W.C., et al., 'Biostratigraphic evidence relating to the age-old question of Hannibal's invasion of Italy, II: chemical biomarkers and microbial signatures.' *Archaeometry* 59; 1 (2017): 179–90. https://doi.org/10.1111/arcm.12228

Malkin, I. (ed.), *Mediterranean Paradigms and Classical Antiquity* (London: Routledge, 2005)

Malkin, I., *A Small Greek World: Networks in the Ancient Mediterranean* (Oxford: Oxford University Press, 2011)

Maraoui Telmini, B., 'Découverte de latrines puniques du 5ème siècle av. J.-C. à Carthage (Bir Massouda).' *BABESCH: Annual Papers on Mediterranean Archaeology* 86 (2011): 53–70

Maraoui Telmini, B., et al., 'Defining Punic Carthage.' In J. Quinn and N. Vella (eds.) *The Punic Mediterranean: Identities and Identification from Phoenician Settlement to Roman Rule* (Cambridge: Cambridge University Press, 2014), pp. 113–47

McCarty, M.M., 'The Tophet and infant sacrifice.' In C. López-Ruiz and B.R. Doak (eds.) *The Oxford Handbook of the Phoenician and Punic Mediterranean* (Oxford: Oxford University Press, 2019). https://doi.org/10.1093/oxfordhb/9780190499341.013.21, accessed 1 April 2024

McDonnell, M., 'Rome aesthetics and the spoils of Syracuse.' In K. Welch (ed.) *Representations of War in Ancient Rome* (Cambridge: Cambridge University Press, 2006), pp. 68–90

Mederos Martín, A., 'The Exploration of the North African Atlantic Coast According to the Periplus of Hanno of Carthage', *Gerion – Revista de Historia Antigua* 33 (2015): 15–45

Melchiorri, V., 'The iconography of children as cultic characters in Mediterranean tophet precincts' *Journal of Ancient History* 11; 2 (2023): 259–76

Melliti, K., *Carthage: Histoire d'une métropole méditerranéenne* (Paris: Perrin, 2016)

Miles, R., *Carthage Must Be Destroyed: The Rise and Fall of an Ancient Civilisation* (London: Allen Lane, 2010)

Miles, R., 'Hannibal and propaganda.' In D. Hoyos (ed.) *A Companion to the Punic Wars* (Malden, MA: Wiley-Blackwell, 2011), pp. 260–79

Mineo, B., 'Principal literary sources for the Punic Wars (apart from Polybius).' In D. Hoyos (ed.) *A Companion to the Punic Wars* (Malden, MA: Wiley-Blackwell, 2011), pp. 111–27

Morrison, J., 'The Trireme.' In R. Gardiner (ed.) *The Age of the Galley: Mediterranean Oared Vessels Since Pre-Classical Times* (London: Conway Maritime Press, 1995), pp. 49–65

Morrison, J., *Greek and Roman Oared Warships, 399–30 BC* (Oxford: Oxbow, 1996)

Moscati, S., 'Fenicio o punico o cartaginese.' *Rivista di Studi Fenici* 16; 1 (1988): 3–13

Moscati, S. (ed.), *The Phoenicians* (London: I.B. Tauris, 2001 [1997])

Moscovich, M.J., 'Septimius Severus and the tomb of Hannibal.' *Ancient History Bulletin* 4; 5 (1990): 108–12

Murray, W., *The Age of Titans: The Rise and Fall of the Great Hellenistic Navies* (Oxford: Oxford University Press, 2012)

Naso, A., 'Etruscan and Italic finds in North Africa, 7th–2nd century BC.' In A. Villing and U. Schlotzhauer (eds.) *Naukratis: Greek Diversity in Egypt* (London: The British Museum Press, 2006), pp. 187–98

Naso, A. (ed.), *Etruscology*, vol. 1 (Boston, Berlin: de Gruyter, 2017)

Neville, A., *Mountains of Silver and Rivers of Gold: The Phoenicians in Iberia* (Oxford: Oxbow, 2007)

Niemeyer, H., 'Expansion et colonisation.' In V. Krings (ed.) *La civilization phénicienne et punique: Manuel de recherche* (Leiden: Brill, 1995), pp. 247–67

O'Bryhim, S., 'Hannibal's elephants and the crossing of the Rhône.' *Classical Quarterly*, New Series, 41; 1 (1991): 121–5

Palmer, R., *Rome and Carthage at Peace* (Stuttgart: F. Steiner, 1997)

Papadopoulos, J.K., 'The Motya Youth: Apollo Karneios, art, and tyranny in the Greek West.' *Art Bulletin* 96; 4 (2014): 395–423

Peters, S. (ed.), *Hannibal ad Portas: Macht und Reichtum Karthago* (Stuttgart: Theiss, 2004)

Picard, C., Sacra Punica: Études sur les *masques et rasoirs* de Carthage. *Karthago* 13 (Paris, 1967a: 1–115)

Picard, C. and Picard, G.-C., *Vie et mort de Carthage* (Paris: Hachette, 1970)

Picard, C., *Hannibal* (Paris, 1967b)

Picard, C., 'Les réprésentations du sacrifice molk sur les ex-voto de Carthage.' *Karthago* 17 (1975): 67–138

Picard, G.-C., 'Est-il possible d'écrire une histoire de Carthage?' Atti del i Congresso Internazionale di Studi Fenici e Punici, Rome, 1 (1983): 279–83

Picard, G.-C., 'Hannibal hégémon hellénistique.' *Rivista Storica dell'Antichità*, 14 (1984), pp. 75–81

Picard, G.-C. and Picard, C., *La vie quotidienne à Carthage au temps d'Hannibal* (Paris: Hachette, 1958)

Pietilä-Castrén, L., *Magnificentia Publica: The Victory Monuments of the Roman Generals in the Era of the Punic Wars*, Commentationes Humanarum Litterarum 84 (Helsinki, 1987)

Pilkington, N., *The Carthaginian Empire: 550–202 BCE* (Lanham, MD: Lexington Books, 2019)

Plon, H. and Dumaine, J. (eds.), *Correspondance de Napoléon Ier publiée par ordre de l'empereur Napoléon III, vol. 1–32* (Paris: Henri Plon, 1858–1870)

Potter, D., 'The Roman army and navy.' In H. Flower (ed.) *The Cambridge Companion to the Roman Republic* (Cambridge: Cambridge University Press, 2004), pp. 66–88

Prag, J., '*Poenus plane est* – but who were the "Punickes"?' *Papers of the British School at Rome* 74 (2006): 1–37

Prag, J., 'Tyrannizing Sicily: the despots who cried "Carthage!"' In *Private and Public Lies* (Leiden: Brill, 2010)

Prag, J. and Quinn, J.C. (eds.), *The Hellenistic West: Rethinking the Ancient Mediterranean* (Cambridge: Cambridge University Press, 2013)

Quinn, J.C., 'The cultures of the Tophet: identification and identity in the Phoenician diaspora.' In E.S. Gruen (ed.) *Cultural Identity in the Ancient Mediterranean* (Los Angeles: Getty Research Institute, 2011), pp. 388–413

Quinn, J.C., 'Translating empire from Carthage to Rome.' *Classical Philology* 112; 3 (2017): 312–31

Quinn, J.C., *In Search of the Phoenicians* (Princeton: Princeton University Press, 2018)

Quinn, J.C., 'Phoenicians and Carthaginians in Greco-Roman literature.' In B.R. Doak and C. López-Ruiz (eds.), *The Oxford Handbook of the Phoenician and Punic Mediterranean* (Oxford Handbooks, 2019; online edn, Oxford Academic, August 2019)

Quinn, J.C., 'Une frontière dans la mer? Les autels des frères Philènes entre Carthage et Cyrène.' In A. Ferjaoui and T. Redissi (eds.) *La vie, la mort et la religion dans l'univers phénicien et punique*, Actes du VIIème congrès international des études phéniciennes et puniques (Tunis: Institut national du patrimoine, 2019a): 217–22

Quinn, J.C. and Vella, N.C. (eds.), *The Punic Mediterranean: Identities and Identification from Phoenician Settlement to Roman Rule* (Cambridge: British School at Rome Studies, Cambridge University Press, 2014)

Rakob, F., 'The making of Augustan Carthage.' In E. Fentress and S.E. Alcock (eds.) *Romanization and the City: Creation, Transformations and Failures: Proceedings of a Conference to Celebrate the 50th Anniversary of the Excavations at Cosa, 14–16 May, 1998, Journal of Roman Archaeology* (2000): 72–82

Ramallo Asensio, S., 'Carthago Nova: arqueología y epigrafía de la muralla urbana.' In A. Morillo, F. Cadiou and D. Hourcade (eds.) *Defensa y territorio en Hispania de Los Escipiones a Augusto* (Casa de Velázquez, León: Universidad de León, 2003), pp. 325–62

Rance, P., 'Hannibal, elephants and turrets in Suda Θ 438 (Polybius Fr. 162^B – an unidentified fragment of Diodorus.' *Classical Quarterly* 59; 1 (2009): 91–111

Rankov, B., 'The Second Punic War at sea.' In T. Cornell et al. (eds.) *The Second Punic War: A Reappraisal* (London: Institute of Classical Studies, University of London, 1996), pp. 49–57

Rankov, B., 'A war of phases: strategies and stalemates 264–241 BC.' In D. Hoyos (ed.) *A Companion to the Punic Wars* (Malden, MA: Wiley-Blackwell, 2011), pp. 149–66

Rawlings, L., 'Celts, Spaniards, and Samnites: warriors in a soldiers' war.' In T. Cornell et al. (eds.), *The Second Punic War: A Reappraisal* (London: Institute of Classical Studies, University of London, 1996), pp. 81–95

Rawlings, L., 'Hannibal and Hercules.' In L. Rawlings and H. Bowden (eds.) *Herakles and Hercules: Exploring Graeco-Roman Divinity* (Swansea, 2005), pp. 153–84

Rawlings, L., 'The Carthaginian navy: questions and assumptions.' In G. Fagan and M. Trundle (eds.) *New Perspectives on Ancient Warfare* (Leiden, Boston: Brill, 2010), pp. 253–87

Reitsema, L., et al., 'The diverse genetic origins of a classical period Greek army.' *PNAS* 119; 41 (2022)

Rich, J., 'The origins of the Second Punic War.' In T. Cornell et al. (eds.) *The Second Punic War: A Reappraisal* (London: Institute of Classical Studies, University of London, 1996), pp. 1–37

Richardson, J.S., 'The triumph, the praetors and the senate in the early second century BC.' *Journal of Roman Studies* 65 (1975): 50–63

Ridley, R., 'To be taken with a pinch of salt: the destruction of Carthage.' *Classical Philology* 81; 2 (1986): 140–6

Ridley, R., 'Livy and the Hannibalic war.' In C. Bruun (ed.) *The Roman Middle Republic: Politics, Religion and Historiography c. 400–133 BC*, Acta Instituti Romani Finlandiae, vol. 23 (Rome, 2000), pp. 13–40

Robinson, E., 'Punic coins of Spain and their bearing on the Roman republican series.' In *Essays in Roman Coinage Presented to H. Mattingly* (London: Oxford University Press, 1956), pp. 34–62

Robinson, E., 'Carthaginian and other South Italian coinages of the Second Punic War.' *Numismatic Chronicle* 37 (1964): 37–64

Rollinger, R., 'The Persian Empire in contact with the world.' In K. Radner, N. Moeller and D.T. Potts (eds.) *The Oxford History of the Ancient Near East, Volume V: The Age of Persia* (New York: Oxford University Press, 2023), pp. 887–948

Rood, T., 'Geographical and historical patterning in Diodorus Siculus.' *Histos Supplement 8* (2018): 23–68

Rosenstein, N., 'Marriage and manpower in the Hannibalic war: "Assidui", "Proletarii" and Livy 24.18.7–8.' *Historia* 51; 2 (2002): 163–91

Rossi, A., 'Parallel lives: Hannibal and Scipio in Livy's third decade.' *Transactions of the American Philological Association* 134; 2 (2004): 359–81

Roth, J., *The Logistics of the Roman Army at War 264 BC to AD 235* (Leiden: Brill, 1999)

Sabin, P., 'The mechanics of battle in the Second Punic War.' In T. Cornell et al. (eds.), *The Second Punic War: A Reappraisal* (London: Institute of Classical Studies, University of London, 1996), pp. 59–79

Sabin, P., van Wees, H. and Whitby, M. (eds.), *The Cambridge History of Greek and Roman Warfare*, 2 vols (Cambridge: Cambridge University Press, 2007)

Sala Sellés, F., 'Nuevas perspectivas sobre las relaciones púnicas con la costa ibérica del sureste peninsular.' *Mainake: Los Púnicos de Iberia: Proyectos, Revisions, Síntesis* 32; 2 (2010): 933–50

Scheid, J. and Svenbro, J., 'Byrsa. La ruse d'Elissa et la foundation de Carthage.' *Annales. Histoire, Sciences Sociales* 40; 2 (1985): 328–42

Schepens, G., 'Polybius on the Punic Wars: the problem of objectivity in history.' In H. Devijver and E. Lipiński (eds.) *Studia Phoenicia X: Punic Wars*, Orientalia Lovaniensia Analecta 33 (Leuven, 1989), pp. 317–28

Schettino, M., 'Pyrrhos en Italie: la construction de l'image du premier ennemi venu de l'Orient grec.' *Pallas* 79 (2009): 173–84

Schmitt, A., 'The significance of Sidon and Tyre during the Iron Age on a regional and supra-regional level.' *Die Welt des Orients* 54; 1 (2024): 78–100

Schwartz, J., et al., 'Bones, teeth and estimating age of perinates: Carthaginian infant sacrifice revisited.' *Antiquity* 86; 333 (2012): 738–45

Schwartz, J.H., et al., 'Two tales of one city: data, inference, and Carthaginian infant sacrifice.' *Antiquity* 91; 356 (2017): 442–54

Scullard, H., *Scipio Africanus in the Second Punic War* (Cambridge: Cambridge University Press, 1930)

Scullard, H., *Scipio Africanus: Soldier and Politician* (London: Thames & Hudson, 1970)

Scullard, H., *The Elephant in the Greek and Roman World* (London: Thames & Hudson, 1974)

Seibert, J., *Hannibal* (Darmstadt: Wissenschaftliche Buchgesellschaft, 1993a)

Seibert, J., *Forschungen zu Hannibal* (Darmstadt: Wissenschaftliche Buchgesellschaft, 1993b)

Serrati, J., 'Sicily from pre-Greek times to the fourth century.' In C.J. Smith and J. Serrati (eds.) *Sicily from Aeneas to Augustus* (Edinburgh: Edinburgh University Press, 2000a), pp. 9–14

Serrati, J., 'The coming of the Romans: Sicily from the fourth to the first century BC' and 'Garrisons and grain: Sicily between the Punic Wars.' In C.J. Smith and J. Serrati (eds.) *Sicily from Aeneas to Augustus* (Edinburgh: Edinburgh University Press, 2000b), pp. 109–33

Serrati, J., 'Neptune's altars: the treaties between Rome and Carthage (509–226 BC).' *Classical Quarterly* 56; 1 (2006): 113–34

Sheldon, R., 'Hannibal's spies.' *International Journal of Intelligence and Counterintelligence* 1; 3 (1986): 53–70

Smith, P., et al., 'Age estimations attest to infant sacrifice at the Carthage Tophet.' *Antiquity* 87; 338 (2013): 1191–9

Steinby, C., *The Roman Republican Navy, from the Sixth Century to 167 BC*, Commentationes Humanarum Litterarum 123 (Helsinki, 2007)

Stocks, C., *The Roman Hannibal: Remembering the Enemy in Silius Italicus' Punica* (Liverpool: Liverpool University Press, 2014)

Storm, E., *Massinissa: Numidien im Aufbruch* (Stuttgart: Steiner, 2001)

Strootman, R., 'Warrior queens of the Hellenistic world.' In *The Public Lives of Ancient Women (500 BCE–650 CE)* (Leiden: Brill, 2023): 18–45

Świerk, M., 'Roman Carthage – an ethnic conglomeration? A study of the anthroponymy of an African metropolis.' *Antichthon* 56 (2022): 162–79

Tipping, B., '"*Haec tum Roma fuit*": past, present and closure in Silius Italicus' *Punica*.' In S. Heyworth, P. Fowler and S. Harrison (eds.) *Classical Constructions: Papers in Memory of Don Fowler, Classicist and Epicurean* (Oxford: Oxford University Press, 2007), pp. 221–41

Tipping, B., *Exemplary Epic: Silius Italicus' Punica* (Oxford: Oxford University Press, 2010)

Tipps, G., 'The defeat of Regulus.' *Classical World* 96; 4 (2003): 375–85

Toynbee, A.J., *Hannibal's Legacy: The Hannibalic War's Effects on Roman Life*, vols 1 and 2 (Oxford: Oxford University Press, 1965)

Turfa, J.M., 'Evidence for Etruscan–Punic relations.' *American Journal of Archaeology* 81; 3 (1977): 368–74

Tusa, S. and Royal, J., 'The landscape of the naval battle at the Egadi Islands (241 BC).' *Journal of Roman Archaeology* 25 (2012): 7–48

Ustinova, Y., 'Seers and poets.' *Caves and the Ancient Greek Mind: Descending Underground in the Search for Ultimate Truth* (Oxford, 2009; online edn, Oxford Academic, January 2009)

van Dommelen, P., 'Punic persistence: colonialism and cultural identities in Roman Sardinia.' In R. Laurence and J. Berry (eds.) *Cultural Identity in the Roman Empire* (London: Routledge, 1998), pp. 25–48

van Dommelen, P., 'Punic identities and modern perceptions in the western Mediterranean.' In J.C. Quinn and N.C. Vella (eds.) *The Punic Mediterranean: Identities and Identification from Phoenician Settlement to Roman Rule* (Cambridge: British School at Rome Studies, Cambridge University Press, 2014), pp. 42–57

van Dommelen, P. and Gómez Bellard, C., 'Defining the Punic world and its rural contexts.' In P. van Dommelen and G. Gómez Bellard (eds.) *Rural Landscapes of the Punic World, Studies in Mediterranean Archaeology*, vol. II (London, 2008), pp. 1–21

van Regenmortel, C., 'Work, labour, and professions in the Roman world.' *Classical Review* 67; 2 (2017): 470–3. https://doi.org/10.1017/S0009840X17001068

van Regenmortel, C., *Soldiers, Wages, and the Hellenistic Economies* (Cambridge: Cambridge University Press, 2024)

Várhelyi, Z., 'The spectres of Roman imperialism: the live burials of Gauls and Greeks at Rome.' *Classical Antiquity* 26; 2 (2007): 277–304

Verhelst, N., 'The Carthaginian sufetes: (re-)assessing the literary, epigraphical, and archaeological sources.' *Carthage Studies* 12 (2021): 31–80

Visonà, P., 'La Numismatique partim occident.' In V. Krings (ed.) *La civilization phénicienne et punique: Manuel de recherche* (Leiden: Brill, 1995), pp. 166–81

Visonà, P., 'Carthaginian coinage in perspective.' *American Journal of Numismatics* 10 (1998): 1–27

Visonà, P., 'Rethinking early Carthaginian coinage.' *Journal of Roman Archaeology* 31 (2018): 7–29

Viva, S., et al., 'The mass burials from the western necropolis of the Greek colony of Himera (Sicily) related to the battles of 480 and 409 BCE.' *International Journal of Osteoarchaeology* 30; 3 (2020): 307–17

Waal, W., 'Deconstructing the Phoenician myth: "Cadmus and the palm-leaf tablets" revisited.' *Journal of Hellenic Studies* 142 (2022): 219–54

Walbank, F.W., *A Historical Commentary on Polybius*, 3 vols (Oxford: Clarendon Press, 1957, 1967, 1979 [cited as vol. 1, 2 or 3])

Walbank, F.W., 'Some reflections on Hannibal's pass.' In *Selected Papers: Studies in Greek and Roman History and Historiography* (Cambridge: Cambridge University Press, 1985), pp. 107–19

Weech, W.N., Warmington, B.H. and Wilson, R.J.A., 'Utica.' *Oxford Classical Dictionary* (7 March 2016)

Welch, K., '*Domi Militaeque*.' In K. Welch (ed.) *Representations of War in Ancient Rome* (Cambridge: Cambridge University Press, 2006), pp. 91–161

Whittaker, C., 'Carthaginian imperialism in the fifth and fourth centuries.' In P. Garnsey and C. Whittaker (eds.) *Imperialism in the Ancient World* (Cambridge: Cambridge University Press, 1978), pp. 59–90

Wilson, A., 'Romanizing Ba'al: the art of Saturn worship in North Africa' in M. Sanader and A.R. Miočevič (eds.), *Proceedings of the 8th International Colloquium on Problems of Roman Provincial Art* (Zagreb 2003). (Zagreb: Opuscula: archaeologica dissertationes et monographiae, 2005): pp. 403–408

Wilson, R., 'Hellenistic Sicily, *c.* 270–100 BC.' In J. Prag and J.C. Quinn (eds.) *The Hellenistic West* (Cambridge: Cambridge University Press, 2013), pp. 79–119

Wilson, S., 'Urban development in the Severan empire.' In S. Swain, S. Harrison and J. Elsner (eds.) *Severan Culture* (Cambridge: Cambridge University Press, 2007), pp. 290–326

Woolf, G., *Rome: An Empire's Story* (Oxford: Oxford University Press, 2013)

Woolmer, M., 'Tinker, trader, sailor, spy? The role of the mercantile community in Greek intelligence gathering.' In E. Bragg, L. Hau and E. Macaulay-Lewis (eds.) *Beyond the Battlefields: New Perspectives on Warfare and Society in the Greco-Roman World* (Cambridge: Cambridge University Press, 2008), pp. 67–83

Woolmer, M., *A Short History of the Phoenicians*, 2nd edn (London, New York: Bloomsbury Publishing, 2021)

Xella, P. (ed.), *The Tophet in the Phoenician Mediterranean*, Studi Epigraphici e Linguistici, vol. 30 (Verona, 2013)

Xella, P., et al., 'Phoenician bones of contention.' *Antiquity* 87; 338 (2013): 1199–207

Zambon, E., 'From Agathocles to Hieron II: the birth and development of *basileia* in Hellenistic Sicily.' In S. Lewis (ed.) *Ancient Tyranny* (Edinburgh: Edinburgh University Press, 2006), pp. 77–92

Zambon, E., *Tradition and Innovation: Sicily between Hellenism and Rome* (Stuttgart: Franz Steiner Verlag, 2008)

Zimmermann, K., 'Roman strategy and aims in the Second Punic War.' In D. Hoyos (ed.) *A Companion to the Punic Wars* (Malden, MA: Wiley-Blackwell, 2011), pp. 280–98

Zimmermann, L., 'Zur Münzprägung "der Libyer" während des Söldnerkrieges.' In K. Geus and K. Zimmermann (eds.) *Studia Phoenicia XVI: Punica – Libyca – Ptolemaica*, Orientalia Lovaniensia Analecta 104 (Leuven, 2001), pp. 235–52

Zimmerman Munn, M.L., 'Corinthian trade with the Punic west in the Classical period.' *Corinth, The Centenary: 1896–1996*, 20 (2003): 195–217

Primary Bibliography

Ammianus Marcellinus, *The Later Roman Empire*, trans. W. Hamilton (London: Penguin, 1986)

Appian, *Roman History*, 4 vols (referenced in the text by section: vol. 1, Sicelica, Iberica, Hannibalica, Libyca (Punica); vol. 2, Illyrica, Syriaica; vol. 3, Bellum Civile, trans. H. White [Harvard, Cambridge, MA: Loeb Classical Library, 1955–64])

Appian, *Wars of the Romans in Iberia (Iberike)*, trans. with introduction and commentary by J.S. Richardson (Warminster: Aris & Phillips, 2000)

Apuleius, 'Apologia.' In V. Hunink (ed. and commentary), *Apuleius of Madauros, Pro se de Magia (Apologia)*, 2 vols (Amsterdam: Gieben, 1997) (vol. 1, introduction, text, bibliography, indexes; vol. 2, commentary)

Aristophanes, *Birds. Lysistrata. Women at Thesmophoria*, trans. J. Henderson (Harvard, Cambridge, MA: Loeb Classical Library, 2000)

Aristotle, *Politics*, trans. H. Rackham (Harvard, Cambridge, MA: Loeb Classical Library, 1959)

Arrian, *Anabasis and Indica*, vol. 2, trans. P.A. Brunt (Harvard, Cambridge, MA: Loeb Classical Library, 1983)

Aulus Gellius, *Attic Nights*, vol. 2, trans. J.C. Rolfe (Harvard, Cambridge, MA: Loeb Classical Library, 1927)

Aurelius Victor, *De Caesaribus*, Livres de Césars, ed. and trans. P. Dufraigne, Budé edn (Paris, 1975).

Cassius Dio, *Roman History*, trans. E. Cary (Harvard, Cambridge, MA: Loeb Classical Library, 1914–27)

Cato, *De Agricultura*. Cato, V. *On Agriculture*. Trans. W. D. Hooper, Harrison Boyd Ash. Loeb Classical Library 283 (Cambridge, MA: Harvard University Press, 1934)

Cicero, *De Divinatione* (De div.), trans. W.A. Falconer (Harvard, Cambridge, MA: Loeb Classical Library, 1959)

Cicero, *De Finibus* (De fin.), trans. H. Rackham (Harvard, Cambridge, MA: Loeb Classical Library, 1968)

Cicero, *De Lege Agrarian Contra Rullum* (De agr.), trans. J.H. Freese (Harvard, Cambridge, MA: Loeb Classical Library, 1945)

Cicero, *De Officiis* (De off.), trans. W. Miller (Harvard, Cambridge, MA: Loeb Classical Library, 1951)

Cicero, *De Oratore*, vol. 1, trans. E.W. Sutton (Harvard, Cambridge, MA: Loeb Classical Library, 1968)

Cicero, *Orationes*, vol. 6, trans. J.H. Freese (Harvard, Cambridge, MA: Loeb Classical Library, 1930)

Cicero, *Pro Balbo*, trans. R. Gardner (Harvard, Cambridge, MA: Loeb Classical Library, 1958)

Cicero, *Pro Sestio*, trans. R. Gardner (Harvard, Cambridge, MA: Loeb Classical Library, 1958)

Cicero, *The Verrine Orations* (Verr.), trans. L.H.G. Greenwood (Harvard, Cambridge, MA: Loeb Classical Library, 1948)

Cn. Naevius, *Bellum Poenicum*, ed. and trans. E. Flores (Naples: Liguori Editore, 2011)

Cornelius Nepos, *On the Great Generals of Foreign Nations*, trans. J.C. Rolfe (Harvard, Cambridge, MA: Loeb Classical Library, 2005 [1984])

Diodorus Siculus, *Library of History*, trans. F.R. Walton et al., vols 1–13 (Harvard, Cambridge, MA: Loeb Classical Library, 1956–7)

Dionysius of Halicarnassus, *Roman Antiquities*, trans. E. Cary (Harvard, Cambridge, MA: Loeb Classical Library, 1937–50)

Ennius, *Annales*, fragments, ed. E.M. Stewart (Cambridge, 1925)

Eutropius, *Historiae Romanae Breviarium* (abridged Roman History), trans. with introduction and commentary by H.W. Bird (Liverpool: Liverpool University Press, 1993)

Hanno, *Periplus, The Date and Origin of Hanno's Periplus*, trans. J. Bloomqvist (Lund: LiberLäromedel/Gleerup, 1979)

Herodian, *History*, vol. 1, trans. C.R. Whittaker (Harvard, Cambridge, MA: Loeb Classical Library, 1969)

Herodotus, *The Histories*, trans. A.D. Godley (Harvard, Cambridge, MA: Loeb Classical Library, 1946)

Herodotus, *The Histories*, trans. A. De Selincourt, revised with introduction and notes by R.A. Burn (London: Penguin, 1972)

Herodotus, *The Histories*, trans. T. Holland, with introduction by P. Cartledge (London: Penguin, 2013)

Hesiod, *Theogony. Works and Days. Testimonia*, trans. G.W. Most (Harvard, Cambridge, MA: Loeb Classical Library, 2007)

Horace, *Odes and Epodes*, trans. C.E. Bennett (Harvard, Cambridge, MA: Loeb Classical Library, 1914)

Jacoby, F., et al. (eds.), *Die Fragmente der Griechischen Historiker* (FGrH) (Leiden, Brill 1923–58)

Justin, *Epitome of the Philippic History of Pompeius Trogus*, trans. J. Yardley and notes R. Develin (Atlanta: Society for Classical Studies Classical Resources n. 3, APA, 1994)

Juvenal, *The Sixteen Satires*, trans. with introduction by P. Green (London: Penguin, 1974)

Livy, *Ab urbe condita*, Oxford Classical Texts, vols 3–5, Books XXI–XXXV (1950–65)

Livy, *Hannibal's War*, Books 21–30 of *Ab urbe condita*, trans. J. Yardley and D. Hoyos (Oxford: Oxford World Classics, 2006)

Livy, *Rome and the Mediterranean*, Books 31–45 of *Ab urbe condita*, trans. H. Bettenson (Harmondsworth: Penguin Books, 1976)

Livy, *Summaries, Fragments and Obsequens (Periochae)*, vol. XIV, trans. A. Schlesinger (Harvard, Cambridge, MA: Loeb Classical Library, 1959)

Menander, *Aspis*, vol. 1, ed. and trans. W.G. Arnott (Harvard, Cambridge, MA: Loeb Classical Library, 1979)

Ovid, *Fasti*, trans. Sir J.G. Frazer (Harvard, Cambridge, MA: Loeb Classical Library, 1989)

Plato, *Laws*, vols. 1 and 2, trans. R. Bury (Harvard, Cambridge, MA: Loeb Classical Library, 1926–31)

Plautus, *Mostellaria*. In trans. H.T. Riley, *The Comedies of Plautus* (London: G. Bell & Sons, 1912)

Plautus, *Poenulus* [The Little Carthaginian], trans. P. Nixon (Harvard, Cambridge, MA: Loeb Classical Library, 1951)

Pliny, *Natural History*, vols 1–10, trans. H. Rackham, W.H.S. Jones and D.E. Eichholz (Harvard, Cambridge, MA: Loeb Classical Library, 1947–62)

Plutarch, 'Demetrius'. In *The Age of Alexander*, trans. I. Scott-Kilvert and T. Duff (London: Penguin, 1973–2012)

Plutarch, *Life of Alexander*, trans. B. Perrin (Harvard, Cambridge, MA: Loeb Classical Library, 1949)

Plutarch, *Life of C. Gracchus*, trans. B. Perrin (Harvard, Cambridge, MA: Loeb Classical Library, 1921)

Plutarch, *Life of Cato the Elder*, trans. B. Perrin (Harvard, Cambridge, MA: Loeb Classical Library, 1914)

Plutarch, *Life of Fabius Maximus*, trans. B. Perrin (Harvard, Cambridge, MA: Loeb Classical Library, 1951)

Plutarch, *Life of Lycurgus*, trans. B. Perrin (Harvard, Cambridge, MA: Loeb Classical Library, 1914)

Plutarch, *Life of Marcellus*, trans. B. Perrin (Harvard, Cambridge, MA: Loeb Classical Library, 1955)

Plutarch, *Life of Pyrrhus*, trans. B. Perrin (Harvard, Cambridge, MA: Loeb Classical Library, 1920)

Plutarch, *Life of Sertorius*, trans. B. Perrin (Harvard, Cambridge, MA: Loeb Classical Library, 1919)

Plutarch, *Life of Timoleon*, trans. B. Perrin (Harvard, Cambridge, MA: Loeb Classical Library, 1919)

Plutarch, *Life of Titus Flamininus*, trans. B. Perrin (Harvard, Cambridge, MA: Loeb Classical Library, 1921)

Polybius, *The Histories*, vols 1–6, trans. W.R. Paton (Harvard, Cambridge, MA: Loeb Classical Library, 1922)

Polybius, *The Rise of the Roman Empire*, trans. I. Scott-Kilvert, with introduction by F. Walbank (London: Penguin Classics, 1979)

Quintus Curtius Rufus, *History of Alexander*, vol. 1, Books 1–5, trans. by J.C. Rolfe (Harvard, Cambridge, MA: Loeb Classical Library, 1946)

Sallust, *Bellum Catilinae and Bellum Jugurthinum*, trans. J.C. Rolfe, rev. J. Ramsey (Harvard, Cambridge, MA: Loeb Classical Library, 2013)

Servius, *Commentary on Book Four of Virgil's Aeneid*, eds. and trans. C. McDonough, R. Prior and M. Stansbury (Wauconda, IL, 2004)

Silius Italicus, *Punica*, vols 1 and 2, trans. J.D. Duff (Harvard, Cambridge, MA: Loeb Classical Library, 1949–50)

Silius Italicus, 'Punica', Book 3. In A. Augoustakis and R. Joy Littlewood (eds. and trans. with introduction and commentary) *Oxford*

Commentaries on Flavian Poetry (Oxford: Oxford University Press, 2022)

Sosylus, 'Sosylos (176)', trans. D.W. Roller. In I. Worthington (ed.), *Brill's New Jacoby* (Brill, University of Missouri, 2012; Brill Online, University of Edinburgh, 15 March 2012)

Statius, *Silvae*, trans. with introduction and notes by D.A. Slater (Oxford: The Clarendon Press, 1908)

Strabo, *Geography*, Book III, trans. H. Jones (Harvard, Cambridge, MA: Loeb Classical Library, 1969)

Strabo [Estrabón], *Geografía di Iberia*, trans. J. Gómez Espelosín, with commentary by G. Cruz Andreotti, M.V. García Quintela and J. Gómez Espelosín (Madrid, 2007)

Suetonius, *Lives of the Caesars*, vol. 1 (for Tiberius), trans. J.C. Rolf (Harvard, Cambridge, MA: Loeb Classical Library, 1914)

Theocritus, *The Idylls*, ed. with introduction and notes by R.J. Cholmeley (London: George Bell & Sons, 1901)

Thucydides, *History of the Peloponnesian War*, vol. 1, Books 1–2, trans. C.F. Smith (Harvard, Cambridge, MA: Loeb Classical Library, 1919)

'Timaeus of Tauromenium', trans. C. Champion. In I. Worthington (ed.), *Brill's New Jacoby* (Brill Online, 15 April 2014). http://referenceworks.brillonline.com/entries/brill-s-new-jacoby/timaios-566-a566

Tzetses, J., *Chiliades*, ed. P.A.M. Leone (Naples, 1968)

Valerius Maximus, *Memorable Doings and Sayings*, vols 1 and 2, ed. and trans. D.R. Shackleton Bailey (Harvard, Cambridge, MA: Loeb Classical Library, 2000)

Velleius Paterculus, *History of Rome*, trans. F.W. Shipley (Harvard, Cambridge, MA: Loeb Classical Library, 1924)

Virgil, *Aeneid*, trans. J. Dryden (London: Sir John Lubbock's Hundred Books, 1891)

Virgil, *Aeneid*, trans. R. Fagles (London: Penguin, 2006)

Virgil, *Aeneid*, trans. T. C. Williams (Boston: Houghton Mifflin Co., 1910)

Virgil, *Eclogues. Georgics. Aeneid: Books 1–6*, trans. H. Rushton Fairclough, revised by G.P. Goold (Harvard, Cambridge, MA: Loeb Classical Library, 1916)

Xenophon, *Cyropaedia: The Education of Cyrus*, trans. and annotated by W. Ambler (Ithaca, London: Cornell University Press, 2001)

Xenophon, *Memorabilia and Oeconomicus*, trans. E. Marchant (Harvard, Cambridge, MA: Loeb Classical Library, 2013)

Zonaras, *Epitome of Histories*, sections referenced here taken from Cassius Dio, *Roman History*, trans. E. Cary (Harvard, Cambridge MA: Loeb Classical Library, 1914–1927)

Acknowledgements

I am indebted to many people for the writing of this book. My lifelong interest in Carthage – Punic, Roman, medieval, early modern and contemporary – began a long time ago when I went along to excavate at a site there with a team from the University of Alberta, Canada. From that project developed so many things but perhaps most importantly were the life-long friendships with a group that includes Sandra Bingham, Stephen Copp, Elizabeth Pennefather-O'Brien, Bretta Gerecke, Michael MacKinnon and Jeremy Rossiter, among others, who have been so much a part of me and my relationship to Carthage.

My biggest debt is to the amazing work of so many great scholars from Tunisia, Europe, North America and beyond who have transformed our understanding of the history and culture of Carthage and the Mediterranean over the past decades and whose research underlies much of the book. These works have been cited in the Notes and in the Bibliography with the caveat that any errors of interpretation are solely mine. I have had much help from Stephen Copp with images and maps, Maria Clarke with mapping and conceptualizing the Mediterranean space of Carthage, and thank you to Helen Stirling for pulling all of that together. I would like also to acknowledge my students at Cardiff University – especially those who took the South Shore module and whose discussions and ideas on all things North African in the ancient world have been inspirational to me. I want to thank Adam Gauntlett, who thought this book would be a good idea, and Robyn Drury, who agreed, and to all the editors at Ebury who have been so helpful and whose suggestions have made this a much better book, especially Amanda Waters.

There are many friends and family who have always encouraged and supported my interests, listened to my rants and believed in and encouraged my work – all of you beauties, sisters, cousins and colleagues know who you are. As always, I want to thank my life partner Keith Tracey for his support and tolerance for my fascinations and interests in old Mediterranean things. Most of all this book is dedicated to a dear friend no longer with us, Victoria Rowbotham – who constantly inspires me.

Permission Acknowledgements

Index

Note: page numbers in **bold** refer to information contained in captions.

ABOUT THE AUTHOR

Dr Eve MacDonald is Senior Lecturer in Ancient History at Cardiff University; she is an archaeologist and ancient historian who has worked and published extensively on the history and material culture of Carthage, North Africa and the Middle East. She is an expert on the region and is the author of *Hannibal: A Hellenistic Life*, which was published in 2015 by Yale University Press. She has also appeared in podcasts (*History Hit: The Ancients, Hannibal's Winter War, The Fall of Carthage*) and documentary films for Channel 4 and PBS's *Secrets of the Dead*. *Carthage* is her first book for the trade.